BIOGRAPHICAL SKETCHES

OF THE

SIGNERS OF THE DECLARATION

OF

AMERICAN INDEPENDENCE

THE

DECLARATION HISTORICALLY CONSIDERED;

AND A SKETCH OF THE LEADING EVENTS CONNECTED WITH
THE ADOPTION OF

THE ARTICLES OF CONFEDERATION,

AND OF

THE FEDERAL CONSTITUTION.

BY B. J. LOSSING,

AUTHOR OF "SEVENTEEN HUNDRED AND SEVENTY-SIX," "LIVES OF THE
PRESIDENTS," &c.

ILLUSTRATED BY FIFTY PORTRAITS
AND OTHER ENGRAVINGS.

PHILADELPHIA:

G. G. EVANS, PUBLISHER,
No. 439 CHESTNUT STREET.
1860.

BIOGRAPHICAL SKETCHES

OF THE

SIGNERS OF THE DECLARATION

OF

AMERICAN INDEPENDENCE

BY   B. J. LOSSING

Digital Scanning and Publishing is a leader in the electronic republication of historical books and documents. We publish many of our titles as eBooks , paperback and hardcover editions. DSI is committed to bringing many traditional and well-known books back to life, retaining the look and feel of the original work.

Trade Paperback ISBN: 1-58218-320-1
Hardcover ISBN: 1-58218-321-X

©2008 DSI Digital Reproduction
First DSI Printing: November 2008

Published by Digital Scanning Inc. Scituate, MA 02066
781-545-2100 http://www.Digitalscanning.com *and*
http://www.PDFLibrary.com

PREFACE.

THERE are lessons of deep, abiding interest, and of inestimable value, to be learned in studying the lives of the men who perilled their all to secure the blessed inheritance of free institutions which we now enjoy. We do not learn merely the dignity and sacredness of pure patriotism, by following them in their career amid the storms of the Revolution, but all the virtues which adorn humanity are presented in such bold relief, in the private and public actions of that venerated company, that when we rise from a perusal of a narrative of their lives, we feel as if all the noble qualities of our common manhood had been passing before us in review, and challenging our profound reverence.

The biography of a great man, is an history of his own times; and when we have perused the record of the actions of the men of our Revolution, we have imbibed a general knowledge of the great events of that struggle for Freedom. If this proposition is true, then we feel that this volume has a claim to the public regard, for we have endeavored to comprise within as small a compass as a penspicuous view of the subject would allow, the chief events in the lives of the men who stood sponsors at the baptism in blood of our Infant Republic.

The memoirs are illustrated by copious notes explanatory of events alluded to in the course of the biographical narrative, and these, we believe, will be found a highly useful feature of the work.

We have made free use of materials long since laid before the public by abler pens than our own. We did not expect to add much that is new to the biographical facts already published; our aim was to condense those facts into the space of a volume so small, that the price of it would make it accessible to our whole population. It is the mission of true patriotism to scatter the seeds of knowledge broad-cast amid those in the humbler walks of society, because adventitious circumstances deny them access to the full granary of information, where the wealthy are filled; for these humbler ones are equal inheritors of the throne of the people's sovereignty, and are no less powerful than others at the ballot-box where the nation decides who its rulers shall be.

The final adoption of the Federal Constitution, and the organization of the present government of the United States under it, formed the climax—the crowning act of the drama of which the Declaration of Independence was the opening scene. We therefore thought it proper to append to the biographies, a brief sketch of the legislative events which led to the formation and adoption of the Constitution. The Declaration is pregnant with grave charges against the King of Great Britain—charges which his apologists have essayed to deny. We have taken them up in consecutive order as they stand in the document, and adduced proofs from historical facts, of the truth of those charges. These proofs might have been multiplied, but our space would not permit amplification.

With these brief remarks, we send our volume forth with the pleasing hope that it may prove useful to the young and humble of our beloved land, unto whom we affectionately dedicate it.

B. J. L.

New York, April, 1848.

CONTENTS.

INTRODUCTION

Independence Hall as it appeared in 1776.

ROM no point of view can the Declaration of American Independence, the causes which led to its adoption, and the events which marked its maintenance, be observed, without exciting sentiments of profound veneration for the men who were the prominent actors in that remarkable scene in the drama of the world's history. Properly to appreciate the true relative position in which those men stood to the then past and future, it is necessary to view the chain of causes and effects, retrospective and prospective, united in them by a brilliant link.

For a long series of years the commercial policy of Great Britain, in her dealings with the American Colonies, was narrow and selfish, and its effects influenced the whole social compact here. The colonists felt the injustice of many laws, but their want of representation in the National Legislature, and their inherent political weakness, obliged them to submit. But when the wars with

the French and Indians called forth their physical energies, and united, in a measure, the disjointed settlements,
scattered in isolated communities along the Atlantic sea-
board, marked by hardly a semblance of union in feeling
and interest, it was then that they perceived the strength
and value of unity, and talked with each other respecting
their common rights and privileges.

The royal governors viewed the interchange of political
sentiments between the colonies with great disfavor, for
they saw therein the harbinger of their own departing
strength. Their representations to the British Ministry,
more than any other single cause, contributed to the enactment of laws respecting the colonies, that finally gene-
rated that rebellious spirit in the hearts of the Anglo-
Americans, which would not, and did not, stop short of
absolute Political Independence.

The enactment of the Stamp Act in 1765, and the
kindred measures that soon followed, made it plain to the
minds of the colonists that even common justice would be
denied them by the Home Government, if its claims inter-
fered with the avaricious demands of an exhausted treasury. They saw plainly that the King and Parliament
were resolved to turn a deaf ear to all petitions and remonstrances that were based upon the righteous assump-
tion that "TAXATION AND EQUITABLE REPRESENTATION
ARE ONE AND INSEPARABLE." As this was a principle too
vital in the very constitution of a free people, to be yielded
the colonists felt the necessity of a General Council to de
liberate upon the solemn questions involved. In this, the
great heart of colonial America seemed to beat with one

pulsation; and almost simultaneously, and without previous concert, the proposition for a General Congress was
put forth in several of the colonies.

The time and place for holding a Congress were designated, and on the fifth of September, 1774, delegates from
the various colonies assembled in Carpenter's Hall, in
Philadelphia. Their deliberations were orderly but firm.
Loyalty to the crown, notwithstanding its oppressions, was
a leading theme in their debates. Not a word was whis-
pered of dismemberment and independence, but they
solemnly consulted with each other upon the best means
of maintaining the integrity of the British realm, compati-
ble with the preservation of their own inalienable rights.
To this end their efforts were directed, and they humbly
petitioned the King, remonstrated with Parliament, and
appealed to their brethren in Great Britain for justice.
But their petitions and remonstrances were in vain. New
oppressions were laid upon them, and the blood of American citizens was shed by British soldiery at Lexington
and Concord!

Another Congress assembled in May, 1775, organized
a temporary general government, made provisions for an
army, and appointed Washington commander-in-chief
And yet they talked not of *independence*. They armed in
defence of rights bestowed by the British Constitution,
and they were still willing to lay them down, and avow
their loyalty, when those rights should be respected.
Even with arms in their hands, and successfully opposing
the force of British bayonets, they petitioned and remonstrated. But their petitions were unheeded; their re-

monstrances were insultingly answered; and their demands for justice were met by swarms of armed mercenaries, purchased by the British Government of petty
German princes, and sent hither to butcher British subjects for asserting the rights of British subjects!

Hope for reconciliation faded away at the opening of
1776, and in June of that year, Richard Henry Lee, of
Virginia, offered a resolution in the General Congress,
declaring all allegiance of the colonies to the British crown,
at an end. This bold proposition was soon after followed
by the appointment of a committee to draft a Declaration
of Independence. This committee consisted of Thomas
Jefferson, John Adams, Benjamin Franklin, Roger Sherman and Robert R. Livingston. The draft was made by
Jefferson, and after a few verbal alterations by Dr. Franklin and Mr. Adams, it was submitted to Congress on the
twenty-eighth of June. It was laid upon the table until
the first of July, when it was taken up in committee of
the whole, and after several amendments were made, nine
States voted for Independence. The Assemblies of Maryland and Pennsylvania refused their concurrence; but
conventions of the people having been called, majorities
were obtained, and on the fourth of July, votes from all
the Colonies were procured in its favor, and the thirteen
united Colonies were declared free and independent States

The Declaration was signed on that day, only by John
Hancock, the President of Congress, and with his name
alone, it was first sent forth to the world. It was ordered
to be engrossed upon the Journals of Congress, and on
the second day of August following, it was signed by all

out one of the fifty-six signers whose names are appended to it. That one was Matthew Thornton, who, on taking his seat in November, asked and obtained the privilege of signing it. Several who signed it on the second of August, were absent when it was adopted on the fourth of July, but, approving of it, they thus signified their approbation.

The signing of that instrument was a solemn act, and required great firmness and patriotism in those who committed it. It was treason against the home government, yet perfect allegiance to the law of right. It subjected those who signed it to the danger of an ignominious death, yet it entitled them to the profound reverence of a disenthralled people. But neither firmness nor patriotism was wanting in that august assembly. And their own sound judgment and discretion, their own purity of purpose and integrity of conduct, were fortified and strengthened by the voice of the people in popular assemblies, embodied in written instructions for the guidance of their representatives.

Such were the men unto whose keeping, as instruments of Providence, the destinies of America were for the time intrusted; and it has been well remarked, that men, other than such as these,—an ignorant, untaught mass, like those who have formed the physical elements of other revolutionary movements, without sufficient intellect to guide and control them—could not have conceived, planned, and carried into execution, such a mighty movement, one so fraught with tangible marks of political wisdom, as the American Revolution. And it is a matter of just pride to the American people, that not one of that noble band who periled life, fortune, and honor, in the cause of freedom, ever fell from his high estate into moral degradation, or dimmed, by word or deed, the brightness of that effulgence which halos the DECLARATION OF AMERICAN INDEPENDENCE.

Their bodies now have all returned to their kindred dust in the grave, and their souls have gone to receive their reward in the Spirit Land.

Congress was assembled in Independence Hall, at Philadelphia, when the Declaration was adopted, and, connected with that event, the following touching incident is related. On the morning of the day of its adoption, the venerable bell-man ascended to the steeple, and a little boy was placed at the door of the Hall to give him notice when the vote should be concluded. The old man waited long at his post, saying, "They will never do it, they will never do it." Suddenly a loud shout came up from below, and there stood the blue-eyed boy, clapping his hands, and shouting, "Ring! Ring!!" Grasping the iron tongue of the bell, backward and forward he hurled it a hundred times, proclaiming "Liberty to the land and to the inhabitants thereof."

Josiah Bartlett

 HE ancestors of JOSIAH BARTLETT were from Normandy, whence they emigrated to England. The name was conspicuous in English History at an early date. Toward the close of the seventeenth century a branch of the family emigrated to America, and settled in the town of Beverley, in Massachusetts. Josiah was born in Amesbury, in Massachusetts, in November, 1729. His mother's maiden name was Webster, and

she was a relative of the family of the great statesman of that name of our time.

Young Bartlett lacked the advantage of a collegiate education, but he improved an opportunity for acquiring some knowledge of the Greek and Latin, which offered in the family of a relative, the Rev. Doctor Webster. He chose for a livelihood the practice of the medical profession, and commenced the study of the science when he was sixteen years old. His opportunities for acquiring knowledge from books were limited, but the active energies of his mind supplied the deficiency, in a measure, and he passed an examination with honor at the close of his studies. He commenced practice at Kingston in New Hampshire, and proving skillful and successful, his business soon became lucrative, and he amassed a competency.

Mr. Bartlett was a stern, unbending republican in principle, yet, notwithstanding this, he was highly esteemed by Wentworth, the royal governor,* and received from him a magistrate's commission, and also the command of a regiment of militia. In 1765 he was elected a member of the provincial legislature of New Hampshire. It was at the time when the Stamp Act† was before the British Parliament, and Mr. Bartlett soon became a prominent leader of a party that opposed the various oppressive measures of the home government. Through Wentworth, magnificent bribes were offered him, but his patriotism was inflexible.

---

* As a general rule the royal governors looked with disfavor upon all democratic movements, and withdrew and withheld their support from those who manifested decided republicanism in their sentiments. The obvious reason for this was, that the voice of republicanism sounded in their ears like the death kneh of their power and place.

† The Stamp Act required all legal instruments of writing, such as wills, deeds, mortgages, marriage certificates, &c., to be written upon paper stamped with the royal arms of Britain. An officer called a "Stamp Master" was appointed to sell them, and-thus Great Britain indirectly taxed her American colonies without their consent.

In 1776 he was appointed a member of the Committee of Safety of his State. The governor was alarmed when this committee was appointed, and to prevent the transaction of other business of a like member he dissolved the Assembly. They re-assembled in side of the governor, and Dr. Bartlett was at the head of this rebellious movement. He was soon after elected a member of the Continental Congress,* and in 1775, Governor Wentworth struck his name from the magistracy list, and deprived him of his military commission. Still he was active in the provincial assembly, and the governor, despairing of reconciliation, and becoming somewhat alarmed for his own safety, left the province. The provincial Congress† assumed the reins of government, and immediately re-appointed Dr. Bartlett colonel of militia.

In August, 1775, he was again chosen a delegate to the Continental Congress, and was again re-elected in 1776. He was one of the committee appointed to devise a plan for the confederation of the States,a as proposed a June, by Dr. Franklin. He warmly supported the 1776. proposition for independence, and when, on the second of August, 1776, the members of Congress signed the Declaration, Dr. Bartlett was the first who affixed his signature, New Hampshire being the first State called.

In 1778, he obtained leave from Congress to visit his family and look after his private affairs, which had become much deranged. He did not resume his seat again in that body. In 1779 he was appointed Chief Justice of the Court of Common Pleas of New Hampshire, and the muster master of its troops. He was afterward raised to the bench of the Supreme Court. He took an active part

* First convened at Philadelphia, on the fourth of September, 1774.

† Before actual hostilities commenced, nearly all the colonies were acting independent of the royal governors and their councils, and provincial Congresses were organized, which performed all the duties of independent State legislatures.

in the Convention of his State, in favor of the Constitution of 1787, and when it was adopted, he was elected a member of the first Senate that convened under it in the city of New York. But he declined the honor, and did not take his seat there. He had been previously chosen President of New Hampshire, and held that responsible office until 1793, when he was elected the first governor of that State, under the Federal Constitution.* He held the office one year, and then resigning it, he retired to private life, and sought that needful repose which the declining years of an active existence required. He had served his country faithfully in its hour of deepest peril, and the benedictions of a free people followed him to his domestic retreat. But he was not permitted long to bless his family with his presence, nor was he allowed to witness his country entirely free from perils of great magnitude, that threatened its destruction, while the elements of the new experiment in government were yet unstable, for in 1795 death called him away. He died on the nineteenth of May of that year, in the sixty-sixth year of his age.

* So jealous were the people of State Rights, that the Federal Constitution was warmly opposed in many parts of the Union, because of its apparent nullification of those rights, and that is the reason why several of the States so long delayed to ratify that instrument. The following table exhibits the dates of the ratification of the Constitution by the thirteen old States.

Delaware, Dec. 7	1787	South Carolina, May 23	1788
Pennsylvania, Dec. 12	1787	New Hampshire, June 21	1788
New Jersey, Dec. 18	1787	Virginia, June 26,	1788
Georgia, Jan. 2,	1788	New York, July 26	1788
Connecticut, Jan. 9,	1788	North Carolina Nov. 21	1789
Massachusetts, Feb. 6,	1788	Rhode Island, May 29	1790
Maryland, April 28,	1788		

Wm Whipple

ILLIAM WHIPPLE was born at Kittery, in New Hampshire (that portion which is now the State of Maine) in the year 1730. His early education was received at a common school in his native town. When quite a lad, he went to sea, in which occupation he was engaged for several years. At the age of twenty nine [a] he quitted the seafaring life, and, with his brother, Joseph Whipple, entered into mercantile pursuits in Portsmouth, New Hampshire.

[a] 759

He early espoused the cause of the colonies and soon

2   17

became a leader among the opposition to British authority In 1775 he was elected a member of the Provincial Congress of New Hampshire, and was chosen by that body, one of the Committee of Safety.* When, in 1775, the people of that State organized a temporary government, Mr. Whipple was chosen a member of the Council. In January, 1776, he was chosen a delegate to the Continental Congress, and was among those who, on the fourth of July of that year, voted for the Declaration of Independence. He remained in Congress until 1777, when he retired from that body, having been appointed a Brigadier General of the New Hampshire Militia. He was very active in calling out and equipping troops for the campaign against Burgoyne. He commanded one brigade, and General Stark the other. He was under Gates at the capture of Burgoyne, and was one of the commissioners to arrange the terms of capitulation. He was afterward selected one of the officers to march the British prisoners to Cambridge, near Boston.

He joined Sullivan in his expedition against the British on Rhode Island in 1778, with a pretty large force of New Hampshire Militia. But the perverse conduct of the French Admiral D'Estaing, in not sustaining the siege of Newport,† caused a failure of the expedition, and General Whipple, with his brigade, returned to New Hampshire.

In 1780, he was offered the situation of Commissioner

---

* These committees were organized in several of the States. Their business was to act as an executive body to regulate the general concerns of the government during the continuance of the war. These committees were of vast importance, and acted efficiently in conjunction with the committees of correspondence. In some instances they consisted each of the same men.

† The Count D'Estaing agreed to assist Sullivan in reducing the town of Newport, but just as he was entering the harbor, the fleet of Lord Howe, from New-York, appeared, and he proceeded to attack him. A storm prevented an engagement, and both fleets were greatly damaged by the gale. D'Estaing, instead of remaining to assist Sullivan, sailed for Boston, under the retence of repairing his shattered vessels.

of the Board of Admiralty, but declined it. In 1782, he was appointed by Robert Morris, financial agent in New Hampshire,* but he resigned the trust in the course of a year. During that year, he was appointed one of the commissioners to settle the dispute between Pennsylvania and Connecticut, concerning the Wyoming domain, and was appointed president of the Court.† He was also appointed, during that year, a side judge of the Superior Court of New Hampshire.‡

Soon after his appointment, in attempting to sum up the arguments of counsel, and submit the case to the jury, he was attacked with a violent palpitation of the heart, which ever after troubled him. In 1785 he was seriously affected while holding court; and, retiring to his chamber, he never left it again while living. He expired on the twenty-eighth day of November, 1785, in the fifty-fifth year of his age. He requested a post mortem examination, which being done, it was found that a portion of his heart had become ossified, or bony. Thus terminated the valuable life of one who rose from the post of a cabin boy, to a rank among the first men of his country. His life and character present one of those bright examples of self-reliance which cannot be too often pressed upon the attention of the young; and, although surrounding circumstances had much to do in the development of his talents, yet, after all, the great secret of his success was doubtless a hopeful reliance upon a conscious ability to perform any duty required of him.

* Robert Morris was then the manager of the finances of the Confederation. and these agents in the various States were a kind of sub-treasurers. Hence it was an office that required honest and faithful incumbents.

† The early western boundary of Connecticut, before the organization of New York, was, like most of the other States on the Atlantic, quite indefinite. A Colony from this province had settled in the Wyoming valley and that region was not included in New York. It was within the bounds of Pennsylvania, hence the dispute.

‡ At that time the Courts in New Hampshire were constituted of four judges, of whom the first or Chief Justice, only, was a lawyer, the others being chosen from among civilians, distinguished for sound judgment, and a good education.

Matthew Thornton

ATTHEW THORNTON was born in Ireland, in 1714, and was brought to this country by his father when he was between two and three years of age. His father, when he emigrated to America, first settled at Wiscasset, in Maine, and in the course of a few years moved to Worcester, in Massachusetts, where he gave his son an academical education, with a view to fit him for one of the learned professions. Matthew chose the medical profession, and at the close of his preparatory studies, he commenced his business career in Londonderry, New Hampshire. He became eminent as a physician, and in the course of a few years acquired a handsome fortune.

In 1745 he was appointed surgeon of the New Hampshire troops, and accompanied them in the expedition against Louisburg.* After his return he was appointed by the royal governor (Wentworth) a Colonel of Militia, and also a Justice of the Peace. He early espoused the cause of the colonists, and soon, like many others, became obnoxious to the governor. His popularity among the people was a cause of jealousy and alarm on the part of the chief magistrate.

When the provincial government of New Hampshire was organized, on the abdication of Governor Wentworth.

* Louisburg was a fortress upon the island of Cape Breton, Nova Scotia, then in possession of the French, and was considered one of the strongest fortifications in America.

20

Dr Thornton was elected president.* When the provincial Congress was organized he was chosen Speaker of the House.[a] In September of the same year, *a* Jan. he was appointed a delegate to the Continental 1776. Congress for one year, and was permitted to sign his name to the Declaration of Independence, when he took his seat in November.† In January, 1776, (prior to his election to the Continental Congress) he was appointed a judge of the Superior Court of his State, having previously been elected a member of the Court of Common Pleas. In December of that year, he was again elected to the general Congress for one year from the twenty-third of January, 1777. At the expiration of the term he withdrew from Congress, and only engaged in public affairs as far as his office as judge required his services. He resigned his judgeship in 1782.

In 1789, Dr. Thornton purchased a farm in Exeter, where he resided until the time of his death, which took place while on a visit to his daughters in Newburyport, Massachusetts, on the twenty-fourth of June, 1803. He was then in the eighty-ninth year of his age.

Dr. Thornton was greatly beloved by all who knew him, and to the close of his long life he was a consistent and zealous Christian. He always enjoyed remarkably good health,‡ and, by the practice of those hygeian virtues, *temperance* and *cheerfulness,* he attained a patriarchal age.

* This provisional government was intrusted to men little experienced in political matters, and only elected for six months, yet they were men of nerve and prudence, and under the advice and direction of the Continental Congress, they succeeded well.

† Dr. Thornton was not the only one to whom this indulgence was granted. There were several members absent when the vote was taken on the adoption of that instrument on the fourth of July, but who, approving of the measure, subsequently signed their names thereto.

‡ At the age of eighty-one he had a severe attack of the hooping cough, which ever afterward caused a weakness of the lungs, and a tendency to pulmonary disease.

John Hancock

NE of the most distinguished person-
ages of the War of Independence,
was John Hancock, who was born
near the village of Quincy, in Massachusetts, in the year 1737. His
father and grandfather were both
ministers of the gospel. His father
is represented as a pious, industrious, and faithful pastor;
a friend of the poor. and a patron of learning. He died

while John was quite an infant, and left him to the care of a paternal uncle, who cherished him with great affection. This relative was a merchant in Boston, who had amassed a large fortune, and after having given John a collegiate education at Harvard College (where at the age of seventeen years he graduated)[a] he took him into his counting-room as clerk. His abilities proved

a 1754

such, that, in 1760, he sent him on a business mission to England, where he was present at the funeral rites of George II., and the coronation ceremonies of George III. Soon after his return to America, his uncle died, and left him, at the age of twenty-six, in possession of a princely fortune—one of the largest in the Province of Massachusetts.

He soon relinquished his commercial pursuits, and became an active politician, always taking sides with those whose sentiments were liberal and democratic. He was soon noticed and appreciated by his townsmen in Boston, and was chosen by them one of its selectmen, an office of much consideration in those days. In 1766, he was chosen a representative for Boston in the General Provincial Assembly, where he had for his colleagues some of the most active patriots of the day, such as Samuel Adams, James Otis, and Thomas Cushing.

Years before Mr. Hancock entered upon public life, the tyrannous measures of the British cabinet had excited the fears of the American colonies, and aroused a sentiment of resistance that long burned in the people's hearts before it burst forth into a flame of rebellion.

These feelings were familiar to the bosom of young Hancock, for he imbibed the principles of liberty with the breath of his infancy, and when circumstances called for a manifestation thereof, they exhibited the sturdy vigor of maturity.

When Parliament adopted those obnoxious measures

toward America, which immediately succeeded the odious
Stamp Act, Mr. Hancock was a member of the Provincial Assembly, and, in union with those patriots before
named, and others, he determined not to submit to them.
He was one of the first who proposed and adopted non-
importation measures, a system which gradually spread
to the other colonies, and produced a powerful effect upon
the home government. Open resistance at length became
common, and the name of Hancock figures conspicuously
in the commotions that agitated Boston for more than eight
years.* He became a popular leader and drew upon
himself the direst wrath of offended royalty.†

At the time of the *Boston Massacre,* and during the
commotion known as the *Tea Riot,* Mr. Hancock was
bold and active; and in March, 1774, on the occasion of
the anniversary of the "Massacre," he boldly delivered
an oration, in which he spoke in most indignant terms of
the acts and measures of the British Government.

In 1767, Mr. Hancock was elected a member of the
Executive Council, but the choice was so displeasing to
the governor, that he rejected him. He was again and
again elected, and as often rejected, and this served to increase his popularity among the people. At last the

---

* One of the earliest acts of open resistance, was on the occasion of the seizure
of the Sloop Liberty, belonging to Mr. Hancock, by the Custom House officers,
under the plea that she was loaded with goods contrary to the revenue laws.
The people were greatly exasperated; they beat the officers with clubs, and
obliged them to fly to Castle William, at the entrance of Boston harbor, for
safety. They also burned the Collector's boat, and committed other acts of violence. These transactions gave the royal governor an excuse he wished for to introduce British troops into the city. This measure excited the indignation of the
people to the highest pitch, and almost daily quarrels took place in the streets between the citizens and the soldiers, which finally resulted in the death of three
Americans, in March, 1770, by shots from the soldiers' muskets—an event known
as *The Boston Massacre.*

† In the terms of general pardon offered in 1775, John Hancock and Samuel
Adams were excluded, as arch rebels. The night preceding the battle of Lexing
ton, Hancock and Adams lodged together, in that village. An armed party was
sent by Governor Gage to arrest them, and they narrowly escaped, for as the soldiers entered one door, they went out through another.

governor, for reasons not easily divined, sanctioned his appointment, and received him into the Council.*

In 1774, the Provincial Congress of Massachustts unanimously elected Hancock their president. The same year he was chosen a delegate to the Continental Con gress; and was re-elected to the same station in 1775. When, during the summer of that year, Peyton Randolph left the presidential chair of that body, John Hancock was elected to the station,—a gift the most exalted, possessed by the American people. In that office he labored arduously, and filled that chair on the ever memorable Fourth of July, 1776. As President, he first signed the Declaration of Independence, and with his name alone, it first went forth to the world. His bold signature, the very index of his character has always excited the admiration of the beholder.

Mr. Hancock resigned the office of President of Congress in 1777, owing to the precarious state of his health† and the calls of his private affairs, which had been necessarily much neglected, and he hoped to pass the remainder of his life in the retirement of the domestic circle.‡ But that pleasure he was not suffered long to enjoy by his fellow citizens. He was elected a member of the Convention of Massachusetts to form a Constitution for the government of that commonwealth. Therein he was assiduous as usual, and upon him was first conferred the honor, under the instrument of their adoption, of being Governor of the Province, or State. He was the first who

* Governor Bernard had tried in vain to win him from the cause of the patriots, In 1767, before his election to the council, he had complimented him wiih a Lieutenant's commission, but Hancock, seeing clearly the nefarious design which it but half concealed, tore up the commission in the presence of the people.

† The ravages of the gout, which was a disease hereditary in his family, made serious inroads upon his general health while engaged in the arduous services of public station.

† He was married in 1773, to Miss Quincy, a relative of the Adams' by whom he had only one son. He died in youth, and consequently Hancock oft no heir to perpetuate his name.

had this dignity conferred by the voluntary suffrages of the people. He held the office five consecutive years, by annual election. For two years he declined the honor, but again accepted it, and held the office until his death, in 1793.

He was governor during that period of confusion which followed the adoption of the Federal Constitution, and its final ratification by the several States, and his wisdom and firmness proved greatly salutary in restraining those lawless acts which a spirit of disaffection toward the general government had engendered in New England, and particularly in Massachusetts and New Hampshire.* Of course his character and motives were aspersed by the interested, but when the agitation ceased, and the clouds passed away, his virtues and exalted character, shone with a purer lustre than before.

He was elected a member of the Convention of Massachusetts to act on the adoption of the Federal Constitution, and was chosen president of that body; but sickness prevented his attendance until the last week of the session. He voted for the adoption of the constitution, and by his influence, a majority voted with him.

Mr. Hancock continued a popular leader until the time of his death, and no one could successfully contend with him for office. He was not a man of extraordinary talent, but was possessed of that tact and peculiar genius fitted for the era in which he lived. He was beloved by all his cotemporaries, and posterity venerates his name, as a benefactor of his country. He died on the eighth of October, 1793, in the fifty-fifth year of his age.

* The theory prevailed to a great extent in New England, that all having contributed to defend the national property, they all had an equal right to possession, thus regarding the matter in the light of personal and individual interest, rather than in that of general welfare. Popular excitements occurred. In Exeter, in New Hampshire, a mob made prisoners of the members of the General Assembly. In Massachusetts, an insurrectionary movement, led by Daniel Shay, (known as Shay's insurrection) was so extensive, that four thousand militia were called act to suppress it

John Adams

O LOFTIER genius nor purer patriot wore the Senatorial robe during the struggle for Independence, than John Adams. He was born at Braintree (now Quincy), in Massachusetts, on the thirtieth of October, 1735, and was a direct lineal descendant, in the fourth generation, from Henry Adams, who fled from the persecutions in England during the reign of the first Charles.* His maternal ancestor was

---

* Archbishop Laud, the spiritual adviser of Charles I. (influenced no doubt by the Roman Catholic Queen, Henrietta Maria) took especial pains to enforce the strictest observance of the Liturgy of the established Church of England in the

John Alden, a passenger in the May-Flower, and thus the subject of our memoir inherited from both parental ancestors, the title of a Son of Liberty, which was subsequently given to him and others.* His primary education was derived in a school at Braintree, and there he passed through a preparatory course of instruction for Harvard University, whence he graduated at the age of twenty years.*a*

a 1753.

Having chosen the law as a profession, he entered upon the study of it with an eminent barrister in Worcester, by the name of Putnam. There he had the advantage of sound legal instruction, and through Mr. Putnam he became acquainted with many distinguished public men, among whom was Mr. Gridley, the Attorney-General. Their first interview awakened sentiments of mutual regard, and young Adams was allowed the free use of Mr. Gridley's extensive library, a privilege of great value in those days. It was a rich treasure thrown open to him, and its value was soon apparent in the expansion of his general knowledge. He was admitted to the bar in 1758, and commenced practice in Braintree.

At an early period, young Adams' mind was turned to the contemplation of the general politics of his country, and the atmosphere of liberal principles in which he had been born and nurtured, gave a patriotic bias to his judgment and feelings. He watched narrowly the movements of the British government toward the American colonies, and was ever out-spoken in his condemnation of its oppressive acts.

He was admitted as a barrister in 1761, and as his professional business increased, and his acquaintance among

Church of Scotland, and also in the Puritan Churches. Those individuals and congregations who would not conform to these requirements were severely dealt with, and these persecutions drove a great many to the western world, where they might worship God according to the dictates of their own consciences.

* This name was given to the American patriots by Colonel Barre, on the floor the British House of Commons.

distinguished politicians extended, he became more publicly active, until in 1765, when the Stamp Act had raised a perfect hurricane in America, he wrote and published his "Essay on the Canon and Feudal Law." This production at once placed him high in the popular esteem; and the same year he was associated with James Otis and others, to demand, in the presence of the royal governor, that the courts should dispense with the use of *stamped paper* in the administration of justice.

In 1766 Mr. Adams married Abigail Smith, the amiable daughter of a pious clergyman of Braintree, and soon afterward he removed to Boston. There he was actively associated with Hancock, Otis, and others, in the various measures in favor of the liberties of the people, and was very energetic in endeavors to have the military removed from the town. Governor Bernard endeavored to bribe him to silence, at least, by offers of lucrative offices, but they were all rejected with disdain.

When, after the *Boston Massacre,* Captain Preston and his men were arraigned for murder, Mr. Adams was applied to, to act as counsel in their defence. Popular favor on one side, and the demands of justice and humanity on the other, were the horns of the dilemma between which Mr. Adams was placed by the application. But he was not long in choosing. He accepted the invitation —he defended the prisoners successfully—Captain Preston was acquitted, and, notwithstanding the tremendous excitement that existed against the soldiers, the patriotism of Mr. Adams was too far above suspicion to make this defence of the enemy a cause for withdrawing from him the confidence which the people reposed in him. His friends applauded him for the act, and the people were satisfied, as was evident by their choosing him, that same year,[a] a representative in the provincial Assem-   [a] 1770
bly.

Mr. Adams became very obnoxious to both Governors Bernard and Hutchinson. He was elected to a seat in the Executive council, but the latter erased his name. He was again elected when Governor Gage assumed authority, and he too erased his name. These things increased his popularity. Soon after the accession of Gage the Assembly at Salem* adopted a proposition for a general Congress, and elected five delegates thereto in spite of the efforts of the governor to prevent it. John Adams was one of those delegates, and took his seat in the first Continental Congress, convened in Philadelphia on the fifth of September, 1774 He was again elected a delegate in 1775, and through his influence, George Washington of Virginia was elected Commander-in-Chief of all the forces of the United Colonies.†

On the sixth of May, 1776, Mr. Adams introduced a motion in Congress "that the colonies should form governments *independent of the Crown.*" This motion was equivalent to a declaration of independence, and when, a month afterward, Richard Henry Lee introduced a motion more explicit to declare the colonies free and independent, Mr. Adams was one of its warmest advocates. He was appointed one of the committee to draft the Declaration of Independence,‡ and he placed his signature to that document on the second of August, 1776. After the battle of Long Island he was appointed by

---

* The "Boston Port Bill," so called, which was adopted by Parliament, closed the port of Boston, removed the Custom House therefrom, its law Courts, &c., and the meeting of the Provincial Assembly was called at Salem. This oppressive act was intended to have a two-fold effect—to punish the Bostonians for the tea riot, and awe them into submission to the royal will. But it effected neither.

† Mr. Adams did not nominate Washington, as has been frequently stated. He gave notice that he should "propose a member of Congress from Virginia," which was understood to be Washington. but, for reasons that do not appear upon the journals, he was nominated by Thomas Johnson, of Maryland.

† The committee consisted of Dr. Franklin, Thomas Jefferson, John Adams Roger Sherman. and Robert R. Livingston

Congress, with Dr. Franklin and Edward Rutledge, to meet Lord Howe in conference upon Staten Island, concerning the pacification of the colonies. According to his prediction, the mission failed. Notwithstanding his great labors in Congress,* he was appointed a member of the council of Massachusetts, while on a visit home, in 1776, the duties of which he faithfully fulfilled.

In 1777 Mr. Adams was appointed a special commissioner to the Court of France, whither Dr. Franklin had previously gone. Finding the subject of his mission fully attended to by Franklin, Adams returned home in 1779. He was immediately called to the duty of forming a Constitution for his native State. While in the discharge of his duty in convention, Congress appointed him a minister to Great Britain, to negotiate a treaty of peace and commerce with that government. He left Boston in the French frigate, La Sensible, in October, 1777, and after a long passage, landed at Ferrol, in Spain, whence he journeyed by land to Paris.[b] He found England *a* Feb. indisposed for peace, if American Independence 1780. was to be the *sine qua non*, and was about to return home, when he received from Congress the appointment of commissioner to Holland, to negotiate a treaty of amity and commerce with the States General. The confidence of Congress in him was unlimited, and he was intrusted at one time, with the execution of no less than six missions, each of a different character.* In 1781 he was associated with Franklin, Jay, and Laurens as a commissioner to conclude treaties of peace with the European powers.

* During the remainder of the year 1776, and until December, 1777 (when he was sent on a foreign mission) he was a member of ninety different committees and chairman of twenty-five!

† These commissions empowered him, 1st: to negotiate a peace with Grea, Britain; 2d, to make a treaty of commerce with Great Britain; 3d, the same with the States General; 4th, the same with the Prince of Orange; 5th, to pledge the faith of the United States to the Armed Neutrality; 6th, to negotiate a loan of ten millions of dollars.

In 1782 he assisted in negotiating a commercial treaty
with Great Britain, and was the first of the American
Commissioners who signed the definitive treaty of peace
_b_ Sept. 3, with that power.[b] In 1784, Mr. Adams returned
1783.   to Paris, and in January, 1785, he was appointed Minister for the United States at the Court of
Great Britain. That post he honorably occupied until
1788, when he resigned the office and returned home.

While Mr. Adams was absent, the Federal Constitution
was adopted, and it received his hearty approval. He
was placed upon the ticket with Washington for Vice
President, at the first election under the new Constitution, and was elected to that office. He was re-elected to
the same office in 1792, and in 1796, he was chosen to
succeed Washington in the Presidential Chair. In 1801
he retired from public life.

In 1816 he was placed on the democratic ticket as
presidential elector. In 1818 he lost his wife, with whom
he had lived fifty-two years in uninterrupted conjugal felicity. In 1824 he was chosen a member of the convention of Massachusetts to revise the Constitution, and was
chosen president of that body, which honor he declined
on account of his great age. In 1825 he had the felicity
of seeing his son elevated to the presidency of the United
States. In the spring of 1826 his physical powers rapidly declined, and on the fourth of July of that year,* he
expired, in the ninety-second year of his age. On the
very same day, and at nearly the same hour, his fellow-
committee-man in drawing up the Declaration of Inde
pendence, Thomas Jefferson, also died. It was the fiftieth anniversary of that glorious act, and the coincidence
made a deep impression upon the public mind.

* On the morning of the fourth it was evident he could not last many hours
On being asked for a toast for the day, the last words he ever uttered—words
if glorious import—fell from his lips Independence for ever!"

Saml Adams

 HIS distinguished patriot of the Revolution, was born in Boston, Massachusetts, on the twenty-second of September, 1722. He was of pilgrim ancestors, and had been taught the principles of Freedom, from his infancy. His father was a man of considerable wealth, and was for a long series of years a member of the Massachusetts Assembly, under the Colonial Government. He resolved to give Samuel a liberal education. After a preparatory course of study, he entered him at Harvard College, Cambridge, where, in

1740, at the age of eighteen years, he took his degree of A. B. He was uncommonly sedate, and very assiduous in the pursuit of knowledge, while a pupil.

His father destined him for the profession of the law, but this design was relinquished, and he was placed as an apprentice with Thomas Cushing, a distinguished merchant of Boston, and afterward an active patriot. His mind, however, seemed fixed on political subjects,* and the mercantile profession presented few charms for him. His father furnished him with ample capital to commence business as a merchant, but his distaste for the profession, and the diversion of his mind from its demands, by politics, soon caused him serious embarrassments, and he became almost a bankrupt.

When Samuel was twenty-five years old, his father died, and the cares of the family and estate devolved on him, as the oldest son. Yet his mind was constantly active in watching the movements of the British government, and he spent a great deal of his time in talking and writing in favor of the resistance of the Colonies to the oppressions of the crown and its ministers. He took a firm and decided stand against the Stamp Act and its antecedent kindred schemes to tax the Colonies. As early as 1763, he boldly expressed his sentiments relative to the rights and privileges of the Colonists; and in some instructions which he drew up for the guidance of the Boston members of the General Assembly, in that year, he denied the right of Parliament to tax the Colonies without their consent—denied the supremacy of Parliament, and suggested a union of all the Colonies, as necessary for their protection against British aggressions. It is asserted that this was the first public expression of

---

* In connection with genial companions, he wrote a series of political essays for a newspaper called the "Independent Advertiser." They incurred the nickname, by way of derision, of the "Whipping Club"

such sentiments in America, and that they were the spark that kindled the flame upon the altar of Freedom here.

In 1765, Mr. Adams was chosen a representative for Boston, in the General Assembly, and became early distinguished in that body, for his intelligence and activity. He became a leader of the opposition to the royal governor, and treated with disdain the efforts made to silence him,* although the offers proffered would have placed him in affluent circumstances. He was chosen Clerk of the House of Representatives; and he originated the "Massachusetts Circular," which proposed a Colonial Congress to be held in New York, and which was held there in 1766.

During the excitement of the *Boston Massacre*, he was among the most active; and chiefly through his influence, and the boldness with which he demanded the removal of the troops from Boston, was that object effected.

Mr. Adams, and Richard Henry Lee, of Virginia, almost simultaneously proposed the system of Committees of Correspondence,[a] which proved such a mighty engine in bringing about a union of sentiment among the several Colonies previous to the bursting out of the Revolution. This, and other bold movements on his part, caused him to be selected as an object of ministerial vengeance, and when Governor Gage issued his proclamation, offering pardon to all who would return to their allegiance, Samuel Adams and John Hancock were alone excepted. This greatly increased their popu-

[a] 1772

---

* When the governor was asked why Mr. Adams had not been silenced by office, he replied, that "such is the obstinacy and inflexible disposition of the man, that he can never be conciliated by any office or gift whatever." And when, in 1774, Governor Gage, by authority of ministers, sent Colonel Fenton to offer Adams a magnificent consideration if he would cease his hostility to government, or menace him with all the evils of attainder, that inflexible patriot gave this remarkable answer to Fenton: "I trust I have long since made my peace with the King of kings. No personal consideration shall induce me to abandon the righteous cause of my country. Tell Governor Gage, it is the advice of Samuel Adams to him, no longer to insult the feelings af an exasperated people."

larity, and fired the people with indignation. Adams was among those who secretly matured the plan of proposing a general Congress, and appointing delegates thereto, in spite of the opposition of Governor Gage.* Mr. Adams was one of the five delegates appointed, and he took his seat in that body on the fifth of September, 1774. He continued an active member of Congress until 1781,† and was among those who joyfully affixed their signatures to the Declaration of Independence.

Mr. Adams retired from Congress in 1781, but not from public life. He was a member of the Convention to form a Constitution for Massachusetts, and was on the committee who drafted it. He was successively a member of the Senate of that Commonwealth, its President, Lieutenant-governor, and finally Governor. To the latter office he was annually elected, until the imfirmities of age obliged him to retire from active life. He expired on the third day of October, 1803, in the eighty-second year of his age.

* The governor hearing of the movement in the General Assembly, then sit ting at Salem, sent his Secretary to dissolve them, but he found the door locked, and the key was safely lodged in Samuel Adams' pocket.

† The journals of Congress during that time show his name upon almost every important committee of that body. And probably no man did more toward bringing about the American Revolution, and in effecting the independence of the Colonies, than Samuel Adams. He was the first to assert boldly those political truths upon which rested the whole superstructure of our confederacy—he was the first to act in support of those truths—and when, in the General Council of States, independence was proposed, and the timid faltered, and the over-prudent hesitated, the voice of Samuel Adams was ever loudest in denunciations of a temporizing policy, and also in the utterance of strong encouragement to the faint-hearted. "I should advise," said he, on one occasion, "persisting in our struggle for liberty, though it were revealed from Heaven that nine hundred and ninety-nine were to perish, and only one of a thousand were to survive and retain his liberty! One such freeman must possess more virtue, and enjoy more happiness, than a thousand slaves; and let him propagate his like, and transmit to them what he hath so nobly preserved."

Rob' Treat Paine

THIS distinguished patriot was born in Boston, Massachusetts, in 1731. His father was a clergyman, and his mother was the daughter of the Reverend Mr. Treat, of Barnstable county. His maternal grandfather was Governor Treat, of Connecticut, Thus connected with the honored and pious, the early moral education of Mr. Paine was salutary in the extreme, and he enjoyed the advantage of instruction in letters, from Mr. Lovell, who was also the tutor of John Adams and John Hancock.

Young Paine entered Harvard College at the age of fourteen years, and graduated with the usual honors. For a time after leaving college he taught school. He then made a voyage to Europe, and on his return he prepared himself for the ministry, in which calling he was engaged as chaplain in a military expedition to the north in 1755. Not long afterward he relinquished theology, studied law with Mr. Pratt, (afterward Chief Justice of New York,) and was admitted to practice at the bar.

He commenced law practice in Boston, but after a short residence there he removed to Taunton, where he became a powerful opponent and rival of the celebrated Timothy Ruggles.* He early espoused the popular cause, but so prudently did he conduct himself, that he retained the full confidence of the Governor. In 1768, after Governor Bernard had dissolved the Assembly,† and a provincial Convention was called, Mr. Paine attended as a delegate from Taunton. In 1770, when the trial of Captain Preston and his men occurred, the District Attorney being sick, Mr. Paine was chosen his substitute, and he conducted the case with great ability. He was chairman of the Committee of Vigilance in Taunton, in 1773. The same, and the following year (1774) he was elected a member of the Provincial Assembly, and was one of the commissioners appointed to conduct the proceedings in the case of the impeachment of Chief Justice Oliver.‡

Mr. Paine was an advocate for a Continental Congress. He was a member of the Assembly, when, in spite of

* Timothy Ruggles was President of the Colonial, or "Stamp Act Congress," in 1765. He was opposed to some of its measures, and when the Revolution broke out, he took sides with the King and Parliament.

† The governor dissolved the Assembly, because with closed doors they adopted a circular to be sent to all the other colonies, inviting them to send delegates to a General Colonial Congress, to be held in New York.

‡ Justice Oliver was impeached on the ground that he received his salary directly from the crown, and not from the people of the province, and thus was made independent of them.

Governor Gage, it elected delegates to the General Congress, of whom Mr. Paine was one. He was elected a member of the Provincial Congress of Massachusetts, in the autumn of 1774, where he was very active. He was deputed by the General Congress, with two others, to visit the army of General Schuyler at the north for the purpose of observation. It was a delicate commission, but one which Mr. Paine and his colleagues performed with entire satisfaction. The same year, John Adams was appointed Chief Justice of the province of Massachusetts, and Mr. Paine was chosen a side judge. He declined the honor, and in December was again elected to the General Congress, where he was very active, and on the fourth of July, the following year, (1776,) he voted for the Declaration of Independence, and was one of its signers. In 1777, he was chosen Attorney-General of Massachusetts, by a unanimous vote of the council and representatives, which office he held until 1790, when he was appointed a Judge of the Supreme Court. He was a member of the Convention that framed the Constitution of his native State, which was adopted in 1780. For fourteen years, he discharged his duties as judge, and in 1804, he left the bench, on account of the approaching infirmities of age. He died in 1814, at the age of eighty-four years. His long and active life was devoted to the public service, and his labors were duly appreciated by a grateful people.

Elbridge Gerry

LBRIDGE GERRY was born in Mar-
blehead, Massachusetts, on the sev-
enteeth of July, 1744. His father
was a merchant in extensive business, and he resolved to give his son
an excellent education. When his
preparatory studies were concluded,
he entered Harvard College, and graduated with the title
of A. B., in 1762. He soon after entered into commercial pursuits, amassed a handsome fortune, and by his intelligence and good character, won for himself the esteem

40

of his fellow-citizens. He watched with much solicitude the rapid strides which the oppressions of Great Britain were making in this country, and having expressed his sentiments fearlessly, his townsmen elected him a member of the General Court of the province, in 1773. There he soon became a bold and energetic leader, ingenious in devising plans of operation, and judicious and zealous in their execution. He was connected with John Adams and others in carrying through resolutions that had been offered in the General Court, having reference to the removal of Governor Hutchinson from office.*

Mr. Gerry was active in all the leading political movements in Massachusetts until the War broke out. He was a member of the first Provincial Congress of that province, and was one of the most efficient opposers of Governor Gage. He was a member of the Provincial Congress at the time of the battle of Bunker Hill. The night preceding that event, he and General Warren slept together in the same bed. They bade each other an affectionate farewell in the morning, and separated, Mr. Gerry to go to the Congress, sitting at Watertown, and Dr. Warren to be slain upon the battle-field.

In January, 1776, Mr. Gerry was elected a delegate to the Continental Congress. There his commercial knowl edge proved very useful, and he was put upon many com

---

* Governor Hutchinson, who had already become very obnoxious to the people, became insupportable after the discovery of some letters of his to the English Ministers, recommending the enforcement of rigid measures against the Americans, and the curtailment of the privileges of the colonies. These letters were put into the hands of Dr. Franklin, then Colonial Agent in England, and by him they were immediately transmitted to the General Court of Massachusetts. They produced great excitement, and a petition was adopted and forwarded to the Ministers, asking for the removal of Hutchinson. It was on the occasion of Dr. Franklin's presenting this petition to the English Privy Council, thas he was so violently assailed by Wedderburn, the Solicitor General. Franklin made no reply, but on going to his lodgings, he took off his suit of clothes, and declared that he would never put it on again until he had signed "America's Independence, and England's degradation." When, nearly ten years afterward, he signed the treaty of peace between the two governments, he again put on that suit of clothes.

mittees where such knowledge was needed. He had been previously elected a Judge of the Court of Admiralty, but preferring a more active life, he declined the appointment. He was a warm supporter of the resolution of Mr. Lee, declaring the United States free and independent, and he signed his name to the Declaration on the second of August, following its adoption.

In 1777, Mr. Gerry was appointed one of a committee to visit Washington at his headquarters at Valley Forge. The report of that committee had a great effect upon Congress, and caused more efficient measures to be taken for the relief and support of the army. In 1780 he retired from Congress to look after his private affairs, but was re-elected in 1783. In all the financial operations of that body, Mr. Gerry was indefatigably engaged. In 1785 he again retired from Congress, and fixed his residence in Cambridge.

Mr. Gerry was a member of the Convention of Massachusetts which adopted the present Constitution of the United States. He was so opposed to many of its leading features that he never subscribed his name to it, but when it became the fundamental law of the land, he did all in his power to carry out its provisions. He was twice elected a member of the House of Representatives of the United States under it, and after faithful services he again retired to private life.

Mr. Adams, when President, knew and appreciated the abilities of Mr. Gerry, and he called him forth from his domestic quiet, by nominating him one of three envoys to the Court of France.[a] The joint mission was

a 1798.

not received by that government, but Mr. Gerry was accepted, and this made him very unpopular with a large portion of the people of the United States.* Mr.

* The joint commission consisted of Elbridge Gerry, Charles Cotesworth Pinckney, and John Marshall, (the late Chief Justice.) The relations between the two

Gerry considered it his duty to remain, and did so. After his return from France, the Republicans* of Massachusetts nominated him for Governor. He failed the first time, but was elected the next.[a] In 1811, he was nominated for, and elected, Vice President of the United States.

[a] 1810.

While in the performance of his duties at the seat of government, he was suddenly seized with illness, and died on the twenty-third of November, 1814, at the age of seventy years. He was entombed in the Congressional Cemetery, and a handsome monument was erected to his memory by Congress.

governments were not at all friendly at that time, and Messrs. Pinckney and Marshall were ordered to leave the country. Mr. Gerry was desired to remain. The Federalists of the United States, who were opposed to the French, strongly condemned Mr. Gerry for remaining, while the Republicans, who sympathized with the French Revolutionists, applauded him. At that time, however, the Federalists were a powerful majority, and hence Mr. Gerry disappointed the great majority of his intelligent countrymen. The feeling of hostility toward France, at that time, was very acrimonious on the part of the Federalists; for the meddling impertinence of Citizen Genet, the French Minister, had roused a feeling of indignation against him and his people that can hardly be conceived at the present day. Hoping to gain for his country the aid and friendly alliance of the United States, he sought to involve us in a war with Great Britain; and he actually issued *Letters of Marque* to vessels of war, to sail from American ports and cruise against the English and other enemies of France. This brought forth from President Washington a proclamation of neutrality. Genet then threatened to appeal to the people of the United States. Finally, Washington became tired of his officiousness, and demanded and obtained his recall. But he left behind him a violence of party spirit between the Federalists and Republicans, unknown until then.

* At this time party spirit continued to run very high between the Federalists and Republicans, the two great political parties of the Union. The more *progressive* policy of the republican party, was so consonant with the spirit of the people, that it increased rapidly from its birth, and finally became so powerful, that Federalism, as a watchword of party, and in truth the Federal party became extinct in 1819.

TEPHEN HOPKINS was born in the town of Providence,* Rhode Island, on the seventh of March, 1707. His mother was the daughter of one of the first Baptist ministers of Providence. The opportunities for acquiring education at the time of Mr. Hopkins' childhood, were rare, but his vigorous intellect, in a measure, became a substitute for these opportunities, and

* The town was subsequently divided, and the portion in which Mr. Hopkins was born is now called Scituate.

44

he became self-taught, in the truest sense of the word, Mr. Hopkins was a farmer until 1731, when he removed to Providence and engaged in mercantile business. In 1732, he was chosen a representative for Scituate in the General Assembly, and was re-chosen annually until 1738. He was again elected in 1741, and was chosen Speaker of the House of Representatives. From that time until 1751, he was almost every year a member and speaker of the assembly. That year he was chosen Chief Justice of the Colony.

Mr. Hopkins was a delegate to the Colonial Convention held in Albany in 1754.* He was elected Governor of the Colony in 1756, and continued in that office almost the whole time, until 1767. During the French war, Governor Hopkins was very active in promoting the enlistment of volunteers for the service, and when Montcalm seemed to be sweeping all before him at the north,† Hopkins raised a volunteer corps, and was placed at its head; but its services were not needed, and it was disbanded.

He early opposed the oppressive acts of Great Britain, and in 1774, he held three offices of great responsibility, which were conferred upon him by the patriots—namely: Chief Justice of Rhode Island, representative in the Provincial Assembly, and delegate to the Continental Congress. At this time he introduced a bill into the Assembly of Rhode Island, to prevent the importation of slaves; and to show that his professions, on this point,

---

* This Convention was called for the purpose of concerting measures to oppose more effectually the encroachments of the French settlers, and to hold a conference with the Six Nations of Indians. Dr. Franklin was a member of that Convention and submitted a plan of union for the colonies which contained all the essential features of our present Constitution.

† Montcalm was commander of the French force that invaded the northern portions of New York, in 1757. He was driven back to Canada, and was attacked by the English, under Wolfe, upon the Plains of Abraham, at Quebec, where he was mortally wounded.

were sincere, he manumitted all of those which belonged to himself.

In 1775, he was a member of the Committee of Public Safety, of Rhode Island, and was again elected a delegate to the General Congress. He was re-elected in 1776, and had the privilege of signing the glorious Declaration of Independence.* He was chosen a delegate to the General Congress for the last time, in 1778, and was one of the committee who drafted the ARTICLES OF CONFEDERATION for the government of the States. Notwithstanding he was then over seventy years, he was exceedingly active, and was almost constantly a member of some important committee. He died on the nineteenth of July, 1785, in the seventy-eighth year of his age.†

The life of Mr. Hopkins exhibits a fine example of the rewards of honest, persevering industry. Although his early education was limited, yet he became a distinguished mathematician,‡ and filled almost every public station in the gift of the people, with singular ability. He was a sincere and consistent Christian, and the impress of his profession was upon all his deeds.

---

* The signature of Mr. Hopkins is remarkable, and appears as if written by one greatly agitated by fear. But fear was no part of Mr. Hopkins' character. The cause of the tremulous appearance of his signature, was a bodily infirmity, called "shaking palsy," with which he had been afflicted many years, and which obliged him to employ an amanuensis to do his writing.

† He was twice married; the first time to Sarah Scott, a member of the Society of Friends (whose meetings Mr. Hopkins was a regular attendant upon through life), in 1726; she died in 1753. In 1755 he married a widow, named Anna Smith.

‡ He rendered great assistance to other scientific men, in observing the transit of Venus which occurred in June, 1769. He was one of the prime movers in forming a public library in Providence, in 1750. He was a member of the American Philosophical Society, and was the projector and patron of the Free Schools in Providence.

William Ellery (signature)

 ILLIAM ELLERY, the colleague of Stephen Hopkins, of Rhode Island, in the Continental Congress of 1776, was born at Newport, on the twenty-second of December, 1727. His father paid particular attention to his early education, and when qualified, he placed him in Harvard College, where he was distinguished as a close student, particularly of the Greek and Latin languages.

He graduated in 1747, at the age of twenty years, with the most honorable commendations of the faculty. He chose the profession of the law as a business, and when he had completed his studies, he commenced practice in Newport, then one of the most flourishing places in the British American Colonies.

For twenty years, Mr. Ellery practised law successfully, and acquired a fortune. When the troubles of the Revolution began, and, as an active patriot,* he enjoyed the entire confidence of his fellow-citizens—he was called into public service. Rhode Island, although not so much oppressed as Massachusetts and New York at the beginning, was all alive with sympathy; and the burning of the Gaspee,† in Providence Bay, in 1772, and the formal withdrawal of the allegiance of the Province from the British crown, by an act of her legislature, as early as May, 1776, are an evidence of the deep, patriotic feeling with which her people were imbued. She promptly responded to the call for a general Congress, and Stephen Hopkins and William Ellery were sent as delegates.

Mr. Ellery was a very active member of Congress, and on the second day of August, 1776, he signed the Declaration of Independence.

In 1778, Mr. Ellery left Congress for a few weeks, and repaired to Rhode Island, to assist in a plan to drive the British from the island.‡ It proved abortive, and many

* The active patriotism of Mr. Ellery excited the ire of the British, and when Newport was taken possession of by the enemy they burnt Mr. Ellery's house, and nearly all of his property was destroyed.

† The Gaspee, a British armed vessel, was, iu 1772, placed in Providence harbor for the purpose of enforcing the revenue laws. The commander, like another Gesler, demanded the obeisance of every merchant vessel that entered, by lowering their flags. One vessel refused, and the Gaspee gave chase. The merchantman so manœuvred as to cause the Gaspee to run aground, and before she could be got off, she was boarded at night by the crews of several boats from Providence, and all on board were made prisoners and sent ashore; after which the vessel was set on fire, and burned to the water's edge.

‡ Rhode Island was taken possession of by the British in 1778, on the very day

of the inhabitants were reduced to great distress. Mr. Ellery exerted his influence in Congress, successfully, for their relief. About the same time he was one of a committee to arrange some difficulties in which Silas Deane, and other commissioners sent to Europe, were involved.* He was also a member of another committee to arrange some difficult matters connected with the admiralty courts. In each capacity, his wisdom and sound discretion made him successful.

In 1782, Mr. Ellery was designated by Congress to communicate to Major General Greene, their estimate of his valuable services in the Southern Campaigns. In 1784, he was one of a committee to whom the definitive Treaty of Peace with Great Britain was referred. At this time, he was a judge of the Supreme Court of Rhode Island. In connection with Rufus King, of New York, he made strong efforts in 1785, to have slavery in the United States abolished. After the new constitution was adopted in 1788, and the new government was put in operation, he was appointed collector for the port of Newport, which office he retained until his death, which occurred on the fifteenth of February, 1820, in the seventy-third year of his age.† As a patriot and a Christian, his name will ever be revered.

that Washington crossed the Delaware. The British troops were commanded by Sir Henry Clinton, and the squadron by Sir Peter Parker. Rhode Island remained in possession of the enemy three years.

* Thomas Paine and others charged Mr. Deane with the crime of prostituting his official station to selfish purposes. The investigation proved the falsity of the charge, yet it was apparent that Mr. Deane, in his zeal, had been very injudicious, and therefore he was not again sent abroad.

† He was always fond of reading the classics in the Latin and Greek languages. He perused *Tully's Offices* on the morning of his death, while sitting in a chair. He soon afterward commenced reading *Cicero,* when his attendants discovered that he was dead, but still holding the book in his hand.

4

Roger Sherman

NE of the most remarkable men of the Revolution, was Roger Sherman. He was born in Newton, Massachusetts, on the nineteenth of April, 1721. In 1723, the family moved to Stonington, in that State, where they lived until the death of Roger's father, in 1741. Roger was then only nineteen years of age, and the whole care and support of a large family devolved on him. He had been apprenticed to a

50

shoemaker, but he now took charge of the small farm his father left. In 1744, they sold the farm, and moved to New Milford, in Connecticut, where an elder brother, who was married, resided. Roger performed the journey on foot, carrying his shoemaker's tools with him, and for some time he worked industriously at his trade there.

Mr. Sherman's early education was exceedingly limited, but with a naturally strong and active mind, he acquired a large stock of knowledge from books, during his apprenticeship.* Not long after he settled in New Milford, he formed a partnership with his brother in a mercantile business, but all the while was very studious. He turned his attention to the study of law, during his leisure hours; and so proficient did he become in legal knowledge, that he was admitted to the bar, in December, 1754.†

In 1755, Mr. Sherman was elected a representative of New Milford, in the General Assembly of Connecticut, and the same year he was appointed a Justice of the Peace. After practising law about five years, he was appointed Judge of the County Court for Litchfield county.[a] He moved to New Haven in 1761, when the same appointments were conferred [a] May, 1759. upon him, and in addition, he was chosen treasurer of Yale College, from which institution, in 1765, he received the honorary degree of A. M. In 1766, he was elected to the senate, or upper house of the legislature of Connecticut; and it was at this time that the passage of the Stamp Act was bringing the politicians of America to a decided stand in relation to the repeated aggressions of

---

* It is said that while at work on his bench, he had a book so placed that he could read when it was not necessary for his eyes to be upon his work He thus acquired a good knowledge of mathematics, and he made astronomical calculations for an almanac that was published in New York, when he was only twenty seven years old.

† Mr. Sherman had no instructor or guide in the study of the law, neither had he any books but such as he borrowed, yet he became one of the most profound jurists of his day.

Great Britain. Roger Sherman fearlessly took part with the patriots, and was a leader among them in Connecticut, until the war broke out. He was elected a delegate from Connecticut to the Continental Congress, in 1774, and was present at the opening on the fifth of September. He was one of the most active members of that body, and was appointed one of the Committee to prepare a draft of a Declaration of Independence; a document to which he affixed his signature with hearty good will, after it was adopted by Congress.

Although his duties in Congress, during the war, were almost incessant, yet he was at the same time a member of the Committee of Safety of Connecticut. In 1783, he was appointed, with Judge Law, of New London, to revise the statutes of the State, in which service he showed great ability. He was a delegate from Connecticut in the Convention in 1787 that framed the present Constitution of the United States; and he was a member of the State Convention of Connecticut which assembled to act upon the ratification of that instrument. For two years after the organization of the government under the Constitution, he was a member of the United States House of Representatives. He was then promoted to the Senate, which office he filled at the time of his death, which took place on the twenty-third of July, 1793, in the seventy-third year of his age. He had previously been elected mayor of New Haven, when it was invested with city powers and privileges, and that office he held until the time of his death.*

* He was twice married, the first time to Elizabeth Hartwell, of Stoughton, and the second time to Rebecca Prescott, of Danvers. By his first wife he had seven children, and eight by his last.

Sam^{ll} Huntington

T H E family of SAMUEL HUNTINGTON was among the earlier settlers of Connecticut, who located at Saybrook. He was born at Windham, Connecticut, on the second of July, 1732. His father was an industrious farmer, and the only education he was able to allow his son, was that to be derived from the common schools in his neighborhood. Samuel was very studious, and the active energies of his mind surmounted many obstacles that stood in the way of intellectual advancement

53

He acquired a tolerable knowledge of the Latin language, and at the age of twenty-two years he commenced
the study of law. Like Sherman he was obliged to pursue it with borrowed books and, without, an instructor.
He succeeded, however, in mastering its difficulties, and
in obtaining a good practice in his native town, before he
was thirty years of age. At the age of twenty-
a 1760.
eight*a* he removed to Norwich, where he had
greater scope for his talents.

Mr. Huntington was elected to the General Assembly
of Connecticut in 1764, and the next year he was chosen
a member of the Council. In the various duties of official
station he always maintained the entire confidence and
esteem of his constituents.

He was appointed Associate Judge of the Superior
Court in 1774; and in 1775 he was appointed one of the
delegates from Connecticut, in the General Congress.
The following year he had the glorious privilege of voting
for, and signing, the Declaration of Independence. He
was a member of the Congress nearly five consecutive
years, and was esteemed as one of the most active men
there. His integrity and patriotism were stern and unbending; and so conspicuous became his sound judgment and untiring industry, that in 1779 he was appointed
President of Congress, then the highest office in the nation.* At length his impaired health demanded his resignation of the office,*b* yet it was with great re-
b 1781.
luctance that Congress consented to dispense
with his services.

On his return to Connecticut he resumed the duties of
the offices he held in the Council and on the Bench, both
of which had been continued while he was in Congress.
He again took his scat in Congress in 1783, but left it

* He was appointed to succeed John Jay, who was sent as Minister Plenipoter-
tiary to Spain, to negotiate a treaty of amity and commerce with that nation.

again in November of that year, and retired to his family. Soon after his return, he was appointed Chief Justice of the Superior Court of his State.*a* In 1785 he was elected Lieutenant Governor, and was promoted to the Chief Magistracy in 1786, which office he held until his death, which occurred at Norwich, on the fifth day of January, 1796, in the sixty-fourth year of his age.

a 1784.

Governor Huntington lived the life of the irreproachable and sincere Christian, and those who knew him most intimately, loved him the most affectionately. He was a thoughtful man, and talked but little—the expression of his mind and heart was put forth in his actions. He seemed to have a natural timidity, or modesty, which some mistook for the reserve of haughtiness, yet with those with whom he was familiar, he was free and winning in his manners. Investigation was a prominent characteristic of his mind, and when this faculty led him to a conclusion, it was difficult to turn him from the path of his determination. Hence as a devoted Christian and a true patriot, he never swerved from duty, or looked back after he had placed his hand to the work. The cultivation of this faculty of *decision* we would earnestly recommend to youth, for it is the strong arm that will lead them safely through many difficulties, and win for them that sentiment of *reliance* in the minds of others, which is so essential in securing their esteem and confidence. It was this most important faculty which constituted the chief aid to Samuel Huntington in his progress from the humble calling of a ploughboy, to the acme of official station, where true greatness was essential, and to which none but the truly good could aspire.

Wm Williams

ALES was the place of nativity of the ancestors of WILLIAM WILLIAMS. They emigrated to America in 1630, and settled at Roxbury, in Massachusetts. His grandfather and father were both ministers of the gospel, and the latter was for more than half a century pastor of a Congregational Society, in Lebanon, Connecticut where the subject of this brief sketch was born on the eighteenth

of April, 1731. He entered Harvard College at the age of sixteen years, and at twenty he graduated with honorable distinction.[a] He then com- *a* 1751.
menced theological studies with his father; but the agita-
tions of the French War attracted his attention, and in
1754 he accompanied his relative, Colonel Ephraim Williams, in an expedition to Lake George, during which the
Colonel was killed. He returned home with settled feelings of dislike toward the British officers in general, who
haughtily regarded the colonists as inferior men, and de-
serving of but little of their sympathy.

He abandoned the study of theology, and entered into
mercantile pursuits in Lebanon. At the age of twenty-
five he was chosen town clerk, which office he held nearly
half a century. He was soon afterward chosen a member of the Connecticut Assembly, and forty-five years he
held a seat there. He was always present at its sessions,
except when attending to his duties in the General Congress, to which body he was elected a delegate in 1775.
He was an ardent supporter of the proposition for Independence, and cheerfully signed the glorious Declaration
when it was adopted.

When, in 1781, Arnold, the traitor, made an attack
upon New London,* Williams, who held the office of colonel of militia, hearing of the event, mounted his horse
and rode twenty-three miles in three hours, but arrived
only in time to see the town wrapped in flames.

Mr. Williams was a member of the State Convention
of Connecticut, that decided upon the adoption of the

* Norwich, fourteen miles from New London, was the native place of Arnold.
On the expedition alluded to, he first attacked Fort Trumbull, at the entrance of
the Tharnes, on which New London stands. The garrison evacuated the Fort at his
approach, and, in imitation of the infamous Governor Tryon, of New York, he
proceeded to lay the town in ashes. Arnold's men were chiefly tories. On the
same day, Fort Grisweld, opposite, was attacked, and after its surrender, all but
about forty of the garrison were butehered in cold blood.

present Constitution of the United States, and voted in favor of it. His constituents were opposed to the measure, but it was not long before they discovered their error, and applauded his firmness.

In 1804, Colonel Williams declined a re-election to the Connecticut Assembly, and withdrew entirely from public life. His life and fortune* were both devoted to his country, and he went into domestic retirement with the love and veneration of his countrymen attending him. He was married in 1772, to Mary, the daughter of Governor Trumbull, of Connecticut, and the excellences of his character greatly endeared him to his family. In 1810 he lost his eldest son. This event powerfully shocked his already infirm constitution, and he never recovered from it. His health gradually declined; and a short time before his death he was overcome with stupor. Having laid perfectly silent for four days, he suddenly called, with a clear voice, upon his departed son to attend his dying father to the world of spirits, and then expired. He died on the second day of August, 1811, at the patriarchal age of eighty-one years.

---

* Many instances are related of the personal sacrifices of Mr. Williams for his country's good. At the commencement of the war he devoted himself to his country's service, and for that purpose he closed his mercantile business, so as not to have any embarrassments. In 1779, when the people had lost all confidence in the final redemption of the continental paper money, and it could not procure supplies for the army, Mr. Williams generously exchanged two thousand dollars in specie for it, and of course lost nearly the whole amount. The Count De Rochambeau, with a French army, arrived at Newport during the summer of 1780, as allies to the Americans, but they did not enter into the service until the next year, and remained encamped in New England. Louzon one of Rochambeau's cavalry officers, encamped during the winter with his legion at Lebanon, and Mr. Wliliams, in order to allow the officers comfortable quarters, relinquished his own house to them, and moved his family to another. Such was the self denial of the Fathers of our Republic, and such the noble examples they present.

Oliver Wolcott

HE name of Wolcott, appeared among the early settlers of Connecticut, and from that day to this, it has been distinguished for living scions, honored for their talents in legislation or literature.* The subject of this brief sketch was born in Windsor, Connecticut, on the twenty-sixth of No-

* The English ancestor, Henry Wolcott, first settled in Dorchester, Massachusetts, after his arrival in 1630. In 1636, he, with a few associates, moved to Windsor, in Connecticut, and formed a settlement there. He was among the first who organized the government of Connecticut, and obtained a sharter from King Charles II.

59

vember, 1726.* He entered Yale College at the age
of seventeen years, and graduated with the usual honors
in 1747. He received a Captain's commission in the
Army the same year, and raising a company immediately,
he marched to the northern frontier to confront the
French and Indians. The Treaty of Aix-la-Chapelle,†
terminated hostilities, and he returned home. He arose
regularly from Captain to Major-General.

Young Wolcott now turned his attention to the study
of medicine, under his distinguished uncle, Dr. Alexander
Wolcott; but when he had just completed his studies, he
was appointed sheriff of the newly-organized county of
Litchfield.

In 1774, he was elected a member of the council of
his native State; and he was annually re-elected until
1786, notwithstanding he was, during that time, a delegate to the Continental Congress, Chief Justice of Litchfield county, and also a Judge of Probate of that district.

Mr. Wolcott was appointed by the first General Congress, one of the Commissioners of Indian Affairs for
the northern department; and he performed excellent
service to the American cause by his influence in bringing
about an amicable settlement of the controversy between
Connecticut and Pennsylvania, concerning the Wyoming
settlement: a controversy at one time threatening serious
effects upon the confederacy.

Toward the close of 1775, Mr. Wolcott was elected a
delegate to the second General Congress, and took his
seat in January, 1776. He took a prominent part in the
debates respecting the independence of the Colonies, and
voted for, and signed that glorious Declaration of Ameri-

* His father was a distinguished man, having been Major General, Judge, Lieutenant Governor, and finally Governor of the State of Connecticut.

† This was a treaty of Peace between Great Britain, France, Spain, Holland
Hungary, and Ganoa. It was concluded in 1748.

can disenthralment. Soon after this act was consummated, he returned home, and was immediately appointed by Governor Trumbull and the Council of Safety; to the command of a detachment of Connecticut militia (con sisting of fourteen regiments) destined for the defence of New York. After the battle of Long Island, he returned to Connecticut, and in November of that year, he resumed his seat in Congress, and was in that body when they fled to Baltimore at the approach of the British toward Philadelphia, at the close of 1776.

During the latter part of the summer of 1776, he was actively engaged in the recruiting service, and after sending General Putnam (then on the Hudson river), several thousands of volunteers, he took command of a body of recruits, and joined General Gates at Saratoga. He aided in the capture of Burgoyne and his army in October, 1777, and soon afterward, he again took his seat in Congress, then assembled at York, in Pennsylvania,* where he continued until July, 1778. In the summer of 1779, he took command of a division of Connecticut militia, and undertook, with success, the defence of the southwestern sea coast of that State, then invaded by a British army.† From that time, until 1783, he was alternately engaged in civil and military duties in his native State, and occasionally held a seat in Congress. In 1784 and 1785, he was an

---

* During the Revolution, Congress held its sessions in Philadelphia, but was obliged on several occasions to retreat to a more secure position. At the close of 1776 it adjourned to Baltimore, when it was expected Cornwallis would attack Philadelphia, after his successful pursuit of Washington across New Jersey. Again, when Howe marched upon Philadelphia, in September, 1777, Congress adjourned to Lancaster, and three days afterward to York, where its sessions were held during the winter the American army were encamped at Valley Forge.

† The British force was led by Governor Tryon, of New York. It was a plundering and desolating expedition. Fairfield and Norwalk were laid in ashes and the most cruel atrocities were inflicted upon the inhabitants, without regard to sex or condition. Houses were rifled, the persons of the females abused, and many of them fled half naked to the woods and swamps in the vicinity of their deserted homes.

active Indian Agent, and was one of the Commissioners who prescribed terms of peace to the Six Nations of Indians who inhabited Western New York.*

In 1786, General Wolcott was elected Lieutenant Governor of Connecticut, and was re-elected every year, until 1796, when he was chosen Governor of the State. He was re-elected to that office in 1797, and held the station at the time of his death, which event occurred on the first day of December, of that year, in the seventy-second year of his age. As a patriot and statesman, a christian and a man, Governor Wolcott presented a bright example; for inflexibility, virtue, piety and integrity, were his prominent characteristics.

* The five Indian Tribes, the *Mohawks*, the *Oncidas*, the *Onondagas*, the *Cayagas*, and the *Senecas*, had formed a confederation long before they were discovered by the whites. It is not known when this confederation was first formed, but when the New England settlers penetrated westward, they found this powerful confederacy strongly united, and at war with nearly all of the surrounding tribes. The *Onondagas* seemed to be the chief nation of the confederacy, for with them the great council fire was specially deposited, and it was kept always burning. Their undisputed domain included nearly the whole of the present area of the State of New York. They subdued the *Hurons* and *Algonquins* in 1657; and in 1665 they almost annihilated the *Eries*. In 1672 they destroyed the *Andastes*, and in 1701 they penetrated as far South as the Cape Fear River, spreading terror and desolation in their path. They warred with the *Cherokees*, and almost exterminated the *Catawbas;* and when, in 1744, they ceded some of their lands to Virginia, they reserved the privilege of a war-path through the ceded domain. In 1714 they were joined by the *Tuscaporas* of North Carolina, and since that time the confederacy has been known as the *Six Nations*. They uniformly took sides with the British, and entered into a compact with them against the French, in 1754. In the war of the Revolution, "The whole confederacy," says De Witt Clinton, "except a little more than half the *Oneidas,* took up arms against us. They hung like the scythe of Death upon the rear of our settlements, and their deeds are inscribed, with the scalping knife, and the tomahawk, in characters of blood, on the fields of Wyoming, and Cherry Valley, and on the banks of the Mohawk."

ALES, in Great Britain, was the father-
land of WILLIAM FLOYD. His grandfather came hither from that country
in the year 1680, and settled at Se-
tauket, on Long Island. He was dis-
tinguished for his wealth, and possessed great influence
among his brother agriculturists.

The subject of this memoir was born on the seventeenth
day of December, 1734. His wealthy father gave him

every opportunity for requiring useful knowledge. He had scarcely closed his studies, before the death of his father called him to the supervision of the estate, and he performed his duties with admirable skill and fidelity. His various excellences of character, united with a pleasing address, made him very popular; and having espoused the republican cause in opposition to the oppressions of the mother country, he was soon called into active public life.

Mr. Floyd was elected a delegate from New York to the first Continental Congress, in 1774, and was one of the most active members of that body. He had previously been appointed commander of the militia of Suffolk County; and early in 1775, after his return from Congress, learning that a naval force threatened an invasion of the Island, and that troops were actually debarking, he placed himself at the head of a division, marched toward the point of intended debarkation, and awed the invaders into a retreat to their ships. He was again returned to the General Congress, in 1775, and the numerous committees of which he was a member, attest his great activity. He ably supported the resolutions of Mr. Lee, and cheerfully voted for and signed the Declaration of Independence.

While attending faithfully to his public duties in Congress, he suffered greatly in the destruction of his property and the exile of his family from their home. After the battle of Long Island, in August, 1776, and the retreat of the American army across to York Island, his fine estate was exposed to the rude uses of the British soldiery, and his family were obliged to seek shelter and protection in Connecticut. His mansion was the rendezvous for a party of cavalry, his cattle and sheep were used as provision for the British army, and for seven years he derived not a dollar of income from his property. Yet he abated not a jot in his zeal for the cause, and labored on hopefully, alternately in Congress and in the Legislature of New York.* Through his skilful management, in connection with one or two others, the State of New York was placed, in 1779, in a very prosperous financial condition, at a time when it seemed to be on the verge of bankruptcy. The depreciation of the continental paper money† had produced alarm and distress wide-spread, and the speculations in bread-stuffs threatened a famine; yet William Floyd and his associates ably steered the bark of state clear of the Scylla and Charybdis.

On account of impaired health, General Floyd asked for and obtained leave of absence from Congress, in April, 1779, and in May he returned to New York. He was at once called to his seat in the Senate, and placed upon the most important of those committees of that body, who were charged with the delicate relations with the General Congress.

In 1780 he was again elected to Congress, and he continued a member of that body until 1783, when peace was declared. He then returned joyfully, with his family, to the home from which they had been exiled for seven years, and now miserably dilapidated. He declined a re-election to Congress, but served in the Legislature of his State until 1778, when, after the newly adopted Con-

---

* After the Declaration of Independence was adopted, the States organized governments of their own. General Floyd was elected a Senator in the first legislative body that convened in New York, after the organization of the new government, and was a most useful member in getting the new machinery into successful operation.

† The amount of paper money issued by Congress before the close of 1779, amounted to about two hundred millions of dollars. The consequence of such an issue was a well grounded suspicion that the bills would not ultimately be redeemed; and this suspicion, at the close of 1779, became so much of a certainty, that the notes depreciated to about one fourth of their value. An attempt was made by Congress to make these bills a legal tender at their nominal value, but the measure was soon perceived to be mischievous, and they were left to their fate.

5

stitution was ratified, he was elected a member of the first Congress that convened under that charter in the city of New York, in 1789. He declined an election the second time, and retired from public life.

In 1784 General Floyd purchased some wild land upon the Mohawk, and when he retired to private life, he commenced the clearing up and cultivation of those lands So productive was the soil, and so attractive was the beauty of that country, that in 1803 he moved thither, although then sixty-nine years old. He directed his attention to the cultivation of his domain, and in a few years, the "wilderness blossomed as the rose," and productive farms spread out on every side.

In 1800 he was chosen a Presidential Elector; and in 1801 he was a delegate in the Convention that revised the Constitution of the State of New York. He was subsequently chosen a member of the State Senate, and was several times a Presidential Elector. The last time that he served in that capacity was a year before his death, which occurred on the fourth day of August, 1821, when he was eighty-seven years of age. Mr. Floyd had always enjoyed robust health, and he retained his mental faculties in their wonted vigor, until the last. His life was a long and active one; and, as a thorough business man, his services proved of great public utility during the stormy times of the Revolution, and the no less tempestuous and dangerous period when our government was settling down upon its present steadfast basis. Decision was a leading feature in his character, and trifling obstacles never thwarted his purposes when his opinion and determination were fixed. And let it be remembered that this noble characteristic, *decision,* was a prominent one with all of that sacred band who signed the charter of our emanci pation, and that without this, men cannot be truly great or eminently useful.

Phil. Livingston

MONG the brilliant names of the Revolutionary era, none shine with a
purer lustre, than that of Livingston.
Like the name of Wolcott, from the
early settlement of our country to
the present time, that name has been
conspicuously honored, and has held a large place in the
public esteem.

Philip Livingston was descended from a Scotch minister of the gospel, of exemplary character, who, in 1663

67

left Scotland and settled in Rotterdam, where he died
His son Robert (the father of the subject of this brief
sketch) soon after his father's decease, emigrated to America, and, under the patroon privileges, obtained a grant
of a large tract of land upon the Hudson River, (now in
Columbia County,) ever since known as Livingston's Manor. He had three sons, of whom Philip was the oldest,
and who became, on the death of his, father, heir to the
manor.*

Philip was born at Albany, on the fifteenth of January,
1716. After completing a preparative course of study,
he entered Yale College, at New Haven, where he graduated with distinguished honor in 1737. He at once
turned his attention to commercial pursuits, and engaged
in an extensive and lucrative business in the city of New
York, where his integrity and upright dealings won for
him the profound respect of the whole community.

Mr. Livingston first entered upon public life in 1754,
when he was elected an Alderman of the East Ward of
the city of New York.† For nine consecutive years he
was re-elected to that office, and always gave entire satis
faction to his constituents.

When Sir Charles Hardy, the Governor of the Colony
of New York, was appointed a rear-admiral in the British navy, the government devolved upon the lieutenant,
Delancey, who at once, on the resignation of the governor, dissolved the General Assembly and ordered new
elections. These contests at that time were very warm,
but the superior education and influence of the Livingston
family secured for Philip and his brother Robert, seats

---

* His two brothers, Robert and Gilbert, were influential men at that time. The
former was the father of Chancellor Livingston, who administered the inaugural
oath to Washington, in 1789; and the latter was the father of the late Rev. John
Livingston, D. D., President of Rutger's College, New Jersey.

† At that time the city contained only about eleven thousand inhabitants and
what is now called Wall street, was quite at the north part of the town

in that body. It was a period of much agitation and alarm,* and required sterling men in legislative councils. Mr. Livingston soon became a leader among his colleagues, and by his superior wisdom and sagacity, measures were set on foot which resulted in the capture from the French of several important frontier fortresses, and finally the subjugation of Canada.

For some time previous to the Revolution, nearly all the Colonies had resident agents in England. The celebrated Edmund Burke was the agent for New York when the war broke out, and it is believed that his enlightened views of American affairs, as manifested in his brilliant speeches in Parliament in defence of the Colonies, were derived from his long continued and constant correspondence with Philip Livingston, who was appointed one of a committee of the New York Assembly, for that purpose. He was very influential in that body, and early took a decided stand against the unrighteous acts of Great Britain. He was the associate and leader of such men as General Schuyler, Pierre Van Cortlandt, Charles De Witt, &c., and so long as whig principles had the ascendency in the Provincial Assembly, he was the Speaker of the House. When toryism took possession of the province he left the Assembly. In 1774, Mr. Livingston was elected a delegate to the first Continental Congress, and was on the committee that prepared the address to the people of Great Britain; an address replete with bold and original thoughts, perspicuous propositions and convincing arguments.† The next year the Assembly presented such an array of tories, that it was impossible to

---

* The "French and Indian War," which was the American division of the famous 'Seven Years' War," was then at its height, and the brilliant successes of Montcalm upon the northern frontier of New York, gave the people great uneasiness.

† William Pitt, the great Earl of Chatham, speaking of that first Congress, and the addressee put forth by it, said: "I must declare and aver, that in all my reading and study—and it has been my favorite study—I have read Thucydides, and

elect delegates to the second Congress. Accordingly several counties* of New York sent delegates to a Provin-

a April, 1775. cial Convention,*a* which body elected delegates to the General Congress, among whom was Philip Livingston, and his nephew, Robert R. Livingston. These delegates were vested with power to act as circumstances should require.

Mr. Livingston warmly supported the proposition for Independence, and he voted for and signed the Declaration thereof. This was sanctioned by the Provincial Assembly of New York.

When the State governments were formed, after the Declaration of Independence, Mr. Livingston was elected a member of the first Senate of New York, which met on the tenth of September, 1777. In 1778, although his health was in a precarious state, occasioned by dropsy in the chest, he obeyed the calls of duty, and took his seat in Congress, to which he had been elected. He had a presentiment that he should not return to his family, and accordingly on his departure, he bade his family and

b May, 1778. friends a final adieu.*b* On the twelfth of June following, his presentiment became a reality, and his disease then suddenly terminated his life, at the age of sixty-two years. No relative was near to smooth his dying pillow, except his son Henry, a lad of eighteen years, then residing in the family of General Washington.

Mr. Livingston was zealous in the promotion of every enterprise conducive to the public welfare,† and has left behind him a name and fame that kings might covet.

have studied and admired the master spirits of the world—that for solidity of reasoning, force of sagacity, and wisdom of conclusion, under such a complica-

General Congress at Philadelphia.
* New York, Albany, Dutchess, Ulster, Orange, Westchester, Kings, and Suffolk,
† He was one of the founders of the New York Society Library: also, of the Chamber of Commerce; and was an active promoter of the establishment of King's (now Columbia) College.

Faan: Lewis

RANCIS LEWIS was born in Wales, in the town of Landaff, in the year 1713. His father was an Episcopal clergyman, his mother was a clergyman's daughter, and Francis was their only child. He was left an orphan when only about five years old, and was taken under the care and protection of a maiden aunt, who watched over him with the appa rent solicitude of a mother. He received a portion of his education in Scotland with another relative, and became proficient not only in his native tongue (the ancient Briton) but in the Gaelic language, then mostly used in Scotland. His uncle, Dean of St. Paul's, in London, afterward sent him to Westminster, where he obtained a good education.

After leaving school he served an apprenticeship with a London merchant. At the age of twenty-one he became the possessor of some money, which he invested in merchandise and sailed for New York, in which city he formed a business partnership. Leaving a portion of his goods with his associate, he proceeded to Philadelphia with the balance, where he resided for two years. He then returned to New York, and made that his place of business and abode. He married the sister of Mr. Annesly, his partner, by whom he had seven children.

Mr. Lewis' business increased, and his commercial pursuits kept him much of his time in Europe until the opening of the "French and Indian War," in which he was an active partisan. He was the aid of Colonel Mercer, at Oswego, when that Fort was captured by Montcalm in August, 1757. Mercer was slain, and Lewis was carried, with other prisoners, to Canada.* Thence he was sent to France, and was finally exchanged. At the close of the war, five thousand acres of land were given him by the British government as a compensation for his services.

Mr. Lewis was distinguished during the administration of Mr. Pitt, for his republican views, and he was elected one of the delegates for New York in the Colonial Congress of 1765. When the Stamp Act became a law, and non-importation agreements nearly ruined commerce, he

---

* Fourteen hundred men were made prisoners; and thirty-four pieces of cannon, a large quantity of ammunition and stores, and several vessels in the harbor, fell into the hands of the French. The Fort was demolished, and was never rebuilt

etired from business to his country residence on Long Island.

In 1775 he was elected a delegate to the General Congress, by the convention of deputies from several counlies of New York.* He was also elected a delegate for 1776, by the Provincial Assembly, and he became one of the signers of the Declaration of Independence, in August of that year. He was a member of Congress until 1778, and was always an active committee man in that body.

Mr. Lewis was a shining mark for the resentment of the British and tories,† and while the former possessed Long Island, they not only destroyed his property, but had the brutality to confine his wife in a close prison for several months, without a bed or a change of raiment, whereby her constitution was ruined, and she died two years afterward.

Having attained to the ripe age of nearly ninety years, and honored by the universal reverence and esteem of his countrymen, Mr. Lewis departed this life on the thirtieth of December, 1803.

---

* See Life of Philip Livingston.

† The party names of *Whig* and *Tory* were first used in New York, in 1774, and rapidly spread throughout the Colonies. The name of Tory was applied to the American royalists, and the name of Whig was assumed by the patriots. The origin of these names, (which were copied from the English) is obscure. According to Bishop Burnett, the term *whig* has the following derivation: The people of the southwestern parts of Scotland, not raising sufficient grain to last them through the winter, generally went to Leith to purchase the superabundance of the North. From the word *Whiggam*, which they used in driving their horses, they were called *Whiggamores*, and, abbreviated, *Whigs*. On one of these occasions, news having reached Leith of the defeat of Duke Hamilton, the ministers invited the Whiggamores to march against Edinburgh, and they went at their head, preaching and praying all the way. The Marquis of Argyle, with a force, opposed and dispersed them. This was called the *"Whiggamore inroad,"* and ever after that, *all that opposed the Court,* came in contempt to be called *Whigs.* The English adopted the name. The origin of the word Tory is not clear. It was first used in Ireland in the time of Charles II. Sir Richard Phillips defines the two parties thus: "Those are *Whigs* who would curb the power of the Crown; those are *Tories* who would curb the power of the people."

Lewis Morris

ᴇᴡɪs Mᴏʀʀɪs was born at Morrisania, Westchester county, New York, in the year 1726. Being the eldest son, he inherited his father's manorial estate,* which placed him in affluent circumstances. At the age of sixteen years he entered Yale College, and under the presidency of the excellent Rev. Mr. Clapp, he received his

* At that time, the English primogeniture law prevailed in America, and over after the Revolution, Virginia and some other States retained it.

education. He graduated with the usual honors at twenty, and returned to the supervision of his large estate.

Mr. Morris was a handsome man; and his personal appearance, connected with a strong intellect and great wealth, made him popular throughout the Colony. When Great Britain oppressed her children here, he hardly felt the unkind hand, yet his sympathy for others was aroused, and he was among the first to risk ease, reputation and fortune, by coalescing with the patriots of Massachusetts and Virginia. His clear perception saw the end from the beginning, and those delusive hopes which the repeal of obnoxious acts held forth, had no power over Lewis Morris. Neither could they influence his patriotism, for he was a stranger to a vacillating, temporizing spirit. He refused office under the Colonial government, for his domestic case and comfort were paramount to the ephemeral enjoyments of place. Hence, when he forsook his quiet hearth, and engaged in the party strife of the Revolution, hazarding fortune and friends, no sinister motive could be alleged for his actions, and all regarded him as a patriot without selfish alloy. He looked upon war with the mother-country as inevitable, and so boldly expressed his opinion upon these subjects, that the still rather lukewarm Colony of New York did not think proper to send him as a delegate to the General Congress of 1774.* But the feelings of the people changed, and in April, 1775, Mr. Lewis was elected a member of the second Congress that met in May following.

During the summer of 1775, Mr. Morris was sent on a mission of pacification to the Indians on the western fron-

---

* New York was so peculiarly exposed to the attacks of the British fleet under Lord Howe, then hovering upon our coast, and so forewarned by the miseries of Boston, and the destruction of Falmouth, that. toryism, or loyalty to the crown, found ample nutriment among the people of the city. It was in the city of New York that the names of whig and tory were first applied to the distinctive political parties.

tier. He was again elected to Congress in 1776, and when the question of Independence came up, he boldly advocated the measure, although it seemed in opposition to all his worldly interests.* Like the others of the New York delegation, he was embarrassed by the timidity of the Provincial Congress, which seemed unwilling to sanction a measure so widely antipodent to all reconciliation with Great Britain. But the conviction of the final necessity of such a step, had been long fixed in the mind of Mr. Morris, and he did not for a moment falter. He voted for and signed the Declaration of Independence, and his State afterward thanked him for his patriotic firmness.† His family seemed to be imbued with his own sentiments, for three of his sons entered the army, served with distinction, and received the approbation of Congress.

Mr. Morris relinquished his seat in the National Council in 1777, but he was constantly employed in public service in his native State, either in its legislature, or as a military commander,‡ until the adoption of the Constitution. When peace was restored, he returned to his scathed and almost ruined estate, where he spent the remainder of his days in agricultural pursuits, amid that happy quiet of domestic life, which an active and virtuous career promotes. He died in January, 1798, in the seventy-second year of his age. His funeral presented a large concourse of citizens, who truly mourned his loss; and the military honors due to his rank of Major General, were rendered, when his body was committed to the family vault.

* He plainly foresaw what actually happened—his house ruined, his farm wasted, his forest of a thousand acres despoiled, his cattle carried off, and his family driven into exile by the invading foe.

† When, in 1777, Mr. Morris left Congress and was succeeded by his brother, Gouverneur Morris, the Convention that elected the latter, adopted a vote of thanks to him for his "long and faithful services rendered to the Colony of New York."

‡ He was raised to the rank of Major General, but his active services were not brought into much requisition.

Richd Stockton

HE great grandfather of RICHARD STOCKTON came from England some time between 1660 and 1670, and first settled upon Long Island, in the Colony of New York. Thence he went into New Jersey, and with his ample means purchased a fine tract of land near Princeton, where, with a few others, he commenced a settlement.

The subject of this memoir was born upon the Stockton manor, on the first of October, 1730. He pursued his studies, preparatory to a collegiate course, at an academy in Maryland, and after two years thus spent, he entered New Jersey college, then located at Newark. He graduated in 1748, and was placed as a student of law, under the Hon. David Ogden, of Newark.

Mr. Stockton was admitted to the bar in 1754, and rose so rapidly in his profession, that in 1763 he received the degree of sergeant-at-law,* a high distinction in the English Courts, and then recognised in the American Colonies.

In June, 1766, Mr. Stockton embarked for London, and during the fifteen months he remained in England he was treated with flattering distinction by the most eminent men in the realm. While there he was not unmindful of his *alma mater,* and he obtained considerable patronage for New Jersey College. His services were afterward gratefully acknowledged by that institution.

At the time Mr. Stockton was in England, American affairs had assumed so much importance, that partisan feeling had sprung up there, and as a consequence, the opinions of so distinguished an American were sought for. By invitation, Mr. Stockton spent a week at the country seat of the Marquis of Rockingham,† and on his making a tour to Edinburgh, he was entertained by the Earl of Leven and other noblemen. At Edinburgh he was re-

---

* *Sergeant-at-Law* —(*serviens ad legem*)—is the highest degree taken in England in the common law. They are sometimes called sergeants of the *coif,* from the lawn coif they wear on their heads, under their caps, when they are created.— *Treasury of Knowledge.*

† The Marquis of Rockingham was an honorable and liberal statesman. He was elevated to the premiership of England in 1766, as successor of Grenville, the author of the Stamp Act. Edmund Burke, and men of like character were called into his cabinet, and the Americans had some hopes of justice under his administration. But his cabinet was soon dissolved, and he was succeeded by Lord North, author of the Tea Act and kindred measures.

ceived by the Lord Provost, in the name of the citizens, and by a unanimous vote, the freedom of the city was conferred upon him. During his stay there he visited Doctor Witherspoon, at Paisley, who afterward became a resident in the Colonies, and a signer of the instrument declaring their emancipation from British rule.*

Improvement in his profession being his chief object in visiting Great Britain, Mr. Stockton was a constant attendant upon the higher courts when in London, and often visited the theatre to witness the eloquence of Garrick. He returned home in September, 1767, and was escorted to his residence by the people, by whom he was greatly beloved.

In 1768, Mr. Stockton was chosen a member of the royal executive council of New Jersey, and in 1774 he was placed upon the bench of the Supreme Court of that Province. Having been honored by the personal regard of the King, and possessing an ample fortune, it would have seemed natural for him to have remained loyal; but, like Lewis Morris, his principles could not be governed by self-interest, and he espoused the cause of the patriots. The Provincial Congress of New Jersey elected him a delegate to the General Congress in 1776, and he took his seat in time to take part in the debate upon the proposition for Independence. At first, he seemed doubtful of the expediency of an immediate Declaration of Independence, but after hearing the sentiments of nearly all, and the conclusive arguments of John Adams, he voted in favor of the measure, and cheerfully signed the Declaration.

In September of that year, Mr. Stockton received an equal number of votes with Mr. Livingston, for Governor

---

* Dr. Witherspoon had been appointed President of Nassau Hall College, at Princeton, a short time before the visit of Mr. Stockton, but declined its acceptance. It is supposed that the latter persuaded him to reconsider his decision for a short time after his return to America Dr. W. accepted the office.

of New Jersey, but for urgent reasons, his friends gave the election to his competitor. He was at once elected Chief Justice of the State, but he declined the honor, and was re-elected to the General Congress. He was an active and influential member, and with Mr. Clymer, was sent, during the autumn, on a delicate mission to visit the northern army under General Schuyler.* Soon after his return, he was obliged to hasten to his family to prevent their capture by the British army, then pursuing Washington and his little band across New Jersey.† He removed them to the house of a friend about thirty miles distant, but there he was captured by a party of refugees, who were guided to his retreat by a treacherous neighbor of his friend. He remained a prisoner for some time, and, on account of his position as one of the signers of the Declaration of Independence, he was treated with great severity.‡ The hardships he endured shattered his constitution,§ and when he found himself almost a beggar, through the vandalism of the British in destroying his estate, and by the depreciation of the continental paper currency, he was seized with a despondency from which he never recovered. A cancer in his neck also hurried him toward the grave, and he died on the twenty-eighth of February, 1781, in the fifty-first year of his age.

* From causes which seem never to have been fully explained, the army of the north was then in a wretched condition, and the object of the mission of Mr. Stockton and his colleagues, was to inquire into the causes and propose a remedy.

† After the success of Cornwallis in capturing Fort Washington, on York Island, Washington crossed the Hudson with the main army of Americans, and for three weeks he was closely pursued by the British General across New Jersey to Trenton, where the memorable crossing of the Delaware took place.

‡ He was first placed in the common jail at Amboy, and afterward he was carried to the old Provost prison in New York, which stood where the present Hall of Records, in the Park, now stands.

§ He suffered greatly from cold, and at one time he was kept twenty-four hours without a particle of food. Congress took up his cause, and threatened Lord Howe with retaliation upon British prisoners. This had its effect, and he was soon afterward exchanged.

Jns Witherspoon

OHN WITHERSPOON was born in the parish of Yester, near Edinburgh, Scotland, on the fifth of February, 1722. He was a lineal descendant of the great reformer John Knox. His father was a minister in the Scottish church, at Yester, and was greatly beloved. He took great pains to have the early education of his son based upon sound moral and religious principles, and early determined to fit him for the gospel ministry. His primary education was received

6

in a school at Haddington, and at the age of fourteen years he was placed in the University of Edinburgh. He was a very diligent student, and, to the delight of his father, his mind was specially directed toward sacred literature. He went through a regular theological course of study, and at the age of twenty-two years he graduated, a licensed preacher. He was requested to remain in Yester, as an assistant of his father, but he accepted a call at Beith, in the west of Scotland, where he labored faithfully for several years.*

From Beith he removed to Paisley, where he became widely known for his piety and learning. He was severally invited to take charge of a parish and flock, at Dublin, in Ireland; Dundee, in Scotland; and Rotterdam, in Holland; but he declined them all. In 1766 he was invited, by a unanimous vote of the trustees of New Jersey College, to become its president, but this, too, he declined, partly on account of the unwillingness of his wife to leave the land of her nativity. But being strongly urged by Richard Stockton (afterward his colleague in Congress, and fellow signer of the Declaration of Independence), then on a visit to that country, he accepted the appointment, and sailed for America. He arrived at Princeton with his family, in August, 1768, and on the seventeenth of that month he was inaugurated president of the College. His name and his exertions wrought a great change in the affairs of that institution, and from a low condition in its finances and other essential elements of prosperity, it soon rose to a proud eminence among the institutions of learning in America.†

* While he was stationed at Beith, the battle of Falkirk took place, between the forces of George the Second, and Prince Charles Stuart, during the commotion known as the Scotch rebellion, in 1745–6. Mr. Witherspoon and others went to witness the battle, which proved victorious to the rebels: and he, with several others were taken prisoners, and for some time confined in the castle of Doune.

† For a long time party feuds had retarded the healthy growth of the College, and its finances were in such a wretched condition that resuscitation seemed al-

When the British army invaded New Jersey, the College at Princeton was broken up, and the extensive knowledge of Dr. Witherspoon was called into play in a vastly different arena. He was called upon early in 1776, to assist in the formation of a new Constitution for New Jersey,* and his patriotic sentiments and sound judgment were there so conspicuous, that in June of that year, he was elected a delegate to the General Congress. He had already formed a decided opinion in favor of Independence, and he gave his support to the resolution declaring the States free forever.† On the second of August, 1776, he affixed his signature to the Declaration.

Doctor Witherspoon was a member of Congress from the period of his first election until 1782, except a part of the year 1780, and so strict was he in his attendance, that it was a very rare thing to find him absent. He was placed upon the most important committees, and intrusted with delicate commissions. He took a conspicuous part in both military and financial matters, and his colleagues were astonished at the versatility of his knowledge.

After the restoration of peace in 1783, Doctor Witherspoon withdrew from public life, except so far as his duties as a minister of the gospel brought him before his flock. He endeavored to resuscitate the prostrate institution over which he had presided. Although to his son-in-law, Vice President Smith, was intrusted the active du-

---

most hopeless. But the presence of Doctor Witherspoon silenced party dissensions, and awakened new confidence in the institution; and the province of New Jersey, which had hitherto withheld its fostering aid, now came forward and endowed professorships in it.

* After the abdication of the Colonial Governors, in 1774 and 1775, provisional governments were formed in the various States, and popular Constitutions were framed, by which they were severally governed under the old confederacy.

† He took his seat in Congress, on the twenty-ninth of June, 1776. On the first of July, when the subject of the Declaration of Independence was discussed, a distinguished member remarked, that "the people are not ripe for a Declaration of Independence." Doctor Witherspoon observed: "In my judgment, sir we are not only ripe, but rotting."

ties in the effort, yet it cannot be doubted that the name and influence of Doctor Witherspoon were chiefly instrumental in effecting the result which followed. After urgent solicitation, he consented to go to Great Britain and ask for pecuniary aid for the college. In this movement his own judgment could not concur, for he knew enough of human nature to believe that while political resentment was still so warm there against a people who had just cut asunder the bond of union with them, no enterprise could offer charms sufficient to overcome it. In this he was correct, for he collected barely enough to pay the expense of his voyage.

About two years before his death, he lost his eye-sight, yet his ministerial duties were not relinquished. Aided by the guiding hand of another, he would ascend the pulpit, and with all the fervor of his prime and vigor, break the Bread of Life to the eager listeners to his message.

As a theological writer, Doctor Witherspoon had few superiors, and as a statesman he held the first rank. In him were centred the social elements of an upright citizen, a fond parent,* a just tutor, and humble Christian; and when, on the tenth of November, 1794, at the age of nearly seventy-three years, his useful life closed, it was widely felt that a "great man had fallen in Israel."

* Doctor Witherspoon was twice married. By his first wife, a Scottish lady, he had three sons and two daughters. One of the latter (Frances) married Doctor David Ramsay, of South Carolina, one of the earliest historians of the American Revolution. She was a woman of extraordinary piety, and the memoirs of but few females have been more widely circulated and profitably read, than were hers, written by her husband.

RANCIS HOPKINSON was born of English
parents, at Philadelphia, in the year 1737
His mother was the daughter of the
Bishop of Worcester, and, like her husband, was well educated, and moved
in the polite circles of England. They
maintained the same standing in Philadelphia, and the
subject of this sketch had every advantage in early life
which social position could give him.

Francis was only fourteen years old when his father
died, and then the whole care of a large family of chil

85

dren devolved upon his mother, whose income was not
very ample. She imparted to Francis his primary education until he was fitted for the college of Philadelphia,
wherein he was placed. On leaving that institution, he
commenced the study of law, and was admitted to practice in 1765. He went to England the same year for the
purpose of visiting his relatives and improving his mind.
He returned in 1768, and was soon after married to Miss
Ann Borden, of Bordentown, New Jersey.

Mr. Hopkinson was a poet and a wit;* and a knowledge of his superior talents having reached the ears of
the British ministers, he was appointed to a lucrative office in the State of New Jersey, soon after his marriage.
This he held until his republican principles were too manifest, by both word and deed, for the minions of British
power here to mistake, and he was deprived of his
office. In the meanwhile, he had been growing rapidly
in the esteem of the people of New Jersey, and in 1776
he was elected by them a delegate to the General Congress. He supported there, by his vote, the Declaration
of Independence, and joyfully placed his signature to it.

Mr. Hopkinson held the office of Loan Commissioner
for a number of years; and on the death of his friend and
colleague in Congress, George Ross, he was appointed
Judge of Admiralty for the State of Pennsylvania. He
held that office until 1790, when President Washington,
properly appreciating his abilities, appointed him District
Judge of the same State, which office he filled with singular fidelity.

Mr. Hopkinson was one of those modest, quiet men,

* His pen was not distinguished for depth, but there was a genuine humor in
his productions, which made him widely popular. A majority of his poetical ef-
fusions were of an ephemeral nature, and were forgotten, in a degree, with the
occasion which called them forth; yet a few have been preserved, among which
may be mentioned *"The Battle of the Kegs,"* a ballad, or sort of epic, of inimi
table humor,

on whom the mantle of true genius so frequently falls. Although ardent in his patriotism and keenly alive to the events in the midst of which he was placed, yet he seldom engaged in debate; and his public life is not marked by those varied and striking features, so prominently displayed in the lives of many of his compatriots.

For several years Judge Hopkinson was afflicted with gout in the head, which finally caused a fit of apoplexy that terminated his life in two hours after the attack, in May, 1791. He was in the fifty-third year of his age. He left a widow and five children.

John Hart

NE of the most unbending patriots of the Revolution was JOHN HART, the New Jersey farmer. His father, Edward Hart, was also a thrifty farmer, and a loyal subject of his King. In 1759 he raised a volunteer corps, which he named "The Jersey Blues," and joined Wolfe at Quebec in time to see that hero fall, but the English victorious. He then retired to his farm, and ever afterward held a high place in the esteem and confidence of the people. The time of the birth of his son John is not on record, and but few incidents of his early life are known.*

---

* His contemporaries represent him as about sixty years of age when first elected to Congress. If so, he must have been born about the close of its reign of Queen Anne, 1714.

Mr. Hart pursued the avocation of his father, and was in quite independent circumstances when the Stamp Act and its train of evils attracted his attention, and aroused his sympathies for his oppressed countrymen in Boston, and elsewhere, where the heel of tyranny was planted. Although living in the secluded agricultural district of Hopewell, in Hunterdon county, yet he was fully conversant with the movements of public affairs at home and abroad, and he united with others in electing delegates to the Colonial Congress that convened in New York city, in 1765. From that time, until the opening scenes of the war, Mr. Hart was active in promoting the cause of freedom; and his fellow citizens manifested their appreciation of his services, by electing him a delegate to the first Continental Congress, in 1774. He was re-elected in 1775, but finding that his estate and family affairs needed his services, he resigned his seat, and for a time retired from public life. He was, however, elected a member of the Provincial Congress of New Jersey, and was Vice President of that body.

The talents of Mr. Hart were considered too valuable to the public, to remain in an inactive state, and in February, 1776, he was again elected a delegate to the General Congress. He was too deeply impressed with the paramount importance of his country's claims, to permit him to refuse the office; and he took his seat again in that body, and voted for and signed the Declaration of Independence.

Nothing would have seemed more inimical to Mr. Hart's private interests, than this act, which was the har binger of open hostilities, for his estate was peculiarly ex posed to the fury of the enemy. Nor was that fury with held when New Jersey was invaded by the British and their mercenary allies, the Hessians. The signers of the Declaration everywhere were marked for vengeance, and when the enemy made their conquering descent upon New Jersey,* Mr. Hart's estate was among the first to feel the effects of the desolating inroad.† The blight fell, not only upon his fortune, but upon his person, and he did not live to see the sunlight of Peace and Independence gladden the face of his country. He died in the year 1780 (the gloomiest period of the War of Independence), full of years and deserved honors.

* After the capture of Fort Washington, on York Island, in November, 1776, Lord Cornwallis crossed the Hudson at Dobb's Ferry, with six thousand men, and attacked Fort Lee opposite. To save themselves, the Americans were obliged to make a hasty retreat, leaving behind them their munitions of war and all their stores. The garrison joined the main army at Hackensack which for three weeks fled across the level country of New Jersey, before the pursuing enemy, at the end of which time a bare remnant of it was left. The troops dispirited by late reverses, left in large numbers as fast as their term of enlistment expired, and returned to their homes; and by the last of November the American army num bered scarcely three thousand troops, independent of a detachment left at White Plains, under General Lee. The country was so level that it afforded no strong position to fortify; indeed, so necessarily rapid had been the retreat, that no time was allowed for pause to erect defences. Newark, New Brunswick, Princeton, Trenton, and smaller places, successively fell into the hands of the enemy, and so hot was the pursuit, that the rear of the Americans was often in sight of the van of the British. On the eighth of December, Washington and his army crossed the Delaware in boats, and Cornwallis arrived at Trenton just in time to see the last boat reach the Pennsylvania shore.—"1776, *or the War of Independence,*" page 209.

† Mr. Hart's family, having timely warning of the approach of the enemy is pursuit of Washington, fled to a place of safety. His farm was ravaged, his tim ber destroyed, his cattle and stock butchered for the use of the British army, and he himself was hunted like a noxious beast, not daring to remain two nights under the same roof. And it was not until Washington's success in the battle of Trenton, that this dreadful state of himself and family was ended.

BRAHAM CLARK was born at Eliza
bethtown, in New Jersey, on the
fifteenth of February, 1726. He
was the only child of his parents,
and was brought up in the employment of his father, a farmer. He
was quite studious, but his early education was considerably neglected. In fact, being an only child, he was, as is

too frequently the case, petted, and allowed to follow the guide of his inclinations; and hence his education might be termed miscellaneous.

A slender constitution warned him that he could not pursue, successfully, the rough labor of a farm, and he turned his attention to the study of mathematics, and of law. He became a good practical surveyor; and though he never went through a course of legal study, yet he transacted a good deal of law business in Elizabethtown for a number of years, particularly in the drawing up of deeds, mortgages, and other legal papers. He acquired the universal esteem and confidence of the people, and received the enviable title of "Poor man's Counsellor."

Mr. Clark held several offices under the royal government, among which was that of sheriff of Essex county; and in all of them he exhibited great fidelity. But when the question of political freedom or slavery was presented to his mind, he did not for a moment hesitate in his choice, but boldly espoused the republican cause. He was placed upon the first committee of vigilance organized in New Jersey, and was distinguished for his watchfulness and untiring activity.

In 1776, Mr. Clark was elected a delegate to the Continental Congress, and having ample instruction from the Provincial Congress of New Jersey, he was not at all at a loss to know how to vote for his constituents, when the proposition of Independence was brought forth. He first look his seat in that body, in June, and he voted for and signed the Declaration of Independence, although, like the rest of his colleagues from New Jersey, he was thus jeoparding the safety of his property, and lives of himself and family.* He remained an active member of the Gen-

* Although Mr. Clark did not suffer in person and estate, like Mr. Stockton and Mr. Hart, yet his property was much reduced in value, by his necessary neglect of it. His two sons took up arms and were captured. They were for a time in

eral Congress until peace was proclaimed, in 1783, with
the exception of one term,

In 1788, Mr. Clark was again elected to the General Congress. In the interim he was a member of the State Legislature, and an active politician. He early perceived the
defects of the old confederation, and was one of the delegates elected by New Jersey to the Convention that framed
the present Constitution of the United States, in 1787.
He was, however, prevented from attending by ill health.
He was appointed one of the commissioners for settling
the accounts of New Jersey with the General Government, and ably did he discharge the arduous duty. He
was elected a member of the first Congress under the
present Federal Government, and continued an active
member of that body until near the close of his life.

When Congress adjourned, in June, 1794, Mr. Clark
retired from public life; and early in the autumn of that
year, he died of inflammation of the brain, (caused by a
coup de soliel, or "stroke of the sun,") in the sixty-ninth
year of his age. He was buried in the church-yard, at
Rahway, New Jersey.

Mr. Clark was a warm partisan, and his feelings of attachment or repulsion were very strong. He had witnessed so much of the cruelty and oppressions of Great
Britain, in her war upon the declared freedom of the
Colonies, that his feelings of hatred could not be soothed
by the treaty of peace, although he patriotically acquiesced
in whatever tended to his country's good. He therefore
took sides with France when questions concerning her
came up in Congress; and, early in 1794, he laid before
Congress a resolution for suspending all intercourse with
Great Britain, until every item of the treaty of peace should
be complied with. It was not sanctioned by Congress.

carcerated in the Jersey prison-ship, and suffered all the horrors of that confine
ment, until released by a final exchange of prisoners.

Rob't Morris

OBERT MORRIS, the distinguished patriot and financier of the Revolution, was born in Lancashire, England, in January, 1733. His father was a Liverpool merchant, extensively engaged in the American trade, and when Robert was but a small child, he left him in the care of his grandmother, came to this country, and settled at Oxford on the eastern shore of Chesapeake Bay. He finally sent for his family, and Robert was thirteen years old when he arrived. He was placed in a school at Philadelphia, but the defi ciencies of his teacher allowed him but slight advantage in the obtainment of knowledge.*

Young Morris was placed in the counting room of Mr. Charles Willing, one of the leading merchants of Philadelphia, when he was fifteen years old, and about the same time he became an orphan by the sudden death of his father.† He was greatly esteemed by Mr. Willing, who gave him every advantage his business afforded; and at the death of his master and friend, he was a finished merchant.‡

In 1754, Mr. Morris formed a mercantile business partnership with Mr. Thomas Willing. The firm soon became the most extensive importing-house in Philadelphia, and rapidly increased in wealth and standing. After the passage of the Stamp Act and the Tea Act, and non-importation agreements became general in the commercial cities of the colonies,§ Willing and Morris, notwithstanding the great loss of business it would occasion, not only cheerfully entered into the plan, but did all in their power to induce others to do likewise. But it was not until the tragedy at Lexington aroused the fiercest indignation of the colonists, and extinguished all hope of reconciliation, that Mr. Morris took an active part in public affairs.‖ That

---

* On being chid by his father for his tardiness in learning, he remarked: "Why, sir, I have learned all that he could teach me."

† A ship having arrived from Liverpool, consigned to Mr. Morris the elder, he invited several friends to an entertainment on board. When they retired, a salute was fired, and a wad from one of the guns hit Mr. Morris upon the arm. The wound was severe, mortified, and in a few days terminated his life.

‡ As an evidence of the general good conduct of Mr. Morris, it is related, that Mr. Willing, on his death-bed, said to him: "Robert, always continue to act as you have done."

§ One of the measures adopted by the Colonists to force Great Britain to do them justice, was that of American merchants everywhere agreeing not to import anything from the mother-country. This had a powerful effect upon Parliament (for in the lower House the mercantile interest was strongly represented) and led to the modification of several stringent measures. These agreements, of course, seriously affected merchants here, and therein their patriotism was made peculiarly manifest.

‖ It is said that Mr. Morris, and a number of others. members of the St.

event called him forth, and in November of the same year,[a] he was elected by the Legislature of Pennsylvania, a delegate to the General Con- a 1775. gress. His business talents were at once appreciated in that body, and he was placed upon the "secret committee,"* and also a committee to devise ways and means for providing a naval armament. In the spring of 1776 Congress chose him a special commissioner to negotiate bills of exchange, and to take other measures to procure money for the Government.

Mr. Morris was again elected to Congress on the eighteenth of July, 1776, fourteen days after the Declaration of Independence was adopted; and being in favor of the measure, he affixed his signature thereto on the second of August following. His labors in Congress were incessant, and he always looked with perfect confidence to the period when peace and independence should crown the efforts of the patriots. Even when the American army under Washington, had dwindled down to a handful of half-naked, half-famished militia, during the disastrous retreat across New Jersey at the close of 1776, he evinced his confidence that final success would ensue, by loaning at that time, upon his individual responsibility, ten thousand dollars. This materially assisted in collecting together and paying that gallant band with which Washington recrossed the Delaware, and won the glorious victory at

George's Society, were at dinner, celebrating the anniversary of St. George's day, when the news of the battle of Lexington reached them. Astonishment and indignation filled the company, and they soon dispersed. A few remained and discussed the great question of American freedom: and there, within that festive hall, did Robert Morris and a few others, by a solemn vow, dedicate their lives, their fortunes, and their honor, to the sacred cause of the Revolution.

* The duties of the secret committee consisted in managing the financial affairs of the government. It was a position of great trust, for they frequently had funds placed in their hands to be disposed of according to their discretion—like the "secret service money" of the present day, placed in the hands of the President, with discretionary powers, it being inimical to the general good to take public action upon such disbursements.

Trenton.* Many instances of a similar nature are related, where the high character of Mr. Morris enabled
him to procure money when the government could not,
and his patriotism never faltered in inducing him to apply
it to the public benefit.

In 1781, the darkest period of the war, Mr. Morris, in
connection with other citizens, organized a banking institution in Philadelphia, for the purpose of issuing paper
money that should receive the public confidence, for the
government bills were becoming almost worthless. This
scheme had the desired effect, and the aid it rendered to
the cause was incalculable. During that year, upon the
urgent solicitation of Congress, Mr. Morris accepted the
appointment of general financial agent of the United
States, in other words, Secretary of the Treasury. It
was a service which no other man in the country seemed
competent to perform, and that Congress well knew. His
business talent, and his extensive credit at home and
abroad, were brought to bear in this vocation, and upon
him alone, for a long time, rested the labor of supplying
a famished and naked army and furnishing other necessary supplies for the public service. Congress, at that
time, could not have obtained a loan of one thousand dollars, yet Robert Morris effected loans upon his own
credit, of tens of thousands. The Bank of North America
was put in successful operation, and there is no doubt that
these patriotic services of Robert Morris present the chief

---

* When Congress fled to Baltimore, on the approach of the British across New
Jersey, Mr. Morris, after removing his family into the country, returned to, and
remained in Philadelphia. Almost in despair, Washington wrote to him, and informed him that to make any successful movement whatever, a considerable sum of
money must be had. It was a requirement that seemed almost impossible to
meet. Mr. Morris left his counting-room for his lodgings in utter despondency. On
his way he met a wealthy Quaker, and made known his wants. "What security
can'st thou give?" asked he. "My note and my honor," promptly replied Mr.
Morris. The Quaker replied: "Robert, thou shalt have it." —It was sent le
Washington, the Delaware was crossed, and victory won!

reason why the Continental army was not at that time disbanded by its own act. And it has been justly remarked, that: "If it were not demonstrable by official records, posterity would hardly be made to believe that the campaign of 1781, which resulted in the capture of Cornwallis, and virtually closed the Revolutionary War, was sustained wholly on the credit of an individual merchant."*

After the conclusion of peace, Mr. Morris served twice in the Legislature of Pennsylvania; and he was a delegate to the Convention that framed the Constitution of the United States. He was elected a Senator under that instrument, and took his seat at the first meeting of Congress in New York to organize the government in accordance with its provisions.

In the selection of his cabinet, President Washington was very anxious to have Mr. Morris Secretary of the Treasury, but he declined. Washington asked him to name a candidate, and he at once mentioned General Alexander Hamilton.

Mr. Morris served a regular term in the United States Senate, and then retired forever from public life. By his liberal expenditures and free proffers of his private obligations for the public benefit, he found his ample fortune very much diminished at the close of hostilities; and by embarking the remainder in the purchase of wild lands,

---

* At the time Washington was preparing, in his camp upon the Hudson, in Westchester county, to attack Sir Henry Clinton in New York, in 1781, Mr. Morris and Judge Peters of Pennsylvania were then at headquarters. Washington received a letter from Count de Grasse, announcing his determination not to sail for New York. He was bitterly disappointed, but almost before the cloud had passed from his brow, he conceived the expedition against Cornwallis, at Yorktown. "What can you do for me?" said Washington to Mr. Peters. "With money, everything, without it, nothing," he replied, at the same time turning with anxious look toward Mr. Morris. "Let me know the sum you desire," said Mr. Morris; and before noon Washington's plan and estimates were complete. Mr. Morris promised him the amount, and he raised it upon his own responsibility.

7

in the State of New York,* under the impression that emigrants from the old world would flow in a vast and cease-
less current to this "land of the free," he became greatly
embarrassed in his pecuniary affairs, and it preyed seriously upon his mind. This misfortune, and the inroads
which asthma had made upon his constitution, proved a
canker at the root of his bodily vigor, and he sunk to rest
in the grave, on the eighth day of May, 1806, in the seventy-third year of his age, leaving a widow with whom he
had lived in uninterrupted domestic happiness for thirty-
seven years.†

* In consequence of some old claims of Massachusetts to a large portion of the
territory of the State of New York, the latter State, in 1786, in order to settle the
matter, ceded to the former more than six millions of acres, reserving, however,
the right of sovereignty. Massachusetts sold the larger portion of this tract to
Oliver Phelps and Nathaniel Gorham, for one million of dollars: and in 1790, they
in turn sold to Mr. Morris 1,204,000 acres, for sixteen cents per acre. He afterward
resold this tract to Sir William Pultney. The original purchasers from Massachusetts, unable to fulfil their contract, surrendered to the State a large tract, to which
the Indian titles had been extinguished. This tract Mr. Morris bought in 1796,
and after selling considerable portions lying upon the Genesee river, he mort-
gaged the residue to Wilhelm Willink, of Amsterdam, and eleven associates, who
styled themselves the *"Holland Land Company."* Mr. Morris was unable to
meet his engagement, and the company foreclosed, and acquired full title to the
land. They opened a sales office in Batavia, Genesee county, which now exists;
and they still own large tracts of land in Western New York.

† In 1769, Mr. Morris married Miss Mary White, sister of the ate venerable
Bishop White, of Pennsylvania.

Benjamin Rush

OCTOR BENJAMIN RUSH was born at Berberry, about twelve miles northeast of Philadelphia, on the twenty-fourth day of December, 1745. He was descended from an officer of that name in Cromwell's army, who, after the death of the Protector, emigrated to America, and settled in Pennsylvania. Benjamin was his grandson.

The father of Benjamin Rush died when he was only six years old, and he and a brother were left entirely to the care of his mother. She was anxious to give Benjamin a classical education, but the earnings from her small farm did not supply her with adequate means. Intent upon her purpose, she sold her land and moved into Philadelphia, where she commenced some commercial pursuit. She was successful; and her wish to give her eldest son a liberal education, was gratified. At the age of nine years he was placed under the care of the Rev. Dr. Findlay, who was the principal of an academy at Nottingham, in Maryland. After completing his preparatory studies, young Rush entered Princeton College,[a] where he took his degree in 1760, at the age of sixteen years.

a 1759.

The study of the law was the voluntary choice of young Rush, but by the advice of Dr. Findlay, he selected the practice of medicine as a profession, and placed himself under the direction of the celebrated Doctor Redman, of Philadelphia. In 1766 he went to England with the view of professional improvement, where he remained two years, attending the lectures at the best hospitals and medical schools in London. In the summer of 1768, he went to Paris, where he added much to his stock of knowledge; and in the autumn of that year he returned to America, bearing the title of "Doctor of Medicine," for which a diploma was conferred at Edinburgh.

Doctor Rush commenced practice in Philadelphia, and before the first year of his professional career was completed, he was called in consultation with some of the most eminent practitioners of that city. His polished manners, superior intellect, kind deportment in the sick room, and unwearied attention to the calls of the poor made him very popular, and he soon had an extensive and lucrative practice. Students from all parts of the

United States, after the war, flocked to Philadelphia to avail themselves of his lectures.*

Doctor Rush espoused the patriot cause immediately after his return to America, in 1768, and his pen proved a powerful instrument, in connection with his personal exertions, in arousing the people to action. He was solicited to take a seat in the General Congress of 1775, but declined; but when, in 1776, some of the Pennsylvania delegates in Congress refused to vote for Independence and withdrew from their seats, he was elected to fill one of them, and obeyed the call of duty by accepting it. He was not a member when the Declaration was adopted, but was present and signed it on the second of August following.

In 1777, Congress appointed Doctor Rush to the office of physician-general of the military hospitals of the middle department, in which he was of great utility. He did not serve again in Congress after that appointment; in fact, with the exception of being a member of the Convention of Pennsylvania, which adopted the Federal Constitution, he did not actively participate in any public duties. He was appointed president of the mint in 1788, which office he held fourteen years.

Although the services of Doctor Rush were eminently useful as a statesman, yet as a medical practitioner and writer, he was most distinguished and is more intimately known. He was appointed professor of chemistry in the Medical College of Philadelphia, in 1769, the year after his return from Europe. He was made professor of the theory and practice of medicine in 1789; and at that time he also held the professorship of the Institutes of Medi-

---

* Students came even from Europe, to attend his lectures; and in 1812, the year before he died, those in the class who attended his lectures, amounted to four hundred and thirty. Within the last nine years of his life, the number of his private pupils exceeded fifty. It is stated by his biographer, that during his life he gave instruction to more than two thousand pupils.

icine and of Chemical Science, in the Medical College of Pennsylvania. On the resignation of Doctor Kuhn, in 1796, he succeeded that gentleman in the professorship of the practice of medicine. These three professorships he held during his life.

Doctor Rush's eminent qualities as a medical practitioner, a philanthropist, and a Christian, were fully developed when the yellow fever rapidly depopulated Philadelphia, in 1793. It was so malignant, that all the usual remedies failed, and the best medical skill was completely foiled. Many physicians became alarmed for their own safety and fled from the city; but Doctor Rush, and a few of his attached pupils and friends, remained to aid the sick and dying, and, if possible, check the march of the destroyer. He at length had a severe attack of the fever, and some of his pupils fell victims; but so long as he was able to get from his bed, he did not remit his labors.*

The impress of Dr. Rush's mind and energy is upon several public institutions. He formed the Philadelphia Dispensary in 1786, and he was one of the principal founders of Dickerson College, at Carlisle, Pennsylvania. In addition to honorary membership in many literary and scientific societies abroad, he held various offices in benevolent and philosophical institutions at home.†

* When alarm seized upon many of the resident physicians of Philadelphia, and they fled from the danger, Doctor Rush called together some of his pupils and professional friends, and in an impressive manner laid before them their solemn responsibilities to their profession and to the public. He portrayed the effects upon the public mind which the flight of physicians would produce—predisposing the system, through fear, to take the disease—and he conjured them to remain. He concluded his earnest appeal, by saying: "As for myself, I am determined to remain. I may fall a victim to the epidemic, and so may you, gentlemen. But I prefer, since I am placed here by Divine Providence, to fall in performing my duty, if such must be the consequence of staying upon the ground, than to secure my life by fleeing from the post of duty allotted in the Providence of God. I will remain, if I remain alone." He and a few of his noble-hearted pupils remained and performed their duty faithfully. His written description of that dreadful epidemic, is one of the most thrilling pieces of composition in our language.

† Among others, he was President of the American Society for the abolition of slavery; President of the Philadelphia Medical Society; Vice President of the

As a patriot, Doctor Rush was firm and inflexible; as a professional man he was skilful, candid, and honorable; as a thinker and writer, he was profound; as a Christian, zealous and consistent; and in his domestic relations, he was the centre of a circle of love and true affection. Through life the Bible was a "lamp to his feet"—his guide in all things appertaining to his duty toward God and man. Amid all his close and arduous pursuit of human knowledge, he never neglected to "search the Scriptures" for that knowledge which points the soul aright in its journey to the Spirit Land. His belief in revealed religion, and in the Divine inspiration of the Sacred Writers, is manifested in many of his scientific productions; and during that period, at the close of the last century when the sentiments of infidel France were infused into the minds of men in high places here, Doctor Rush's principles stood firm, and his opinions never wavered.

The life of this truly great man terminated on the nineteenth day of April, 1813, when he was in the sixty-eighth year of his age. During his last illness, the public mind was greatly affected, and his house was constantly thronged with people inquiring concerning the probable result of the disease that was upon him. When death closed his eyes, every citizen felt that a dear friend had been taken away, and a general gloom overspread the community.

Philadelphia Bible Society; one of the Vice Presidents of the American Philosophical Society, &c., &c.

Benj. Franklin

ROBABLY a greater man than BENJA-
MIN FRANKLIN never lived, regarded
with that analytical discrimination which
distinguishes true greatness in inherent
qualities rather than in brilliant exter-
nal displays; and in almost every par-
ticular characteristic of a man, he presented a model of
excellence of the highest standard.

Benjamin Franklin was born in Boston, Massachusetts, on the seventeenth day of January, 1706. His father was a true Puritan, and emigrated hither from England, in 1682. He soon afterward married Miss Folger, a native of Boston. Being neither a mechanic nor farmer, he turned his attention to the business of a soap-boiler and tallow-chandler, which was his occupation for life.

The parents of Benjamin wished him to be a minister of the gospel, and they began to educate him with that end in view, but their slender means were not adequate for the object, and the intention was abandoned. He was kept at a common school for a few years, and then taken into the service of his father. The business did not please the boy, and he was entered, on probation, with a cutler. The fee for his admission to apprenticeship was too high,* and he abandoned that pursuit also, and was put under the instruction of an elder brother, who was a printer. There he continued until he became quite proficient, and all the while he was remarkable for his studiousness, seldom spending an hour from his books, in idle amusement. At length the harmony between himself and brother was interrupted, and he left his service and went on board of a vessel in the harbor, bound for New York. In that city he could not obtain employment, and he proceeded on foot to Philadelphia, where he arrived on a Sabbath morning.† He was then but seventeen years old, friendless and alone, with but a single dollar in his pocket. He soon found employment as compositor in one of the two

---

* At that time, as in England at the present day, apprentices, instead of receiving any pay for their services, were obliged to pay a bonus, or fee, for the privilege of becoming an apprentice.

† It is said that his first appearance in Philadelphia attracted considerable attention in the streets. With his spare clothing in his pocket, and a loaf of bread under each arm, he wandered about until he came to a Quaker meeting, where he entered, sat down, want to sleep, and slept soundly until worship was closed. He was then awakened by one of the congregation, and he sought some other place of rest.

printing establishments then in Philadelphia, and was at once noticed and esteemed by his employers, for his industry and studious habits.

Having written a letter to a friend at New Castle, in Delaware, in which he gave a graphic account of his journey from Boston to Philadelphia, which letter was shown to Governor Keith, of that province, that functionary became much interested in the young journeyman printer, and invited him to his mansion. Friendship succeeded the first interview, and the governor advised him to set up business for himself, and offered his patronage. The plan of operation was rather an extensive one, and involved the necessity of making a voyage to England for materials. Franklin went to London, but found Sir William Keith's patronage of so little avail, that he was obliged to seek employment for his daily bread. He obtained a situation as journeyman printer in one of the principal offices there, and by the same line of industry, studiousness, punctuality, and frugality, he soon won to himself numerous friends.* Unfortunately he was thrown in the way of some distinguished infidels while he was in London, (among whom was Lord Mandeville,) and received flattering attentions from them. His mind became tinctured with their views, and he was induced to write a pamphlet upon deistical metaphysics, a performance which he afterward regretted, and candidly condemned.

With the fruits of his earnings Franklin resolved to take a trip to the Continent, but just as he was on the point of departure, he received an offer from a mercantile friend about to sail for America, to accompany him as a clerk. He accepted it, and embarked for home in July, 1726.

With his new employer, at Philadelphia, Franklin had before him a prospect of prosperity and wealth, but soon

* We have seen the identical Printing Press which was worked by Franklin when in London. It is now in the National Museum at Washington city.

a heavy cloud obscured the bright vision. His friend died, and once more Franklin became a journeyman printer with his old employer. In a short time he formed a partnership with another printer, and commenced business in Philadelphia, where his character, habits, and talents, soon gained him warm friends, public confidence, and a successful business.* So multifarious were the public and private labors of usefulness of this great man, from this period until his death, that our circumscribed limits will permit us to notice them only in brief chronological order.

In 1732, Franklin began his useful annual, called "Poor Richard's Almanac." It was widely circulated in the Colonies, and in England, and was translated into several Continental languages of Europe. It continued until 1757. About the same time he commenced a newspaper, which soon became the most popular one in the Colonies. By constant, persevering study, he acquired a knowledge of the Latin, French, Spanish, and Italian languages. He projected a literary club, called the Junto, and the books which they collected for their use, formed the nucleus of the present extensive Philadelphia Library. He wrote many pamphlets containing essays upon popular subjects, which were read with avidity, and made him very popular. With his popularity, his business increased, and his pecuniary circumstances became easy in a few years.

In 1734, he was appointed government printer for Pennsylvania, and in 1736 he received the appointment of Clerk of the General Assembly. The next year he was made postmaster of Philadelphia. The income arising from these offices, and from his business, relieved him from constant drudgery, and left him leisure for philo-

---

* In 1730, he married a young widow lady, whose maiden name was Read. He had sought her hand before going to England, but she gave it to another, Her husband died while Franklin was absent, and their intimacy was renewed soon after his return.

sophical pursuits, and the advancement of schemes for the public good.*

In 1741, he commenced the publication of the "General Magazine and Historical Chronicle, for the British Plantations," which had a wide circulation. In 1744 he was elected a member of the General Assembly,† and was annually re-elected, for ten consecutive years. It was about this time that he made some of his philosophical discoveries, upon the mysterious wings of which his fame spread world-wide.‡

In 1753 he was appointed a commissioner to treat with the Indians at Carlisle. In 1754, he was a delegate from Pennsylvania to a Convention of representatives of the Colonies that met at Albany to consult upon the general defence and security against the French. He there proposed an admirable plan of union.§ About this time he was appointed deputy Postmaster General. He was also active in improving the military affairs of the colony, and rendered General Braddock distinguished service in providing material for his expedition against Fort Du Quesne.

* He organized fire companies in Philadelphia, the first on the Continent, and he devised means for paving the streets and lighting the city with gas. All military discipline in the Province had become entirely neglected, but Franklin saw the utility of a thorough knowledge of tactics, and he applied himself to the task of instruction. He projected the "American Philosophical Society," the "Pennsylvania Hospital," and the "Pennsylvania University." In 1742, he published a treatise on the improvement of chimneys, and invented the celebrated stove which bears his name. This invention he gave to the public.

† He had previously held the office of Justice of the Peace, and an Alderman of the city.

‡ His attention was powerfully drawn to the subject of electricity, in consequence of some experiments which had been exhibited by Europeans in Boston; and he not only repeated them all with success, but he was led to such investigations of the nature and effects of electricity, as to discover many astounding truths such as the identity of lightning and the electrical spark of a machine.

§ This plan for a confederation of the several Colonies, contained all the essential features of the present Constitution of the United States, and exhibited the powers of a great mind. But it had the singular fortune to be rejected, both by the home government and by the Colonies; the former contending that it had too much *democracy* in it, and the latter, that it had too much *prerogative* in it.

In 1757, Franklin was sent by the General Assembly of the Province, to London, as its counsel in a dispute with the governor; and he so managed the case as to obtain a verdict for the Assembly. He remained a resident agent for the Colony, in England, for five years, and formed many valuable acquaintances while there. On his return, he was publicly thanked by the General Assembly, and the sum of twenty thousand dollars was presented to him as compensation for his important services.

In 1764, he was again sent to England as agent for the Colony, upon business similar to that for which he was first sent, and he was there when the Stamp Act was passed, loudly and boldly protesting against it. His opinions had great weight there; and, having been appointed agent for several of the Colonies, the eyes of statesmen at home and abroad were turned anxiously to him, as the storm of the Revolution rapidly gathered in dark and threatening clouds. He labored assiduously to effect conciliation, and he did much to arrest for a long time the blow that finally severed the Colonies from the mother country. Satisfied at length that war was inevitable, he returned home in 1775, and was at once elected a delegate to the General Congress. He was again elected in 1776, and was one of the committee appointed to draft a Declaration of Independence, voted for its adoption, and signed it on the second of August.

In September[a] Franklin was appointed one of three commissioners to meet Lord Howe in conference on Staten Island, and hear his propositions for peace. The attempt at conciliation proved abortive, and hostilities commenced.* About this time a Convention was

[a] 1776.

* Franklin had formed a personal acquaintance with Lord Howe, in England. At the conference in question, when his lordship expressed his kind feelings toward the Americans, and his regret that they would not share in the protection of British power, Doct. Franklin told him plainly that he need not give himself any trouble on their account as the Americans were fully able to take care of themselves.

called in Pennsylvania, for the purpose of organizing a State government, according to the recommendation of the General Congress. Franklin was chosen its President, and his wisdom was manifested in the Constitution which followed. He was appointed by Congress a Commissioner to the Court of France, to negotiate a treaty of alliance. Although then over seventy years of age, he accepted the appointment, and sailed in October, 1776. He was received with distinguished honors, and strong expressions of sympathy in behalf of his country were made; yet the French ministry were so cautious, that it was not until af-

a Oct. 1777. ter the news of the capture of Burgoyne*a* reached them, and American affairs looked brighter, that they would enter into a formal negotiation. A treaty was finally concluded, and was signed by Franklin and the French Minister, in February, 1778. America was acknowledged independent, and the French government openly espoused her cause. Franklin was invested by Congress with almost unlimited discretionary powers, and his duties were very arduous and complex; yet he discharged them with a fidelity and skill which excited the admiration of Europe. Great Britain at length yielded, and consented to negotiate a treaty of peace upon the basis of American independence; and on the third day of September, 1783, Doctor Franklin had the pleasure of signing a definitive treaty to that effect.*

Franklin now asked leave of Congress to return home to his family,† but he was detained there until the arrival

---

* It was on this occasion, that Doctor Franklin again put on a suit of clothe which ten years before, on the occasion of his being insulted before the English Privy Council, he declared he would never wear again until he had "signed England's degradation and America's independence."

† Doctor Franklin had two children, a son and daughter. The former was a royal governor of New Jersey before the Revolution, and adhering to the government, he went to England, where he died. His daughter married Mr. Bache, of Philadelphia, whose descendants are among the first families of that city at the present time.

of Mr. Jefferson, his successor, in 1785. His return to America was received with every demonstration of joy and respect, not only from the most distinguished individuals, but from nearly every public body in the country. Notwithstanding his great age (eighty years) the public claimed his services, and he was appointed President of Pennsylvania, which office he held three years. In 1787, he was in the Convention which framed the present Constitution of the United States, and this was the last public duty he performed. The gout and stone, with which he had been afflicted many years, terminated his life on the seventeenth day of April, 1790, in the eighty-fourth year of his age. A vast concourse of people followed his body to the grave, and the whole country, nay the whole civilized world, mourned his loss.*

* Congress directed a universal mourning throughout the United States for thirty days. In France, and indeed throughout Europe, the news of his death was received with profound grief. In the National Assembly of France, the eloquent Mirabeau announced his death, and in a brief but brilliant eulogium, he used these words: " Franklin is dead!" [a profound silence reigned throughout the hall.] "The genius which gave freedom to America, and scattered torrents of light upon Europe, is returned to the bosom of the Divinity! The sage, whom two worlds claim; the man disputed by the history of the sciences, and the history of empires, holds, most undoubtedly, an elevated rank among the human species. Political cabinets have too long notified the death of those who were never great but in their funeral orations; the etiquette of courts have but too long sanctioned hypocritical grief. Nations ought only to mourn for their benefactors; the representatives of freemen ought never to recommend any other than the heroes of humanity to their homage.   *   *   *   *   *

"Antiquity would have elevated altars to that mortal, who, for the advantage of the human race, embracing both heaven and earth in his vast and extensive mind, knew how to subdue thunder and tyranny Enlightened and free Europe at least owes its rememorance and its regrets, to one of the greatest men who has ever served the cause of philosophy and of liberty.' The Deputies adopted a resolution to wear mourning for three days.

John Morton

OHN MORTON descended from ancestors of Swedish birth, who emigrated to America in the early part of the seventeenth century, and settled upon the Delaware River, not far below Philadelphia. He was the only child of his father, who died before his son was born, which event occurred in the year 1724. His mother, who was quite young, afterward married an English gentleman, who became greatly attached to his infant charge. Being highly educated, and a good practical surveyor, he instructed young Morton in mathematics, as well as in all the common branches of a good education. His mind was of unusual strength, and at an early age it exhibited traits of sound maturity.

Mr. Morton first accepted official station, in 1764, when he was appointed justice of the peace under the Provincial government of Pennsylvania. He was soon afterward chosen a member of the General Assembly of that Province, and for a number of years was Speaker of the House. So highly were his public services appreciated, that the people were loath to dispense with them.

He was a delegate to the "Stamp Act Congress," in 1765; and in 1766, he was made high sheriff of the county in which he resided. He warmly espoused the cause of the patriots, and on that account, when, after the Lexington tragedy, military corps were formed in Pennsylvania, he was offered the command of one. This he declined, on account of other engagements, for he then held the office of presiding Judge of the Quarter Sessions and Common Pleas, and about the same time he

112

was elevated to the bench of the Supreme Court of the Province.

In 1774, the Assembly of Pennsylvania appointed Mr. Morton a delegate to the General Congress. He was ze-elected for 1775 in December of the same year, and he was also elected in 1776 to the same office. His election did not take place until some days after the Declaration of Independence was adopted, but he had the privilege of signing it in August.* He was very active while in Congress, and the committee duties which he performd, were many and arduous. Among other committees on which he served, he formed one of that which reported the Articles of Confederation for the States, which were adopted, and remained the organic law of the nation until the adoption of the present Constitution in 1787.

Mr. Morton did not live to see the blessings of peace and independence descend upon his country. He died in April, 1777, in the fifty-fourth year of his age, leaving a widow and a large family of children. His death was a great public calamity, for men of his genius and patriotism were much needed at that time, His career presented another instance of the triumph of virtue and sound principles, in rising from obscurity to exalted station.

* By virtue of his previous election, Mr. Morton was in his seat on the memorable fourth of July, 1776. The delegation from Pennsylvania then present were equally divided in opinion upon the subject of independence, and Mr. Morton was called upon officially to give a casting vote for that State. This was a solemn responsibility thrown upon him—it was for him to decide whether there should be a unanimous vote of the Colonies for independence—whether Pennsylvania should form one of the American Union. But he firmly met the responsibility, and voted YES; and from that moment the United Colonies were declared Independent States. We have said the delegation from Pennsylvania were divided. It was thus: Morris and Dickenson were absent, and Franklin and Wilson were in favor of, and Willing and Humphrey were opposed to, the Declaration; and Morton gave the casting vote.

Geo Clymer

EORGE CLYMER was born in Philadelphia, in the year 1739. His father was from Bristol, England, and died when George was only seven years old. His wife died before him and George was left an orphan. William Coleman, his mother's brother, a wealthy and highly-esteemed citizen of Philadelphia, took George into his family, and in his education, and all other things, he treated him as a son. Having completed a thorough English education, he was taken into the counting-room of his uncle, and prepared for commercial life,

Mr. Clymer was not partial to a mercantile business, for he deemed it a pathway beset with many snares for the feet of pure morality, as sudden gains and losses were apt to affect the character of the most stable. For himself he preferred literature and science, and his mind was much occupied with these subjects.

At the age of twenty-seven years he married a Miss Meredith, and entered into mercantile business with his father-in-law, and his son, under the firm of Meredith and Sons. His uncle died about the same time, and left the principal part of his large fortune to Mr. Clymer. Still he continued in business with his father-in-law, until his death; and with his brother-in-law afterward, until 1782.

Even before his marriage, when none but old commercial grievances were complained of by the Colonies, Mr. Clymer expressed decided republican principles; and when the Stamp Act aroused the resistance of the American people, he was among the most ardent defenders of the republican cause. He was a zealous actor in all the public meetings in Philadelphia; and when, in 1774, military organizations took place preparatory to a final resort to arms, which seemed inevitable, Mr. Clymer accepted the command of a volunteer corps belonging to General Cadwallader's brigade.

When the oppressions which Boston experienced at the hands of British power, after the "Tea Riot,"*

---

* When the British ministry became convinced that the Americans would never submit to be taxed without their consent, they repealed several acts which were most obnoxious to the Colonies, but retained a duty upon tea. This, it was well understood in Parliament, was intended merely as a salvo for British honor, for the government had declared its right to tax the Colonies; and it was urged, that if it should, because of the opposition of the Americans, relinquish that right, it would be a virtual abdication of government in the Colonies. On the other hand, although the duty was but little more than nominal, the Americans saw involved in it a principle they could not sacrifice, and therefore they manfully re

aroused the strong sympathy of the people of the com
mercial cities, Mr. Clymer was placed at the head of a
large and responsible Committee of Vigilance in Philadelphia, to act as circumstances should require. He was
also placed upon the first Council of Safety that was organized in Philadelphia; and early in 1775, he was appointed by Congress one of the Continental treasurers.

In 1776, after two of the Pennsylvania delegates in the
General Congress declined voting for the Declaration of
Independence, and withdrew from their seats, Mr. Clymer and Dr. Rush were appointed to succeed them, and
they both joyfully affixed their signatures to that instrument. Mr. Clymer was soon afterward appointed one of
a committee to visit the northern army at Ticonderoga;
and when the British approached Philadelphia at the close
of 1776, and Congress retired to Baltimore, he was put
upon a committee with Robert Morris and others, to remain as a Committee of Vigilance in that city. He was
again elected to Congress in 1779, and was one of a committee sent by that body to Washington's head-quarters at
Valley Forge, to inquire into the alleged abuses of the
commissary department.

Mr. Clymer was peculiarly obnoxious to the British,*
an evidence of his patriotic zeal and unwavering attachment to the Republican cause. While the enemy were
in possession of Philadelphia in the winter of 1778, they
surrounded a house which they thought was Mr. Clymer's,

---

sisted the exercise of the assumed right. The duty being so light, the East
Indian Company believing the Colonists would not complain, at once sets large
cargoes of tea to America. In Boston the people would not allow it to be landed,
and ordered the vessel out of port. Refusing to comply, a party (some disguised
as Indians) went on board on the night of the sixteenth of December, 1773, and
broke open, and cast into the harbor, more than three hundred chests of tea.

* After the defeat of the Americans at the Brandywine, and the British were
marching triumphantly toward Philadelphia, Mr. Clymer moved his family into
the country for safety. But their retreat was discovered, and the British soldiers
sacked the house, destroyed the furniture, and wasted every sort of property
which they could find.

with the intention of demolishing it, but they discovered it to belong to a relative of his of the same name, and they spared the edifice.

In 1778, Mr. Clymer was sent by Congress to Pittsburgh to endeavor by negotiation to quiet the savages, who, influenced by British emissaries, were committing dreadful ravages on the frontier. In this he was successful, and for his arduous services he received the thanks of Congress. In the autumn of 1780 he was elected to Congress for the third time, and he continued an attentive and active member until 1782. During that year, he joined with Robert Morris and others in the establishment of a bank in Philadelphia, designed for the public good. Mr. Clymer was a considerable subscriber, and was made one of its first directors.*

In 1782, Mr. Clymer and Edward Rutledge were ap pointed by Congress to visit the Southern States, and urge the necessity of a prompt contribution of their assessed quota of funds for the public Treasury. The individual States were slow to respond to the calls of Congress, and this tardiness very much embarrassed the operations of government. On his return, Mr. Clymer moved his family to Princeton, for the purpose of having his children educated there. Public interest soon called him back to Pennsylvania, and he took a seat in its Legislature. It was while he was a member of that body, that the criminal code of that State was modified, and the penitentiary system introduced. It is conceded that the credit of maturing this wiser system of punishment, is chiefly due to Mr. Clymer, and for this alone he is entitled to the veneration due to a public benefactor.

Mr. Clymer was a member of the Convention that

---

* Two years before, he, with Mr. Morris and others, established a private bank, which was designed for the public good, and was of great utility. The bank es tablished in 1782 was of a national character.

framed the Federal Constitution, and was elected one of the first members of Congress, convened under that instrument. He declined a re-election, and was appointed, by President Washington, supervisor of the revenue for the State of Pennsylvania. This was an office in which great firmness and decision of character were requisite, in con sequence of the spirit of resistance to the collection of revenue which was then abroad. In fact, open rebellion at length appeared, and the movement known as the "Whiskey Insurrection"* in Pennsylvania, at one time threatened serious consequences to the whole framework of our government. But Mr. Clymer was unawed, and amid many personal dangers, he passed forward in the performance of his duty. At length, when things became quiet, he resigned. In 1796, he was appointed, with Colonels Hawkins and Pickens, to negotiate a treaty with the Cherokee and Creek tribes of Indians, in Georgia. This they effected to the mutual satisfaction of the contending parties. This mission closed the public life of Mr. Clymer, and the remainder of his days were spent in acts of private usefulness,† and a personal preparation for another world. He died on the twenty-fourth day of January, 1813, in the seventy-fourth year of his age. His long life was an active and useful one, and not a single moral stain marked its manifested purity.

* A portion of the people of the interior of Pennsylvania, violently opposed the excise law, it being a region where much whiskey was distilled, and hence the tax or duty amounted to a considerable resource. This excise law was adopted by Congress in 1790. In 1792, so insurrectionary had the people become in relation to the duty on distilled liquor, that Congress passed an act authorizing the President of the United States to call out the militia of the State, if necessary to enforce the laws. He withheld his power for nearly two years, but at length the "Whiskey Insurrection" assumed such a formidable aspect, that an army of fifteen thousand men were placed in the field. The rebellion ceased without a conflict.

† Mr. Clymer was one of the projectors of the Academy of Arts and Sciences in Philadelphia, and was its first President, which office he held until his decease He was also one of the founders of the Philadelphia Agricultural Society; and his name appears conspicuous in many of the benevolent movements of his day

AMES SMITH was born in Ireland, and was quite a small child when brought by his father to this country. The date of his birth is not recorded, and Mr. Smith himself could never be induced to tell it. It is supposed to be somewhere about 1720. His father, who had a numerous family of children, settled upon the Susquehanna river, in Pennsylvania, and died there in 1761. James was his second son, and, discovering a strong intellect at

an early age, his father determined to give him a liberal education. For this purpose he placed him under
the charge of Reverend Doctor Allison, provost of the
college of Philadelphia. He there acquired a knowledge
of Latin and Greek, and what proved more useful to
him, practical surveying.

After completing his tuition, he began the study of law
in Lancaster, and when admitted to the bar, he removed
westward, and practised both law and surveying. The
place where he located was very sparsely populated, and
indeed was almost a wilderness. The flourishing town of
Shippensburg has since sprung up there. After a short
continuance in his wilderness home, Mr. Smith moved to
the flourishing village of York, where he found no business competition for many years. He married Miss
Eleanor Amor of Newcastle, Delaware, and became a
permanent resident of York, where he stood at the head
of the bar until the opening of the Revolution.

Mr. Smith early perceived the gathering storm which
British oppressions were elaborating here; and when men
began to speak out fearlessly, he was among the first in
Pennsylvania to take sides with the patriots of Massachusetts and Virginia. He heartily seconded the proposition
for non-importation agreements, and for a General Congress. He was a delegate from the county of York to the
Pennsylvania convention (which was styled the "Committee of Pennsylvania"*), whose duty it was to ascertain the
sentiments of the people, and publish an address. Mr.
Smith was a member of the sub-committee chosen to
prepare the address, which was in the form of instructions
to the representatives of the people in the General Assembly of the state. He was earnest in endeavor-

---

* These committees formed in other Colonies, and were distinct from the
Colonial Assemblies authorized by the Royal Governors. In 1775 they superseded
those Assemblies, and assumed general legislative powers which they exercised
as Provincial Congresses, until the Confederation of the States took place.

ing to arouse the people to positive resistance, and as early as 1774, he was in favor of cutting the bond that held the colonies to the British throne.*

When Congress passed a resolution, recommending the several colonies to "adopt such governments as in the opinion of the representatives of the people, might best conduce to the happiness and safety of their constituents," the Pennsylvania Assembly was slow to act accordingly. In fact its instructions to its delegates in Congress were not favorable to independence, and it was not until the people of that state spoke out their sentiments in a general convention, that Pennsylvania was truly represented there. The seats of her delegates, who refused to vote for the Declaration of Independence, and withdrew from Congress, were filled with bold men, and one of these was James Smith, who, with George Clymer and Benjamin Rush, took his seat some days after that glorious instrument was adopted. He was there in time, however, to place his signature to the parchment on the second day of August ensuing.

Mr. Smith, was a member of the convention of Pennsylvania convened to form a constitution for the state, after the Declaration of Independence. There he was very active, and it was not until October, 1776, that he was a regular attendant in the General Congress. He was soon after appointed one of a most important committee whose business was to aid Washington in opposing the

---

* He was convinced that reconciliation was out of the question, and that war was inevitable. He accordingly raised and drilled a volunteer corps at York, (the first ever raised in the State,) which was the commencement of a general organization of the militia in that Province. Other companies were formed, and when a sufficient number were organized to form a regiment, Mr. Smith was elected Colonel. His age, however, precluded his entering upon active service, and he held the office as an honorary boon. According to the testimony of Mr. Penn before Parliament, the body of military "Associators" thus founded by Mr. Smith amounted in number, before the Declaration of Independence, to twenty thousand, whose services were pledged to the State.

progress of General Howe's army.* They were intrusted with almost unlimited discretionary powers, and the scope of their operations included the whole business of advi sing and superintending the military movements.

In the spring of 1777, Mr. Smith declined a re-election to Congress, and resumed his professional business at York; but the unfortunate defeats of the Americans at the Brandywine and at Germantown, and the capture of Philadelphia by the British, called for his valuable presence in the national council, and he obeyed the voice of duty. Congress adjourned to Lancaster when Howe's army took Philadelphia, and afterward it adjourned to York, the place of Mr. Smith's residence. When the battle of Monmouth, in 1778, made the hope of American triumph beam brightly, Mr. Smith retired again from Congress, and resumed his professional business. In 1779 he was called to a seat in the Legislature of Pennsylvania, where he served one term, and then withdrew. This closed his public career, and he lived in the enjoyment of domestic happiness until his death, which occurred on the eleventh day of July, 1806. He is supposed to have been nearly ninety years of age.

Mr. Smith was quite an, eccentric man, and possessed a vein of humor, coupled with sharp wit, which made him a great favorite in the social circle in which he moved. He was always lively in his conversation and manners except when religious subjects were the topics, when he was very grave and never suffered any in his presence to sneer at or speak with levity of Christianity. Although not a professor of religion, he was a possessor of many of its sublimer virtues, and practised its holiest precepts.

* His associates were James Wilson, Samuel Chew, George Clymer, and Rich and Stockton

Geo Taylor

EORGE TAYLOR was born in Ireland, in
the year 1716, and came to this country when he was about twenty years of
age. He was the son of a clergyman
hut whether Roman Catholic or Protes
tant, is not known. He was well edu
cated, but was poor on his arrival, and performed menial
service for a livelihood. He afterward became a clerk in
the iron establishment of Mr. Savage, at Durham, in Penn-

sylvania; and sometime after the death of his employer he married that gentleman's widow, by which he came into possession of considerable property and a thriving business.

After pursuing the business for some time, at Durham, and acquiring a handsome fortune, Mr. Taylor purchased an estate on the Lehigh, in Northumberland county, and erected iron works there. His wealth, education, and business talents, and his urbanity of manner, soon gained for him the esteem and confidence of the people, and he was elected by them a member of the Colonial Assembly in 1764. In that body he soon became a distinguished actor, and was placed upon its most important committees.

It was during Mr. Taylor's membership in the Colonial Assembly of Pennsylvania, that that body received the circular letter from Massachusetts, proposing a General Colonial Congress at New York, in 1765.* The Assembly accepted the invitation, and Mr. Taylor was one of the committee to whom was assigned the duty of drawing

---

* The passage of the Stamp Act, in March, 1765, excited a spirit of resistance in the Colonies, that threatened open rebellion. The Massachusetts Assembly sent forth a circular letter to the other Colonies, proposing a General Congress of delegates from them, to be held in the city of New York in October following, for he purpose of consulting upon the public good. At the opening of the Convention, the following delegates appeared and took their seats. From *Massachusetts,* James Otis, Oliver Partridge, Timothy Ruggles; *Rhode Island,* Metcalf Bowler, Henry Ward; *Connecticut,* Eliphalet Dyer, David Rowland, William S. Johnson; *New York,* Robert R. Livingston, John Cruger, Philip Livingston, William Bayard, Leonard Lispenard; *Pennsylvania,* John Dickenson, John Morton, George Bryan; *Maryland,* William Murdock, Edward Tilghman, Thomas Ringgold *New Jersey,* Robert Ogden, Hendrick Fisher, Joseph Borden; *Delaware,* Thomas McKean, Cæsar Rodney; *South Carolina,* Thomas Lynch, Christopher Gadsden, John Rutledge. Timothy Ruggles, of Massachusetts, (who was a royalist during the Revolution), was, by ballot, elected President. They adopted a "Declaration of Rights," a "Petition to the King," and a "Memorial to Parliament." The "Declaration of Rights" was penned by John Cruger, delegate from New York. He was at that time speaker of the Provincial Assembly, and Mayor of the city of New York. The "Petition to the King," was written by Robert R. Livingston, also a member from New York, who afterward had the high honor of administering the oath of office to Washington when he was inaugurated the that President of the United States.

up instructions for the delegates from that Province. Those instructions were supposed to be from his pen, and evinced much wisdom and sound judgment.

Mr. Taylor was a member of the Provincial Assembly five consecutive years, when, finding his private interests suffering in consequence of his absence, he declined a re-election, and for sometime withdrew from public life. He was elected to the Provincial Congress in 1775, and was one of the committee appointed to draw up instructions for the delegates to the General Congress, which convened in May of that year. These instructions, which were not sanctioned by the Assembly until November, contained a clause strictly prohibiting the delegates from concurring in any proposition for political independence, a reconciliation being still hoped for. But public feeling very materially changed on this point during the spring of 1776 and in June that prohibition was removed, and the delegates were left to act according to their own direction. Still, a portion of the delegates remained firm in their opposition to the measure, and Mr. Taylor was one of those appointed to fill their places. He was therefore not present in Congress when the Declaration of Independence was adopted, but was there in time to sign it on the second day of August.

Mr. Taylor remained in Congress one year, and then withdrew from public life and settled in Easton. He died on the twenty-third day of February, 1781, aged sixty-five years.

James Wilson

his distinguished patriot was born in Scotland in 1742, and emigrated to this country in 1766. He had received his education under some of the best teachers in Edinburgh, and he brought with him such strong recommendations to eminent citizens of Philadelphia, that he soon obtained a situation as an assistant teacher in the Philadelphia college, then under the supervision of the Reverend Doctor Peters. In the course of a few months he commenced the study of law in the office of the eminent John Dickenson,* and after two years' close application, he established himself in business, first in Reading and afterward in Carlisle, Pennsylvania. He finally fixed his permanent residence in Philadelphia. He rapidly rose to eminence in his profession, and became distinguished as an ardent supporter of the republican cause whenever an opportunity presented itself.

Having adopted America as his home, Mr. Wilson espoused her cause with all the ardor of a native born citizen. This gave him great popularity, and in 1774, he was elected a member of the Provincial Assembly of Pennsylvania. In May, 1775, he was chosen a delegate to the General Congress, together with Benjamin Franklin and Thomas Willing. He was again elected for the session of 1776, and warmly supported the motion of Richard Henry Lee for absolute independence. He voted for and signed the Declaration of Disenthralment and remained an active member of Congress until 1777, when he and Mr. Clymer were not re-elected in consequence of the operations of a strong party spirit which at that time existed in the Pennsylvania Assembly.

Mr. Wilson, however, continued actively engaged for the public good, even in private life, nor did he allow that jealousy of his rising fame, which had interposed a barrier to his re-election, in the least to repress his zeal for his adopted country's welfare. He had been an indefatigable coadjutor with Mr. Smith in the organization of volunteer military corps, and was elected colonel of a regiment in 1774. The energy he there displayed was now again exerted in raising recruits for the Continental army, and through

* Mr. Dickenson was at that time one of the most eminent lawyers in America. He was a powerful writer, and his "Letters of a Pennsylvania Farmer" were very instrumental in bringing on that crisis in public affairs in the Colonies which brought about the Revolution. He was always opposed to the proposition for independence, and would have voted against it if he had been in his seat on the fourth of July, 1776. His earnest desire was to obtain justice for America, without dismembering the British empire.

his influence, the Pennsylvania line was much strengthened.

In 1777, difficulties having arisen with the Indians
within the bounds of the state, Mr. Wilson was sent
as a commissioner to treat with them, and he was successful in his undertaking. Soon after the arrival of Mr
Gerard, the French minister,* Mr. Wilson formed an acquaintance with him, which ripened into friendship, and
Mr. Gerard was so struck with the versatility of his ta
lents, that in 1780 he appointed him the Advocate General of the French nation in the United States, an office
which required a thorough knowledge of international
and commercial laws. The appointment was confirmed
by the French King in 1781.†

Toward the close of 1782, Mr. Wilson was again elected a delegate to the General Congress, and took his
seat in January, 1783. During that year, the executive
council of Pennsylvania, appointed him an agent and
counsellor in the controversy of that state with Connecticut, respecting the Wyoming domain. In this important
service he was very successful, and the matter was
brought to an amicable settlement. He was again elected
to Congress toward the close of 1785, and took his seat in
March following. He was an active member of the convention that framed the Federal Constitution in 1787, and
was chairman of the committee that reported the first
draft. He was also a member of the state convention
that ratified it, and was chosen to deliver an oration on

---

* As soon as France, by the treaty of February, 1778, openly deelared in favor
of the United States, she promptly commenced the fulfilment of her agreement, by
fitting out a fleet of twelve sail of the line, and sent them to America, under Count
D'Estaing. She also appointed a minister (Mr. Gerard) to Congress, and he came
with the French fleet, and was landed at Sandy Hook, in July of that year.

† Mr. Gerard stipulated with Mr. Wilson, that an annual salary should be
allotted him; but after his devotion to his duties for some time, he received a no-
tification from the French King, that it was not his pleasure to sanction that stipulation. Mr. Wilson at once resigned the office, justly complaining of bad treatment.

the occasion of a celebration of the event in Philadelphia. He was also a member of the convention that framed a new constitution for Pennsylvania in 1788. In the arrangement of the judiciary under the Federal Constitution, President Washington appointed Mr. Wilson one of the judges of the Supreme Court of the United States.

He was appointed the first Professor of Law in the College of Philadelphia, in 1790, and when, in 1792, that institution and the University of Pennsylvania were united, he was appointed to the same professorship there, which office, as well as that of Judge of the Supreme Court, he held until his death.

In 1791, the Pennsylvania House of Representatives chose him, by a unanimous vote, to revise and properly digest the laws of the state. He at once entered upon the duties assigned him, and had made a considerable progress in the arduous work, when his labors were arrested by the Senate refusing to concur in the object for which the appointment had been made. His task was never resumed.

In his official capacity as judge of the United States Supreme Circuit Court, he frequently made long journeys into other states. It was while on a judicial circuit in North Carolina, that his death occurred on the twenty-eighth day of August, 1798, at the house of his friend, Judge Iredell of Edenton. He was in the fifty-sixth year of his age.

For many years, Mr. Wilson stood at the head of the Philadelphia bar, and so popular was he as an advocate, that nearly every important case that came before the higher tribunals of that State was defended by him. As a patriot none was firmer; as a Christian none sincerer; and as a husband, father, neighbor and friend, he was beloved and esteemed in the highest degree.

9

EORGE Ross was born in New Castle, Delaware, in the year 1730. His father was a highly esteemed minister of the Episcopal Church in that town, and he educated his son with much care, having himself experienced the great advantage of a liberal education. He soon became very proficient in Latin and Greek, and at the age of eighteen years entered, as a student, the law office of his brother then a respectable member of the Philadelphia bar. He

130

was admitted to practice at the age of twenty-one years, and fixed his residence in Lancaster, where he married a highly respectable young woman named Lawler.

Mr. Ross first appeared in public life in 1768, when he was elected a member of the Pennsylvania Assembly for Lancaster. He was much respected in that body, and was re-elected several successive years. And when the enactments of the British Cabinet for enslaving the Colonies were causing the public men of America to define their positions, Mr. Ross very readily took sides with the patriots, and heartily commended the proposed measure of calling a General Congress. He was chosen one of the seven delegates which represented Pennsylvania in that august Convention, and was present at the opening in September, 1774. And, strange as it may appear, Mr. Ross was directed by the Assembly of Pennsylvania, to draw up the instructions which were to govern himself and his colleagues in the Continental Congress. And so highly was he esteemed by his fellow-citizens, that during the whole time that he was in Congress, from 1774 to 1777, he was regularly elected a member of the Assembly of Pennsylvania, as a representative for Lancaster. Nearly his whole time was consumed by attention to public duties in one or the other of these legislative councils, yet he freely gave it "without money and without price."* He was a warm supporter of the resolution of Mr. Lee, proposing independence, and joyfully signed the Declaration thereof, on the second of August, 1776.

The benevolent attributes of Mr. Ross's character, led him early to exercise an active sympathy for the remnants of the Indian tribes in his vicinity, and through his influence their condition was ameliorated, and justice meted

* As a testimony of their appreciation of his services in the General Congress, it was voted that the sum of one hundred and fifty pounds sterling should be sent to him as a free gift, from the treasury of Lancaster county. But his stern patriotism made him courteously refuse the proffered donation.

out to them, and their just wrath was frequently appeased by his exertions, when it threatened to burst like a consuming fire upon the frontier settlements.* Both his own State Legislature and the National Council, made him a mediator in difficulties which arose with the Indians, and he acted the noble part of a pacificator, and a true philanthropist. Nor did his humane sentiments flow out toward the oppressed red man alone, but wherever weakness was trodden down by strength, he fearlessly lent his aid. Thus, when Tories or adherents to the Crown, were persecuted and imprisoned, and it was esteemed next to treason to defend their cause, Mr. Ross, Mr. Wilson, and a few others, were ever ready to plead in their behalf.†

In April, 1799, Mr. Ross was appointed a Judge of the Court of Admiralty for Pennsylvania, in which office he would undoubtedly have greatly distinguished himself, had not death suddenly closed his active and highly useful life, in July, 1780, in the fiftieth year of his age.

* It cannot be denied that the treatment of the Indian tribes at the hands of the whites, in a large majority of cases, has been such that it is not to be wondered at that the untutored mind of the savage should, in its excited workings, elaborate schemes of revenge, a sentiment growing out of injuries received, and a jealous foreboding of future expulsion from their hunting grounds and the graves of their fathers. Although unchristian and savage, yet the Indian possesses the sentiment of patriotism, and reveres the land of his fathers; and among no people upon earth is veneration for the resting place of the dead more strongly exhibited than by him. No wonder, then, that the vision of expatriation, perhaps annihilation, which the future revealed, should have made him arise in his might, and by the tomahawk and torch attempt to stay the flood of white settlement, whose surges beat so strongly against the feeble barriers of his already contracted domain. Had the law of kindness and the principle of justice always prevailed, as they did under the mild and prosperous rule of William Penn, the Indian would have been the white man's friend, and those dark pictures of fire and blood would never have appeared among the delineations of our eventful history.

†The tories of the Revolution were far more despised (and justly so) by the patriots, than the mercenary troops of Great Britain. They not only lifted their hands against their own brethren, but in many cases their treachery and cruelty exceeded the worst acts of the British soldiery. During the winter, when the American army was suffering every thing but death at Valley Forge, the interior of Pennsylvania swarmed with tories; and when Washington, by order of Congress proceeded to take, by force, the grain and other food which the tory farmers refused to sell to the army, they, in some instances, burnt their produce, rather than have it feed the starving Americans!

Cæsar Rodney

ÆSAR RODNEY was born at Dover, in the Province of Delaware, in the year 1730. He was descended from English ancestry. His grandfather came from England soon after William Penn commenced the settlement of Pennsylvania.* After remaining a short time in Philadelphia, and forming acquaintances with some of its most esteemed citizens, he went into the county of Kent, on the Delaware, and settled down upon a plantation. He was an active man, and becoming very popular, he held many posts of honor and distinction in that Province. He had several sons, but lost them all except his youngest, Cæsar, the father of the subject of this memoir. Unambitious of public honors, and preferring the quiet of domestic life to the bustle and turmoil of the political field, he declined all offices that were tendered to him; and in the midst of agricultural pursuits he enriched his mind by study, and prepared his children for the duties of life.

* In 1681, William Penn, a member of the Society of Friends, or Quakers, and son of the English Admiral of that name, obtained a grant of Charles II. of all the lands embraced in the present State of Pennsylvania. That region had been colonized by Swedes, nearly forty years before, and Penn issued a proclamation, guarantying to permanent settlers undisputed right to the lands they occupied. The great aim of that good man was to establish an empire in the new world, upon the sacred principles of peace and brotherly love, where men of all nations, creeds, and hues, might live together as one harmonious family. Had the policy of William Penn, in conciliating the Indians by uniform kindness of treatment, been followed in the other colonies, much bloodshed might have been prevented, and the settlements would sooner have become permanent and prosperous. During the entire time that William Penn was proprietor of Pennsylvania, not a single dispute occurred with the natives.

133

He married the daughter of an esteemed clergyman, and, Cæsar being the first born, received their special attention in the matter of education of mind and heart.

On the death of his father, Mr. Rodney as the eldest male heir inherited the paternal estate, and with it, the distinguished consideration with which the family had ever been regarded. There are no records to show at what precise time he appeared in public life, but as he seems to have been a leader in the recorded proceedings of the Legislature of that Province in 1762, it is quite probable that he had done service there some years earlier.

When the Stamp Act excited the jealousy and alarm of the colonies, Mr. Rodney boldly proclaimed his sentiments in opposition to it and several antecedent acts of injustice which the British government had inflicted upon her colonies in America. He acted as well as thought and spoke, and when the "Stamp Act Congress" met in New York, in 1765, Mr. Rodney, together with Mr. M'Kean and Mr. Rollock, was chosen delegate thereto by a unanimous vote.

Mr. Rodney was a member of the Provincial Assembly in 1769, and was chosen its Speaker. He continued a member, and the Speaker of that body until 1774, and as chairman of the corresponding committee, he was arduous in plying his pen in the interchange of political sentiments with his compatriots in other colonies. He was elected a delegate to the General Congress, by a convention of the people of the three counties of Delaware, in Auguss, 1774, and took his seat at the opening of Congress, on the fifth of September following. His colleagues were Thomas M'Kean and George Read, and three more devoted and active men than these could hardly be found. He was one of a committee who drew up a Declaration of Rights and set forth, in an address, the causes for complaint, under which the colonists groaned.

Mr. Rodney was elected a delegate for 1775 and while attending to his duties in Congress, he was appointed Brigadier General of his province. This appointment imposed heavy additional duties upon him, yet he did not shrink from their performance, and he was alternately in Congress and at home, attending at the latter place to the duties of his military station. He was there during the closing debates upon the proposition for a Declaration of Independence in 1776, but was sent for by his colleague, Mr. M'Kean, so as to secure the vote of Delaware for that important measure. He arrived in time to give his voice for independence, and enjoyed the high privilege of signing the revered parchment. On his return to his constituents they approved, by acclamation, of his acts in the National Council.

In the autumn of 1776, the people of Delaware called a convention to frame a State Constitution, and to elect delegates to the next Congress. Through the machinations of tory members of that convention, whose principles to a great extent leavened it, Mr. Rodney and Mr. M'Kean were not re-elected. But this only tended to increase his ardor, and his pen was constantly busy in correspondence. He was also enabled by this defeat, to attend to his private affairs which had suffered much by his absence.

After the battle of Princeton at the beginning of 1777, in which Colonel Haslet, who belonged to General Rodney's brigade, was killed, the latter immediately started for the army, and meeting Lord Stirling at Philadelphia, received orders to remain at Princeton, and make it a sort of recruiting station. General Rodney remained there for about two months, when his services became no longer necessary and he returned to his family.

Soon after his return home, he was appointed a judge of the Supreme Court. He, however, declined the honor preferring the more active life of his military station. Ho

was soon afterward called to marshal his brigade to a scene
of insurrectionary disorder in Delaware, which he speedily
quelled; and he also joined the main army of Washington
when the British under Lord Howe landed at the mouth of
the Elk river, and directed their march toward Philadelphia.* Not long after this event, toryism became so much in
the minority, that it had but little power to oppose the patriots and General Rodney was again elected to Congress.
But the political agitation of his State demanded his presence there, and he remained. He was chosen President
of the State, and performed the arduous duties of his
office with great faithfulness for about four years. Delaware was peculiarly exposed to the predatory incursions
of the enemy, and it required great sagacity and arduous
toil for those who managed her affairs, to prevent a state
of anarchy.

While thus laboring for his country's good, Mr. Rodney
suffered greatly from the effects of a disease (cancer in the
cheek) that had been upon him from his youth, and it
made dreadful inroads upon his health. Feeling conscious
that he was wasting away, he retired from public life and
calmly awaited the summons for departure to the spirit-
land. He died early in the year 1783, when in the fifty-
third year of his age.

* General Howe, finding it impracticable to reach Philadelphia by land, embarked his troops on board the British fleet, then lying off Sandy Hook, and proceeded to the Chesapeake Bay. His troops were landed at the mouth of Elk
River on the twenty-fifth of August, 1777, and that was the first intimation Washington had of his real destination. The British immediately commenced their march
toward Philadelphia, and the Americans at the same time marched from that city
to meet them. They met upon the river Brandywine, where the battle of that
name, so disastrous to the Americans, occurred. It was there that La Fayette
greatly distinguished himself, and was severely wounded.

Geo. Read

EORGE READ was born in Cecil county, in the Province of Maryland, in the year 1734, and was the eldest of six brothers. He was of Irish descent. His grandfather was a wealthy resident of Dublin, his native city, and his father emigrated to America from Ireland, about 1726. George was placed in a school of considerable repute at Chester, in Pennsylvania, where he made much progress in Latin and Greek, his father having previously instructed

him in all the common branches of a good English education. He was afterward placed under the care of the
Reverend Doctor Allison, who at various times had charge
of several pupils, who were afterward members of the
Continental Congress, or held other high official stations.

At the age of seventeen years young Read commenced
the study of the law in the office of John Morland, a distinguished barrister of Philadelphia. He was very studious, and during his pupilage in the profession, he possessed the entire confidence of his instructor, who also became his warm friend. He was admitted to the bar in
1753, at the early age of nineteen years, and then commenced a career of honor and usefulness to himself and
others.* In 1754, he settled in the county of New Castle,
Delaware, and commenced the practice of his profession.
Although competitors of eminence were all around him,
Mr. Read soon rose to their level, and at the age of
twenty-nine, he succeeded John Ross,† as Attorney General for the "lower counties on the Delaware" of Kent,
Sussex and New Castle. This office he held until elected
a delegate to the Continental Congress, in 1774.

In 1765 Mr. Read was elected a member of the General Assembly of Delaware, and was re-elected to the
office eleven consecutive years. He was one of a committee of that body, who, in view of the odious features
of the Stamp Act, proposed an address to the King in behalf of the people of the Province. Mr. Read clearly
perceived however, that remonstrances from isolated Colo-

---

* We cannot pass unnoticed an act of noble generosity which marked his initial
step in his profession. As soon as he was admitted to the bar a practising attorney, he voluntarily released, by deed, all the legal right which he had in the estate of his father, in behalf of the rest of the children; alleging that he had received
his share in full in the expenses of his education, and that he conscientiously believed that it would be a fraud upon the others, if he should claim an equal share
with them in the final division.

† He was married in 1763 to the accomplished and pious daughter of the Reverend George Ross, the pastor of a Church in New Castle, and a relative at the
Attorney General

nies would have but little effect, and he was one of those patriots of prudence and sound judgment, who looked to a general Convention of representatives of the several Colonies, as the surest means through which the sense of justice in the home government could be reached. He also heartily approved of the system of non-importation agreements, and by assiduous labor, he succeeded in engaging the people of Delaware in the measure.

When the sufferings of the people of Boston, from the effects of the Act of Parliament known as the "Boston Port Bill,"* excited the warmest sympathy throughout the Colonies, and subscriptions for their relief were everywhere made—Mr. Read, with Nicholas Van Dyke, was made the channel of transmission of the donations of the people of Delaware, and he was exceedingly active himself in procuring pecuniary and other aid.

In 1774, Mr. Read, with Cæsar Rodney and Thomas M'Kean for colleagues, was appointed by the Assembly of Delaware, a delegate to the General Congress that met in September of that year, at Philadelphia. He was a delegate also in 1775 and 1776, and during the early part of the latter year, his labors were divided between his duties in Congress, and the affairs of his own State.† He

* On the thirty-first of March, 1774, the British Parliament passed an act for the punishment of the people of Boston for the destruction of tea in the harbor, on the sixteenth of December previous. It provided for the virtual and actual closing of the port. All importations and exportations were forbidden, and vessels were prohibited from entering or leaving that port. The Customs, Courts of Justice, and all government offices, were removed to Salem; and on the arrival of Governor Gage, a few days before the first of June (the time the act was to take effect), he called a meeting of the General Assembly of Massachusetts at Salem. Thus all business was suddenly crushed in Boston, and the inhabitants were reduced to great misery, overawed as they were by large bodies of armed troops. The people of the Colonies deeply sympathized with them, and lent them generous aid. And, strange as it may appear, the city of London subscribed one hundred and fifty thousand dollars for the poor of Boston!

† When, in 1777, soon after the battle of Brandywine, Governor M'Kinley, the President of the State, was taken prisoner by the British, Mr. Read, who was Vice President, was obliged to perform his duties. He discharged them with fidelity and at the same time he was active in the Committee of Safety. On one or two

was an earnest advocate for the Declaration of Independence, and considered it a high privilege when he placed his name upon the parchment. After the Declaration, the people of Delaware formed a State Constitution, and Mr. Read was President of the Convention that framed the instrument.

His arduous duties at length affected his health, and in August, 1779, he resigned his seat in the Assembly of Delaware. He was re-elected, however, the next year. In 1782, he was appointed one of the Judges of the Court of Appeals in Admiralty cases, and he retained the office until that tribunal was abolished. In 1785, Mr. Read was appointed by Congress one of the Justices of a special Court to adjudicate in a case of dispute about territory between Massachusetts and New York. In 1786, he was a member of the Convention that met at Annapolis, in Maryland, to consider and repair the defects in the Articles of Confederation. This Convention was the egg of the one, which, in the following year, framed the Federal Constitution. In 1788, he was elected a member of the Senate of Delaware, under the new Constitution, and he occupied a seat there until 1793, when he was elevated to the bench, as Chief Justice of the Supreme Court of his State. He occupied that station until the autumn of 1798, when death, by sudden illness, closed his useful life, in the sixty-fourth year of his age.

occasions he marched with the militia, musket in hand, to repel invasion. On his return to Delaware at the time Governor M'Kinley was made prisoner, Mr. Read and his whole family narrowly escaped the same fate. His family were with him in Philadelphia, and he was obliged to pass down the Jersey side of the Delaware, and cross at a place where the river is five miles wide. He procured a boat and proceeded within sight of the ships of the enemy. Before reaching the shore the boat grounded, and, being perceived from one of the British vessels, a skiff was sent in pursuit. Mr. Read had time to efface every mark from his baggage that might identify him, and so completely did he deceive the inmates of the skiff, by representing himself as a country gentleman just returning from an excursion with his family, that his pursuers kindly assisted in landing the ladies and the children, and in getting his boat ashore.

THOMAS M'KEAN was born in New London, Chester County, Pennsylvania, in the year 1734. His father was a native of Ireland, and Thomas was the second child of his parents. After receiving the usual elementary instruction, he was placed under the care of the Reverend Doctor Allison, and was a pupil under him with George Read. At the conclusion of his studies, he en tered the office of David Finney, of New Castle, as a law student; and so soon did his talents become manifest, that in the course of a few months after entering upon the study of the law, he was employed as an assistant clerk of the Court of Common Pleas. In fact, he performed all the duties of the principal. He was admitted to the bar before he was twenty-one years of age, and permitted to practise in the three counties of Delaware.

Mr. M'Kean soon rose to eminence in his profession, and attracted the attention of most of the leading men of the day. Without any solicitation, or premonition, he was appointed, by the Attorney General of the Province, his deputy[a] to prosecute all claims for the Crown in the county of Sussex. He was then only twenty-two years old. The next year (1767) he was admitted to practice in the Supreme Court of Pennsylvania, and about the same time the House of Assembly of Delaware, elected him their clerk. He declined a second election in 1758. In 1762, he was appointed, with Cæsar Rodney, to revise and print the laws of the Province enacted during the ten preceding years. He was elected that year a representative for New Castle, to the General Assembly. This promotion to office was a distinguished mark of the confidence of the people of that district, for he had expressed a desire not to be elected, and besides that he had been a resident of Philadelphia six years. Another singular manifestation of confidence in his integrity and judgment was exhibited by the people of the district, when, at his urgent request, he was allowed to relinquish his seat in the Legislature. They appointed a committee to wait on him and request him to nominate seven proper men in the district for their representatives. This delicate office he at first declined, but on the request being urgently repeated, and assurances offered that no offence should be given, he acceded to their desires, and those he named were elected by large majorities.

_a_ 1756.

Mr. M'Kean was a delegate to the "Stamp Act Congress" in 1765, and was the associate upon a committee with James Otis and Thomas Lynch, in preparing an address to the British House of Commons. For their services in that Congress, he and his colleague, Mr. Rodney, received the unanimous thanks of the Assembly of Delaware.

In 1765, he was appointed by the governor sole notary public for the "lower counties on the Delaware," and in rapid succession he received the offices of Justice of the Peace, Judge of the Court of Common Pleas and Quarter Sessions, and of the Orphan Court. He, with his colleagues, defied the Stamp Act, by using unstamped paper in their legal proceedings. In 1766, the governor of New Jersey, upon the recommendation of the Supreme Court of that State, admitted him to practice in any of its Courts. In 1769 the Assembly of Delaware employed him to proceed to New York and obtain copies of historical records, valuable to the former Province. In 1771, he was appointed Collector of the Customs for the port of New Castle, and the following year he was elected Speaker of the Assembly of Delaware.

Mr. M'Kean zealously opposed the encroachments of British power upon American rights, and he heartily concurred in the sentiments of the Massachusetts Circular, recommending a General Congress. He was elected a delegate thereto, was present at the opening on the fifth of September, 1774, and soon became distinguished as one of the most active men in that august body. He continued a member of the Continental Congress from that time, until the ratification of the treaty of peace, in 1783. Impressed with the conviction that reconciliation with Great Britain was out of the question, he zealously supported the measure which led to a final Declaration of Independ ence; and when that Declaration was submitted to Congress for action, he voted for and signed it.*

In September, 1776, (although then at the head of a regiment under Washington in New Jersey,) he was chosen a member of a Convention in Delaware to frame a State Constitution.† That instrument was the production of his pen, and was adopted by a unanimous vote.

Mr. M'Kean was claimed as a citizen by both Pennsylvania and Delaware,‡ and he faithfully served them both, for in 1777, he was Chief Justice of the former, and President of the latter. In addition to these offices he was Speaker of the Delaware Assembly, and delegate to the Continental Congress. In 1781, on the resignation of Mr. Huntington, of Connecticut, of the office of President of Congress, Mr. M'Kean was elected to succeed him. But he resigned the office in November following, and received the thanks of Congress for his able services while presiding over that body.§

* Being called away to aid General Washington in New Jersey, with a regiment of "Philadelphia Associators," (of which he was colonel,) immediately after the vote on the Declaration of Independence was taken, Mr. M'Kean did not sign the instrument until sometime in the month of October following.

† On receiving notice of his appointment, he set off for Dover, and on his arrival was requested by the Convention to draft a Constitution. He acceded to their request, and before the next morning the charter was completed.

‡ We have several times had occasion to mention the three counties which constituted the Province of Delaware, and the political connection which seemed to exist between it and Pennsylvania. The following was the relative position of the former to the latter. Delaware was originally included in the grant made to William Penn, and was a part of Pennsylvania. But, in 1691, the "three Lower counties on the Delaware," dissatisfied with some of the proceedings of the Executive Council, withdrew from the Union, with the reluctant consent of the proprietor, who appointed a deputy governor over them. The next year, the Provincial government was taken from William Penn, by a royal commission to Governor Fletcher, of New York, who re-united Delaware to Pennsylvania, under the name of the "Territory of the three Lower Counties on the Delaware." It remained subordinate to Pennsylvania until 1776, yet having a separate Legislature of its own.

§ During that year he was obliged to move his family five times, to avoid the marauding enemy. The next year (1788) party spirit running very high in Pennsylvania, he found a faction arrayed against him, who made an abortive attempt to impeach him, It was like "the viper biting a file."

From the period of the conclusion of the war, Judge M'Kean was actively engaged in Pennsylvania and Delaware in various services which the arrangement of discordant political elements into a symmetrical form of government required; and his labors in aid of the formation and adoption of the Federal Constitution, were various and arduous.* He continued in the chair of Chief Justice of Pennsylvania until 1799, (a period of twenty years,) when he was elected Governor of that State. To this office he was elected three successive terms, and held it nine years. At the session of 1807-8, of the Pennsylvania Legislature, his opponents presented articles of impeachment for maladministration, which closed with a resolution that "Thomas M'Kean, the Governor of the Commonwealth, be impeached of high crimes and misdemeanors." The charges were brought fully before the House, but by the summary measure of indefinitely postponing their consideration, they were never acted upon.

The last public act of Governor M'Kean, was to preside over the deliberations of the people of Philadelphia, when, during the war with Great Britain in 1812, that city was threatened with an attack from the enemy. He then withdrew into private life, where he remained until his death, which occurred on the twenty-fourth day of June, 1817, in the eighty-fourth year of his age.

* When the war of the Revolution was terminated, and the army disbanded, Congress, which had been powerful through its military arm, was rendered quite impotent, for the authority before concentrated in the National Legislature, returned to the individual States whence it emanated. Congress was burdened with a foreign debt of eight millions of dollars, and a domestic debt of thirty millions, and yet, according to the Articles of Confederation, it possessed no power to liquidate debts incurred during the war; it only possessed the privilege of recommending to the several States the payment thereof. The people lost nearly all regard for Congress, general indifference prevailed, and a disposition to refuse to pay any taxes whatever began to be cherished. General anarchy and confusion seemed to be the tendency of all things, and the leading men of the Revolution felt gloomy forebodings for the future. It was clearly seen that the serious defects of the Articles of Confederation were the root of the growing evil, and these convictions led to those measures which finally wrought out the Federal Constitution.

10

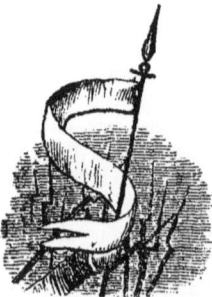

AMUEL CHASE was born on the seventeenth day of April, 1741, in Somerset county, Maryland. His father was a clergyman of the protestant episcopal church, and possessing an excellent education himself, he imparted such instruction to his son in the study of the classics, and in the common branches of an English education, as well fitted him for entering upon professional life. He commenced the study of law at the age of eighteen years, under Messrs. Hammond and Hall

146

of Annapolis, who stood at the head of their profession in that section of the province. At the age of twenty he was admitted to practice before the mayor's court; and at twenty-two he became a member of the bar, and was allowed to practise in the chancery and other colonial courts. He located at Annapolis, where he soon became distinguished as an advocate, and one of the most successful lawyers in the province.

At the early age of twenty years, Mr. Chase was chosen a member of the Provincial Assembly, and there his independence of feeling and action in matters of principle greatly offended those time-serving legislators who fawned at the feet of the royal governor. There he first gave evidence of that stamina of character which he afterward so strongly manifested when called upon to act amid the momentous scenes of the Revolution.

The Stamp Act aroused the energies of his soul to do battle for his country's right, and he was among the first in Maryland who lifted up voice and hand against the oppressor.* He became obnoxious to the authorities of Annapolis, and they attempted, by degrading epithets, to crush his eagle spirit while yet a fledgling. But their persecution extended his notoriety, and he soon became popular with the great mass of the people.

Mr. Chase was one of the five delegates to the first Continental Congress, in 1774, appointed by a convention of the people of Maryland. He was also appointed by the same meeting, one of the "Committee of Correspondence" for that colony.† These appointments made him

---

* He was one of a band of young patriots, who, in imitation of those of Massachusetts, styled themselves "Sons of Liberty." They opposed the operation of the Stamp Act in every form, and even went so far as to assault the Stamp Offices, and destroy the Stamps.

† These committees of correspondence constituted a powerful agent in the great work of the Revolution. Their conception was simultaneous in Massachusetts and Virginia, and both States claim the honor of priority. At first these committees were confined to the larger cities, out very speedily every village and

obnoxious to the adherents to royalty, yet their good opinion was the least thing he coveted. In the General Congress he was bold and energetic, and even at that early
day, he expressed his sentiments freely in favor of absolute
independence. This feeling, however, was not general
in the colonies, and the people were desirous of reconciliation by righteous means, rather than independence.

Mr. Chase was again elected to Congress in 1775, and
with his usual zeal, he was active in promoting every
measure for strengthening the military force of the country, then concentrated in the vicinity of Boston. He was
also a delegate in 1776, and in the meanwhile he had
used his growing influence and popularity to the utter-
most in endeavoring to have the Maryland convention
remove its restrictive instructions by which its delegates
were prohibited from voting in favor of independence.
This restriction was a galling yoke for him to bear, and
he was very restiff under it.

Early in the spring of 1776, he was appointed one of a
committee with Dr. Franklin and Charles Carroll, to go
on a mission to Canada, the chief object of which was to
effect a concurrence, in that province, with the movements
in the other English colonies. The mission, however,
proved a failure, and on his return to his seat in Congress
he found the subject of independence before that body.
He was warmly in favor of the measure, and to his great
joy and satisfaction, Maryland lifted her restrictions and
left her representatives free to vote as they liked. Mr.
Chase of course gave his vote for the Declaration of Independence, and signed the instrument with a willing hand.

hamlet had its auxiliary committees, and the high moral tone evinced by the
Chiefs, ran through all the gradations, from the polished committees appointed by
Colonial Assemblies, to the rustic, yet not the least patriotic ones of the interior
towns; and through these made an impression upon the whole American people.
Thus the patriot heart of America, at this crisis, (1773,) beat as with one pulsation.
and the public mind was fully prepared to act with promptness and decision
when circumstances should call for action.—"1776," page 105.

He continued a member of Congress until in 1778, and was almost constantly employed in the duties of most important committees. Some of these were of a delicate and trying nature, yet he never allowed his sensibility to control his judgment, or shake his firmness of purpose.* His private affairs demanding his attention, Mr. Chase withdrew from Congress toward the close of 1778, and he resumed the practice of his profession in Annapolis. He was engaged but little in public affairs for several years, and it was not until 1788, about ten years after he retired from Congress, that he again appeared in the arena of the political world. He was then appointed Chief Justice of the criminal court for the newly organized judicial district of Baltimore.† He was that year chosen a member of the state convention of Maryland, called to consider the ratification of the Federal Constitution, and about the same time he received and accepted the appointment of Chief Justice of the Supreme Court of the state. In 1796, President Washington nominated him a judge of of the Supreme Court of the United States, which nomination was confirmed by the Senate. He held the office about fifteen years, and no man ever stood higher for honesty of purpose and integrity of motives, than Judge

* He was chairman of a committee appointed by Congress to act in relation to those Americans who gave "aid and comfort to the enemy;" and it was his painful duty to recommend the arrest and imprisonment of various persons of this class, among whom were several wealthy Quakers of Philadelphia. An instance of his fearlessness in the performance of his duty, may be properly mentioned here. During the summer of 1776, Reverend Doctor Zubly was a delegate in Congress from Georgia. By some means Mr. Chase discovered that he was in secret correspondence with the royal governor of Georgia. He immediately rose in his place and denounced Doctor Zubly as a traitor, before all the members of the House. Zubly fled, and was pursued, but without success.

† Mr. Chase had moved from Annapolis to Baltimore, on the urgent solicitation of Colonel Howard, one of the largest property holders in the vicinity of that city. He offered to Mr. Chase one full square for city building lots, if he would make Baltimore his residence. The offer was accepted, the property was conveyed to him, and now, being within the city, is very valuable. It is in the possession of the descendants of Judge Chase.

Chase. Notwithstanding the rancor of such party feeling as dared to charge President Washington with appropriating the public money to his own private use, did all in its power to pluck the ermine from his shoulders,* yet his purity beamed the brighter, as the clouds grew darker, and he lived to hear the last whisper of calumny flit by like a bat in the morning twilight. His useful life terminated on the nineteenth day of June, 1811, when he was in the seventieth year of his age.

Judge Chase was a man of great benevolence of feeling† and in all his walks, he exemplified the beauties of Christianity, of which he was a sincere professor. At the time of his death he was a communicant in St. Paul's church in Baltimore, the parish of which, when he was a child, his father had pastoral charge.

---

* His political and personal opponents procured his impeachment in 1804, for malconduct on the bench. He was tried and honorably acquitted, to the shame and confusion of his enemies.

† We cannot forbear relating an instance in which this characteristic was displayed. Being on a visit to Baltimore, about the close of the Revolution, curiosity led him to a debating society, where he was struck by the eloquence of a young man, a druggist's clerk. He ascertained his name, sought an interview, and advised him to study law. The youth stated frankly that his poverty was an insuperable impediment in the way. Mr. Chase at once offered him a seat at his table and free access to his extensive library. The young man gratefully accepted the kind offer, went though a course of legal studies, and was admitted to the bar, after passing an examination with distinguished ability. That young man was William Pinkney, afterward Attorney General of the United States, and minister for the same at the Court of Great Britain.

Thos Stone

ANY of those bold patriots who pledged life, fortune, and honor, in support of the independence of the United States of America, left behind them but few written memorials of the scenes in which they took a conspicuous part, and hence the biographers who first engaged in the task of delineating the characters and acts of those men, were obliged to find their materials in scattered fragments among public records, or from the lips of surviving relations or compatriots. Such was the case of Thomas Stone, the subject of this brief sketch, whose un assuming manners and attachment to domestic life kept him in apparent obscurity except when called forth by the commands of duty.

Thomas Stone was born at the Pointoin Manor, in the Province of Maryland, in the year 1743. After receiving a good English education, and some knowledge of the classics, he entered upon the study of the law, and at the age of twenty-one years he commenced its practice. Where he began business in his profession, is not certainly known, but it is supposed to have been in Annapolis.

Although quite unambitious of personal fame, he nevertheless, from the impulses of a patriotic heart, espoused the cause of the patriots and took an active part in the movements preliminary to the calling of the first General Congress in 1774. He was elected one of the first five delegates thereto from that state, and after actively performing his duties throughout that first short session,* he again retired to private life. But his talents and patriotism had become too conspicuous for his fellow citizens to allow him to remain inactive, and toward the latter part of 1775, he was again elected to the General Congress. As we have before observed, the people of Maryland, although warmly opposed to the oppressive measures of the British government, and determined in maintaining their just rights, yet a large proportion of them were too much attached to the mother-country, to harbor a thought of political independence. They therefore instructed their delegates not to vote for such a proposition, and thus Mr. Stone, like his colleagues, who were all for independence, felt themselves fettered by an onerous

* The first Continental Congress convened on the fourth day of September, 1774, and adjourned on the twenty-sixth day of October following—a session of only fifty-two days. Yet within that time they organized, or made provisions for those efficient movements which afterward took place in favor of freedom; and they sent forth to the world those able addresses and petitions, which so much excited the admiration of the statesmen of Europe.—*See note, Life of Philip Livingston.*

bond. But the restriction was removed in June, 1776, and Mr. Stone, like Paca and others, voted for and signed the Declaration of Independence. And it is worthy of record that on the fourth of July, the very day on which the vote for Independence was given, Mr. Stone and his colleagues from Maryland, were re-elected by the unanimous voice of the same convention, which, about six weeks previously forbade them thus to act.

The unobtrusive character of Mr. Stone kept him from becoming a very prominent member of Congress, yet his great good sense and untiring industry in the business of important committees, rendered him a very useful one. He was one of the committee who framed the Articles of Confederation, which were finally adopted in November, 1777. He was again elected to Congress that year, and finally retired from it early in 1778, and entered the Legislature of his own State, where he earnestly advocated the adoption, by that body, of the Articles of Confederation. The Maryland Legislature was too strongly imbued with the ultra principles of State rights and absolute independence of action to receive with favor the proposition for a general political Union, with Congress for a Federal head, and it was not until 1781 that that State agreed to the confederation.

Mr. Stone was again elected to Congress in 1783, and was present when General Washington resigned his military commission into the hands of that body. In 1784, he was appointed President of Congress, pro tempore; and had not his native modesty supervened, he would doubtless have been regularly elected to that important station, then the highest office in the gift of the people. On the adjournment of Congress, he returned to his constituents and resumed the duties of his profession at Port Tobacco, the place of his residence, where he died, on the fifth of October, 1787, in the forty-fifth year of his age.

Wm Paca

WILLIAM PACA was the descendant of a wealthy planter on the east shore of Maryland. He was born at Wye Hall, his paternal residence, in the year 1740. His early moral and intellectual training was carefully attended to, and at a proper age he was placed in the Philadelphia College, whence he graduated, after a course of arduous and profitable study, with great credit to himself. He then commenced the study of the law with Mr. Hammond and Mr. Hall, of Annapolis, and Samuel Chase, his subsequent Congressional colleague, was a fellow student.

154

Mr. Paca, was admitted to the bar at the age of twenty, and the next year (1761), he was chosen a member of the Provincial Assembly. When the Stamp Act, in 1765, aroused the people of the colonies to their common danger, Mr. Paca, with Mr. Chase and Mr. Carroll, warmly opposed its operation. And every succeeding measure of the British government, asserting its right to tax the Americans without their consent, was fearlessly condemned by him, and thus he soon obtained the disapprobation of the royal governor of the Province, and of those who adhered to the king and parliament. Like Mr Chase, he became very popular with the people by his patriotic conduct.

He approved of the proposition for a General Congress in 1774, and he zealously promoted the meeting of the people in county conventions to express their sentiments upon this point. He was appointed by a State Convention of Maryland, one of its five representatives in the Continental Congress, who were instructed to "agree to all measures which might be deemed necessary to obtain a redress of American grievances." Mr. Paca was re-elected in 1775, and continued a member of Congress until 1778, when he was appointed Chief Justice of the Supreme Court of his state.

Like Mr. Chase, Mr. Paca was much embarrassed in Congress by the opposition of his constituents to independence, and their loyal adherence to the British Crown, as manifested in their instructions, frequently repeated in the early part of 1776.* Even as late as the middle of May, they passed a resolution prohibiting their delegates from voting for independence; but on the twenty-eighth of the

---

* The people of Maryland, as represented in its State Convention, were alarmed lest their enthusiastic delegates should favor independence, and early in 1776, they sent them instructions, in which they forbade their voting for such a measure. They also passed a resolution "that Maryland would not be bound by a vote of a majority of Congress to declare independence."

same month a remarkable change in their opinions took place, and they *ceased praying for the king and royal family!* This was a sort of half wheel, and toward the latter part of June the convention finished its evolutions by a "right about face" and withdrew their restrictions upon the votes of their delegates. Thus relieved, Mr. Paca and his associates continued their efforts to effect a declaration of independence with more zeal than ever, and recorded their votes for the severance of the political bond of union with Britain, on the fourth of July following. On the second of August, they fearlessly affixed their signatures to the parchment.

About the beginning of 1778, Mr. Paca was appointed Chief Justice of the State of Maryland. He performed the duties with great ability and fidelity until 1782, when he was elected President or Governor of the State, under the old Articles of Confederation. He held the executive office one year, and then retired to private life.

In 1788, he was a member of the convention of Maryland, called to act upon the ratification of the Federal Constitution. He was a firm advocate there for its ratification, which event took place in November. After the New Constitution had gone into effect, and offices under it were to be filled, President Washington nomina-

a 1789.   ted him Judge for the district of Maryland.*a*

This office he held until the period of his death, which was in the year 1799, when he was in the sixtieth year of his age. He was a pure and active patriot, a consistent Christian, and a valuable citizen, in every sense of the word. His death was mourned as a public calamity; and his life, pure and spotless, active and useful, exhibited a bright exemplar for the imitation of the young men of America.

Charles Carroll of Carrollton

HARLES CARROLL was descended from Irish ancestry. His grandfather, Daniel Carroll, was a native of Littemourna, in Ireland, and was a clerk in the office of Lord Powis, in the reign of James the Second. Under the patronage of Lord Baltimore, the principal proprietor of Maryland, Mr. Carroll emigrated to that Colony toward the close of the seventeenth century, and became the possessor of a large plantation. His son Charles, the father of the subject of this memoir, was born in 1702, and lived

157

to the age of eighty years, when he died and left his large estate to his eldest child, Charles, who was then twenty-five years old.

Charles Carroll, the Revolutionary patriot, was born on the twentieth of September, 1737. When he was only eight years of age, his father, who was a Roman Catholic, took him to France, and entered him as a student in the Jesuit College at St. Omer's. There he remained six years, and then went to another Jesuit seminary of learning, at Rheims. After remaining there one year, he entered the College of Louis le Grand, whence he graduated at the age of seventeen years, and then commenced the study of law at Bourges. He remained at Bourges one year, and then moved to Paris, where he continued until 1757. He then went to London for the purpose of continuing his law studies there. He took apartments in the Inner Temple, where he remained until 1765, and then returned to Maryland, a most finished scholar and well-bred gentleman.

The passage of the Stamp Act, about the time that he returned to America, arrested his attention and turned his mind more intently upon political affairs, of which he had not, for some time, been an indifferent spectator. He at once espoused the cause of the American patriots, and became associated with Chase, Paca, Stone, and others, in the various patriotic movements of the day. They became engaged in a newspaper war with the authorities of Maryland, and so powerfully did these patriots wield the pen, that their discomfited opponents soon beat a retreat behind the prerogatives and power of the royal governor. Mr. Carroll was particularly distinguished as a political writer, and in 1771-'72, his name, as such, became familiar in the other Colonies.

In 1772, he wrote a series of essays against the assumed right of the British government to tax the Colonies with out their consent. The Secretary of the Colony wrote in opposition to them, but Mr. Carroll triumphed most emphatically. His essays were signed "The First Citizen," and the name of the author was entirely unknown. But so grateful were the people for the noble defence of their cause which these papers contained, that they instructed the members of the Legislative Assembly of Maryland, to return their hearty thanks to the unknown writer, through the public prints. This was done by William Paca, and Matthew Hammond. When it became known that Mr. Carroll was the writer, large numbers of people went to him and expressed their thanks personally, and he at once stood among the highest in popular confidence and favor.

Mr. Carroll early foresaw that a resort to arms in defence of Colonial rights, was inevitable, and this opinion he fearlessly expressed. His decided character, his stern integrity, and his clear judgment, made him an umpire in many momentous cases,* and in every step he ascended higher and higher the scale of popular favor. He was appointed a member of the first Committee of Safety of Maryland; and in 1775, he was elected a member of the Provincial Assembly. His known sentiments in favor of independence were doubtless the cause of his not being sooner sent to the General Congress, for, as we have already seen, the Maryland Convention were opposed to that extreme measure.

Anxious to witness the men and their proceedings in

---

* As an instance of the entire confidence which the people had in his judgment, it is related, that when, in 1773-'4, the "tea excitement" was at its height, a Mr. Stewart of Annapolis, imported a quantity of the obnoxious article. The people were exasperated, and threatened to destroy the tea if landed. The Provincial Legislature being then in session, appointed a committee of delegates to superintend the unlading of the cargo and see that no tea was landed. With this the people were not satisfied, and Mr. Stewart appealed to Mr. Carroll to interpose his influence. The latter told him it would be impossible to have any effect upon the public mind in this matter, where such an important principle was concerned, and he advised Mr. Stewart to allow the vessel and cargo to be burned. This advice Mr Stewart followed, and by his consent the conflagration took place.

the Continental Congress, he visited Philadelphia for the purpose, early in 1776, and so favorably was he known there, that Congress placed him on a committee, with Doctor Franklin and Samuel Chase, to visit Canada on an important mission, the object of which we have mentioned in the life of Mr. Chase. On his return, finding Mr. Lee's motion for independence before Congress, he hastened to Maryland, to endeavor, if possible, to have the restrictive instructions which governed her delegates in the National Assembly, removed. In this he was successful, and when the prohibition was removed, he was elected a delegate to the Continental Congress. With instructions to vote as the judgment of the delegates should dictate, Mr. Carroll proceeded to Philadelphia, where he arrived on the eighth of July, too late to *vote* for the Declaration of Independence,* but in ample time to affix his signature to the parchment.

Ten days after he took his seat in Congress, Mr. Carroll was placed upon the Board of War, and continued a member of the same during his continuance in that body. He was at the same time a member of the Assembly of Maryland, and all the time which he could spare from his duties at Philadelphia, he spent in the active service of his own State. He was appointed, in 1776, a member of the Convention that framed a Constitution for Maryland as an independent State, and after its adoption, he was chosen a member of the State Senate.

Mr. Carroll continued a member of Congress until 1788, when he relinquished his seat, and devoted himself to the interests of his native State. He was again elected to the

---

*The question naturally arises, Why did Mr. Carroll append to his signature the place of his residence, "Carrollton"? It is said that when he wrote his name, a delegate near him suggested, that as he had a cousin of the name of Charles Carroll, in Maryland, the latter might be taken for him, and he (the signer) es cape attainder, or any other punishment that might fall upon the heads of the patriots. Mr. Carroll immediately seized the pen, and wrote "of Carrollt in" at the end of his name, exclaiming "They cannot mistake me now!"

Senate of Maryland, in 1781, and continued a member of that body until the adoption of the Federal Constitution In December, 1788, he was elected a member of the first United States Senate for Maryland. He remained there two years, and in 1791 he was again elected to the Senate of Maryland, where he continued until 1801, when, by the machinations of the strong party feeling of the day, he was defeated as a candidate for re-election. He then retired from public life, being sixty-four years of age; and he spent the remainder of his days amid the quiet pleasures of domestic retirement, where his children's children, and even their children grew up around him like olive plants. He lived, honored and revered by the Republic with whose existence he was identified, until 1832, and was the last survivor of the fifty-six signers of the Declaration of Independence. He died at Baltimore, on the fourteenth day of November, 1832, in the ninety-sixth year of his age.

For a long term of years, Mr. Carroll was regarded by the people of this country with the greatest veneration, for, when Jefferson and Adams died, he was the last vestige that remained upon earth of that holy brotherhood, who stood sponsor at the baptism in blood of our infant Republic. The good and the great made pilgrimages to his dwelling, to behold, with their own eyes, the venerable political patriarch of America, and from the rich store-house of his intellect, he freely contributed to the deficiencies of others. "His mind was highly cultivated. He was always a model of regularity of conduct, and sedateness of judgment. In natural sagacity, in refinement of taste and pleasures, in unaffected and habitual courtesy, in vigilant observation, vivacity of spirit, and true susceptibility of domestic and social happiness, in the best forms, he had but few equals during the greater part of his long and bright existence.'

11

George Wythe

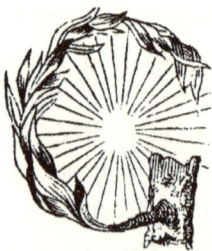

EORGE WYTHE was one of Virginias most distinguished sons. He was born in the year 1726, in Elizabeth county, and being the child of wealthy parents, he had every opportunity given him which the colony afforded for acquiring a good education. His father died when he was quite young, and his education and moral training devolved upon his mother, a woman of superior abilities. She was very proficient in the Latin lauguage, and she aided him much in the study of the classics. But

162

before he was twenty-one years of age, death deprived him
of her guidance and instruction; and he was left at that
early period of life with a large fortune and the entire control of his own actions. His character not having become
fixed, he launched out upon the dangerous sea of pleasure
and dissipation, and for ten years of the morning of his life
he laid aside study and sought only personal gratification

When about thirty years of age, a sudden change was
wrought in him, and he forsook the places of revelry and
the companionship of the thoughtless and gay, and resumed the studies of his youth with all the ardor of one
anxious to make up lost time. He mourned over his mis-
spent days, even in his old age which was clustered round
with honors, and he felt intensely the truth of the assertion that "time once lost, is lost forever." He at once
commenced a course of study, preparatory to entering
upon the profession of the law, and he became a student in the office of Mr. Jones, then one of the most distinguished lawyers in the colony. He was admitted to
the bar in 1757, and rose rapidly to eminence, not only
as an able advocate, but as a strictly conscientious one,
for he would never knowingly engage in an unjust cause.
Strict in all his business relations, and honorable to the
last degree, he was honored with the full confidence of
the people of Virginia, and when that state organized
an independent government pursuant to the recommendations of Congress, Mr. Wythe was appointed Chancellor of the State, then the highest judicial office in the gift
of the people. That office he held during his life.

For several years prior to the Revolution, Mr. Wythe
was a member of the Virginia House of Burgesses, and
when the Stamp Act aroused the patriotic resistance
of the people, he stood shoulder to shoulder in that Assembly with Patrick Henry, Richard Henry Lee, Peyton
Randolph and others, who were distinguished as leaders

in legislation when the storm of the War of Independence burst upon the land.

In 1775, Mr. Wythe was elected a delegate to the Gene ral Congress, and was there in 1776, when his colleague, Mr. Lee submitted his bold resolution for Independence He steadfastly promoted every measure tending toward such a result, and he voted for and signed the Declaration of Independence. During the autumn of that year, he was associated with Thomas Jefferson and Edmund Pendleton in codifying the laws of Virginia, to make them conformable to the newly organized government. This duty was performed with singular ability.

In 1777, he was chosen Speaker of the House of Burgesses of Virginia, and the same year he was elevated to the bench as one of the three judges of the high court of Chancery. When the new court of Chancery was organized, he was appointed sole judge, and occupied that bench with great ability for twenty years. Always firm in his decisions, which were never made without serious investigation and analysis, he seldom gave dissatisfaction, even to the defeated party.* For a while he was professor of law in the college of William and Mary, but when he removed to Richmond, he found it impracticable to attend to its duties, and he resigned the office.†

In 1786, Mr. Wythe was chosen a delegate to the National Convention that framed the Federal Constitution. He was also a member of the Virginia convention called to consider its adoption, and was twice chosen a United States Senator under it. Notwithstanding the constant

---

* He was called upon to make the first decision on the important question whether debts contracted by persons in the United States to men in Great Britain, were or were not recoverable by law. The general feeling in the public mind was with the negative side of the question, but Chancellor Wythe, after patiently investigating the whole matter, fearlessly gave his opinion that such debts were binding and legally recoverable.

† Chancellor Wythe had the honor of being the law instructor of two of the Presidents, and one Chief Justice of the United States.

demand upon his time, which the duties of his official station made, he opened and taught a private school, free to those who chose to attend it. Among other pupils was a negro boy belonging to him, whom he taught Latin, and he was preparing to give him a thorough education, when both he and the boy died. This occurrence took place the eighth day of June, 1800, when Mr. Wythe was in the eighty-first year of his age. His death was sudden and was believed to have been caused by poison placed in his food by a near relative. That person was tried for the crime, but acquitted. The negro boy alluded to, partook of the same food, and died a short time previous to his master.

Mr. Wythe was a man of great perseverance and industry, kind and benevolent to the utmost;* was strict in his integrity, sincere in every word, faithful in every trust; and his life presents a striking example of the force of good resolution triumphing over the seductions of pleasure and vice, and the attainments which persevering and virtuous toil will bring to the practician of these necessary ingredients for the establishment of an honorable reputation, and in the labors of a useful life.

Mr. Wythe was twice married, but he left no offspring, an only child, by his first wife, having died in infancy.

---

* During his lifetime he manumitted all of his adult slaves, and he provided for the freedom of the younger ones, who were his property at the time of his death. He also made provision in his will for the support of a man, woman, and child, unto whom he had given freedom.

Rich ard Henry Lee

ICHARD HENRY LEE was a scion of the noblest stock of Virginia gentlemen. Could ancestral dignity and renown add aught to the coronal that enwreathes the urn of his memory, it is fully entitled to it, for his relations for several generations were distinguished for wealth, intellect and virtue.

Richard Henry Lee was born in the county of Westmoreland, Virginia, on the twentieth day of January, 1732, within a month of time, and within a few miles space

166

of the great and good Washington. According to the fashion of the time in the "Old Dominion," his father sent him to England, at an early age to be educated. He was placed in a school at Wakefield, in Yorkshire, where he soon became marked as a thoughtful and industrious student. Ancient history, especially that part which treats of the republics of the old world, engaged his close attention; and he read with avidity, every scrap of history of that character, which fell in his way. Thus he was early indoctrinated with the ideas of republicanism, and before the season of adolescence had passed, he was warmly attached to those principles of civil liberty, which he afterward so manfully contended for.

Young Lee returned to Virginia when nearly nineteen years of age, and there applied himself zealously to literary pursuits. He was active in all the athletic exercises of the day; and when about twenty years of age, his love of activity led him to the formation of a military corps, to the command of which, he was elected, and he first appeared in public life in 1755, when Braddock arrived from England, and summoned the colonial Governor to meet him in council, previous to his starting on an expedition against the French and Indians upon the Ohio. Mr. Lee presented himself there, and tendered the services of himself and his volunteers, to the British General. The haughty Braddock proudly refused to accept the services of those plain volunteers, deeming the disciplined troops whom he brought with him, quite sufficient to drive the invading Frenchmen from the English domain.*

---

* Braddock did indeed accept the services of Major Washington and a force of Virginia militia, and had he listened to the advice of the young Virginia soldier, he might not only have avoided the disastrous defeat at the Great Meadows, but saved his own life. But when Washington, who was well acquainted with the Indian mode of warfare, modestly offered his advice, the haughty Braddock said: 'What, an American buskin teach a British General how to fight!" The advice was unheeded, the day was lost, and Braddock was among the slain

Lee, deeply mortified, and disgusted with the insolent bear
ing of the British General returned home with his troops.

In 1757 he was appointed, by the royal governor, a
justice of the peace for the county in which he resided;
and such confideuce had the other magistrates in his fit-
ness to preside at the court, that they petitioned the
Governor so to date Mr. Lee's commission, that he might
be legally appointed the President. About the same
time he was elected a member of the House of Burgesses
of Virginia, although then only twenty-five years old.*
He was too diffident to engage in the debates, and it
was not until some time afterward that he displayed those
powers of oratory, which distinguished him in the Gene
ral Congress.†

Mr. Lee fearlessly expressed his sentiments of reproba
tion of the course pursued by the British Government
toward the colonies, and he organized the first association
in Virginia for opposing British oppression in that colony,
when it came in the form of the "Stamp Act." He was

* Such confidence had the people in the judgment and integrity of Mr. Lee, even
though so young, that, it is said, numbers of people on their dying beds, committed
to him the guardianship of their children.

† The first time he ever took part in a debate, sufficiently to make a set speech,
was in the House of Burgesses, when it was proposed to "lay so heavy a duty on
the importation of slaves, as effectually to stop that disgraceful traffic." His feelings were strongly enlisted in favor of the measure, and the speech which he
made on the occasion astonished the audience, and revealed those powers of oratory which before lay concealed. His fearlessness and independence of spirit, as
well as his eloquence, were soon afterward manifested when he undertook the
task of calling to account Mr. Robinson, the delinquent treasurer of the colony.
A large number of the members of the House of Burgesses, who belonged to the
old aristocracy of Virginia, were men, who, by extravagance and dissipation, had
wasted their estates, and resorted to the ruinous practice of borrowing to keep up
an expensive style of living not warranted by their reduced means. Nearly
all of them had borrowed money of Mr. Robinson, and he had even gone so far as
to lend them treasury notes, already redeemed, which it was his duty to destroy,
to secure the public against loss. He believed that their influence and number in
the House of Burgesses, would screen him from punishment, supposing there
were none hardy enough to array himself against them. But Mr. Lee *did* array
himself against all that corrupt power, and in the prosecution of the delinquent
treasurer, carried his point successfully.

the first man in Virginia, who stood publicly forth in opposition to the execution of that measure, and although by birth, education and social station, he ranked with the aristocracy, he was foremost in breaking down those distinctions between the wealthy class and the "common people," as those self-constituted patricians called those who labored with their hands. Associated with him, was the powerful Patrick Henry, whose stormy eloquence strongly contrasted with the sweet-toned and persuasive rhetoric of Lee, but when they united their power the shock was always irresistible.

Mr. Lee was one of the first "Committee of Correspondence"* appointed in Virginia in 1778, and he was greatly aided in the acquirement of knowledge respecting the secret movements and opinions of the British Parliament, by frequent letters from his brother, Arthur Lee, who was a distinguished literary character in London, and an associate with the leading men of the realm He furnished him with the earliest political intelligence, and it was generally so correct, that the Committees of Correspondence in other colonies always received without doubt, any information which came from the Virginia Committee. Through this secret channel of correct intelligence, Richard Henry Lee very early learned that nothing short of absolute political independence would probably arrest the progress of British oppression and misrule, in America. Hence, while other men

---

* To Mr Lee is doubtless due the credit of first suggesting the system of "Committees of Correspondence," although Virginia and Massachusetts both claim the honor of publicly proposing the measure first. So far as that claim is concerned, the proposition was almost simultaneous in the Assembly of both Provinces. It was proposed in the Virginia Assembly, on the twelfth of March, 1773, by Dabney Carr, a brother-in-law of Mr. Jefferson, and a young man of brilliant talents. The plan, however, was fixed on in a caucus at the "Raleigh Tavern," and Richard Henry Lee was one of the number. But in a letter to John Dickenson, of Pennsylvania, dated July twenty-fifth, 1768, Mr. Lee proposed the system of "Corresponding Committees," as a powerful instrument in uniting the sentiments of the colonists on the great political questions constantly arising to view

thought timidly of independence, and regarded it merely as a possibility of the distant future, Mr. Lee looked upon it as a measure that must speedily be accomplished, and his mind and heart were prepared to propose it whenever expediency should favor the movement.

He was very active in promoting the prevalence of non-importation agreements;* and when he heard, through his brother, of the "Boston Port Bill," he drew up a series of condemnatory resolutions to present to the Virginia Assembly.† The Governor heard of them, and dissolved the Assembly before the resolutions could be introduced. Of course this act of royal power greatly exasperated the people, and instead of checking the ball that Mr. Lee had put in motion, it accelerated its speed. The controversy between the Governor and representatives here begun, continued, and the breach grew wider and wider, until at length, in August, 1774, a convention of delegates of the people assembled at Williamsburgh, in despite of the Governor's proclamation, and appointed Richard Henry Lee, Patrick Henry, George Washington and Peyton Randolph, to the General Congress called to meet in Philadelphia on the fifth of September, following. In that Congress, Mr. Lee was one of the prime movers, and his convincing and persuasive eloquence nerved the timid to act and speak out boldly for the rights of the colonists. His conduct there made a profound impression upon the public mind, and he stood be-

---

* Long before non-importation agreements were proposed, Mr. Lee practised the measure. In order to show the people of Great Britain that America was really independent of them in matters of luxury, as well as necessity, he cultivated native grapes, and produced most excellent wine. He sent several bottles to his friends in Great Britain, "to testify his respect and gratitude for those who had shown particular kindness to Americans." He told them that it was the production of his own hills; and he ordered his merchant in London, who had before furnished his wine, not to send any more, nor any other articles on which Parliament had imposed a duty to be paid by Americans.

†One of these resolutions proposed the calling of a General Congress, but even the warmest partisans thought this measure altogether too rash to be thought of.

fore his countrymen as one of the brightest lights of the age.

Mr. Lee was elected a member of the House of Burgesses of Virginia as soon as he returned home from Congress, and there his influence was unbounded. He was again elected a delegate to the General Congress for the session of 1775, and the instructions and commission to General Washington as commander-in-chief of the Continental army were the productions of his pen. He was placed upon the most important committees, and the second "Address" of Congress to the people of Great Britain, which created such a sensation in that country, was written by him. During a short recess in September, he was actively engaged in the Virginia Assembly where he effectually stripped the mask from the "conciliatory measures," so called, of Lord North, which were evidently arranged to deceive and divide the American people. By this annihilation of the last vestige of confidence in royalty, in the hearts of the people of Virginia, he became very obnoxious to Lord Dunmore, the royal governor of the province, and he tried many ways to silence the patriot.

Mr. Lee was a delegate in the Congress of 1776, and on the seventh day of June of that year, pursuant to the dictates of his own judgment and feelings, and in obedience to the express instructions of the Assembly of Virginia, he introduced the resolution so often referred to in these memoirs, for a total separation from the mother-country.* The consideration of the resolution was made the special order of the day, for the first Monday in July, and a committee, of which Thomas Jefferson was chairman, was appointed to draw up a Declaration of Indepen-

---

* The resolution was as follows:- *"Resolved,* That these United Colonies are, and of right ought to be, free and independent States; that they are absolved from all allegiance to the British Crown; and that all political connection between them and the State of Great Britain is, and ought to be, totally dissolved."

dence.* This document was presented to Congress on the first day of July; and after several amendments made in committee of the whole, it was adopted on the fourth, by the unanimous votes of the thirteen United Colonies.

Mr. Lee continued an active and indefatigable member of Congress until 1779, when, as lieutentant of the county of Westmoreland, he entered the field at the head of the militia, in defence of his State. He was occasionally absent from Congress on account of his health, and once on account of being charged with toryism, because he received his rents in produce, instead of the depreciated continental currency! He demanded and obtained an investigation before the Virginia Assembly, and it resulted in the passage of a resolution of thanks for his many services in and out of Congress, and by his immediate re-election to a seat there.

Mr. Lee was again chosen a delegate to Congress in 1783, and was elected President thereof by the unanimous voice of that body. He filled the high station with ability, and at the end of the session received the thanks of that assembly. Although not a member of any legislative assembly when the Federal Constitution was submitted to the several States for action, he wielded a powerful influence, in connection with Patrick Henry and others, in opposing its ratification by Virginia, without amendments. But when it was finally adopted and became the organic law of the Union, he cheerfully united in carrying it into effect, and was chosen the first Senator

---

* The Committee consisted of Thomas Jefferson, Dr. Franklin, John Adams. Roger Sherman, and Robert R. Livingston. It may be asked, why was not Mr. Lee, by common courtesy, at least, put upon that committee, and designated its chairman? The reason was, that on the very day he offered the resolution, an express arrived from Virginia, informing him of the illness of some of his family which caused him to ask leave of absence. and he immediately started for home He was therefore absent from Congress when the committee was formed.

from Virginia under it. He retained the office until the infirmities of age compelled him to retire from public life, and he there enjoyed, amid the quietude of domestic retirement, the fruits of a well-spent existence.

His last days were crowned with all the honor and reverence which a grateful people could bestow upon a benefactor, and when death cut his thread of life, a nation truly mourned. He sunk to his final rest on the nineteenth day of June, 1794, in the sixty-fourth year of his age.

Mr. Lee was a sincere practical Christian, a kind and affectionate husband and parent, a generous neighbor, a constant friend, and in all the relations of life, he maintained a character above reproach. "His hospitable door," says Sanderson, "was open to all; the poor and destitute frequented it for relief, and consolation; the young for instruction; the old for happiness; while a numerous family of children, the offspring of two marriages, clustered around and clung to each other in fond affection, imbibing the wisdom of their father, while they were animated and delighted by the amiable serenity and captivating graces of his conversation. The necessities of his country occasioned frequent absence; but every return to his home was celebrated by the people as a festival; for he was their physician, their counsellor, and the arbiter of their differences. The medicines which he imported were carefully and judiciously dispensed; and the equity of his decision was never controverted by a court of law."

MERICAN history presents few names to its students more attractive and distinguished than that of THOMAS JEFFERSON, and rarely has a single individual, in civil station, acquired such an ascendency over the feelings and actions of a people, as was possessed by the subject of this brief memoir. To trace the lines of his character and career, is a pleasing task for every American whose mind is fixed upon the political destiny of his country, and we regret the narrow limits to which our pen is confined.

174

Mr. Jefferson's family were among the early British emigrants to Virginia. His ancestors came from Wales, from near the great Snowdon mountain. His grandfather settled in Chesterfield, and had three sons, Thomas, Field, and Peter. The latter married Jane, daughter of Isham Randolph, of Goochland, of Scotch descent; and on the thirteenth of April, 1743, she became the mother of the subject of this sketch. They resided at that time at Shadwell, in Albermarle county, Virginia. Thomas was the eldest child. His father died when he was fourteen years old, leaving a widow and eight children—two sons, and six daughters. He left a handsome estate to his family; and the lands, which he called Monticello, fell to Thomas, where the latter always resided when not engaged in public duty, and where he lived at the time of his death.

Thomas entered a grammar school at the age of five years, and when nine years old he commenced the study of the classics with a Scotch clergyman named Douglas. On the death of his father, the Reverend Mr. Maury became his preceptor; and in the spring of 1760, he entered William and Mary College, where he remained two years From Doctor William Small, a professor of mathematics in the college, he received his first philosophical teachings, and the bias of his mind concerning subjects of scientific investigation seemed to have received its initial impetus from that gentleman. Through his influence, in 1762, young Jefferson was admitted as a student-at-law in the office of George Wythe, the intimate friend of Governor Fauquier, at whose table our subject became a welcome guest.

In 1765, while yet a student, Jefferson heard the celebrated speech of Patrick Henry against the Stamp Act; and fired by its doctrines, he at once stood forth the avowed champion of American freedom. So manifest were his rents, that in 1769 he was elected a member of the Virginia Legislature, and became at once active and popular there.* He filled that station until the period of the Revolution, when he was called to the performance of more exalted duties in the national council.

He was married in January, 1772, to Mrs. Martha Skelton, a wealthy widow of twenty-three, who was the daughter of John Wales, an eminent Virginia lawyer.

When the system of committees of correspondence was established in 1773, Mr. Jefferson was a member of the first committee in Virginia, and was very active with his pen. In 1774, his powerfully written pamphlet was published, called "A Summary View of the Rights of British America." It was addressed to the king, and was published in England, under the auspices of Edmund Burke

He was elected a delegate to represent Virginia in the Continental Congress of 1775, and for several years he was one of the most efficient members of that body. He soon became distinguished among the men of talents there, although comparatively young; and when, in the succeeding year, a committee was appointed to draught a DECLARATION OF INDEPENDENCE, he was chosen one of the members. Although the youngest member of the committee, he was appointed chairman, and was requested by the others to draw up the instrument, which he did, and his draught was adopted, with a very few verbal amendments, on the fourth of July, 1776. This instrument forms an everlasting monument to his memory, and gives, by far, a wider range to the fame of his talents and patriotism, than eloquent panegyric or sculptured epitaph.

* He made strong but unsuccessful efforts in the Virginia Assembly for the emancipation of the slaves.

† This pamphlet gave great offence to Lord Dunmore, the royal governor of Virginia, who threatened to prosecute him for high treason. And because his associates in the Virginia Assembly sustained Jefferson, Dunmore dissolved it. They assembled in a private capacity, and drew up a remonstrance, which had a powerful effect upon the people. The governor perceived that his acts were futile and he allowed the matter to rest.

During the summer of 1776, he was elected to a seat in the Virginia Assembly, and, desirous of serving his own State, he resigned his seat in Congress and returned to Virginia. He was soon afterward appointed a joint commissioner with Dr. Franklin and Silas Deane, for negotiating treaties with France, but circumstances caused him to decline the acceptance of the proffered honor, and he continued in Virginia during the remaining period of the Revolution, actively engaged in the service of his State. He received a third election to Congress, but declined it, and was succeeded by Benjamin Harrison, the father of the late President.

From the early part of 1777 to the middle of 1779, Mr. Jefferson was assiduously employed, conjointly with George Wythe and Edmund Pendleton, on a commission for revising the laws of Virginia. The duty was a most arduous one; and to Mr. Jefferson belongs the imperishable honor of being the first to propose, in the Legislature of Virginia, the laws forbidding the importation of slaves; converting estates tail* into fee simple; annulling the rights of primogeniture;† establishing schools for general education; and confirming the rights of freedom in religious opinion.

Congress having resolved not to suffer the prisoners captured at Saratoga, under Burgoyne, to leave the United States until the convention, entered into by Gates and Burgoyne, should be ratified by the British government, they were divided, and sent to the different States, to be provided for during the interval. A division of them was

---

* A law entitled *fee tail* was adopted in the time of Edward I. of England, and at the period in question extended to all the English colonies. It restrained the alienation of lands and tenements by one to whom they had been given, with a limitation to a particular class of heirs. A *fee-simple* estate is one in which the owner has absolute power to dispose of it as he pleases; and if in his possession when he dies, it descends to his heirs general.

† This right belonged to the eldest son, who succeeded to the estate of his ancestor, to the exclusion of his brothers and sisters. This is still the law in England

12

sent, early in 1779, into the interior of Virginia, near the residence of Mr. Jefferson and his benevolent feelings were strongly exhibited by his sympathy for these enemies of his country. The prisoners were in great distress, and Mr. Jefferson and his friends did all in their power to alleviate their sufferings. An apprehended scarcity of provisions, determined Governor Patrick Henry to remove them to another part of the State, or out of it entirely. At this the officers and men were greatly distressed, and Mr. Jefferson wrote a touching appeal to the governor in their behalf, and they were allowed to remain.*

In June, 1779, Mr. Jefferson succeeded Mr. Henry as governor of Virginia, and the close of his administration was a period of great difficulty and danger. His State became the theatre of predatory warfare, the infamous Arnold having entered it with British and tory troops, and commenced spreading desolation with fire and sword along the James river. Richmond, the capital, was partly destroyed, and Jefferson and his council narrowly escaped capture. He tried, but in vain, to get possession of the person of Arnold, but the wily traitor was too cautious for him.

Very soon after his retirement to private life, Tarleton, who attempted to capture the members of the legislature convened at Charlottesville, a short distance from Jefferson's residence, came very near taking him prisoner. Jefferson had sent his family away in his carriage, and remained to attend to some matters in his dwelling, when he saw the cavalry ascending a hill toward his house. He mounted a fleet horse, dashed through the woods, and reached his family in safety.

---

* The officers and soldiers were very grateful to Mr. Jefferson, and when they were about to depart for England, the former united in a letter of thanks to him. Mr. Jefferson, in reply. disclaimed the performance of any great service to them, and said: "Opposed as we happen to be in our sentiments of duty and honor, and anxious for contrary events, I shall, nevertheless, sincerely rejoice in every circumstance of happiness and safety which may attend you personally'

M. de Marbois, secretary of the French legation in the United States, having questioned Mr. Jefferson respecting the resources, &c., of his native State, he wrote, in 1781, his celebrated work entitled "Notes on Virginia." The great amount of information which it contains, and the simple perspicuity of its style, made its author exceedingly popular in Europe as a writer and man of science, in addition to his character as a statesman.

In 1782, he was appointed a minister plenipotentiary to assist others in negotiating a treaty of peace with Great Britain; but information of the preliminaries having been signed, reached Congress before his departure, and he did not go. He was soon after elected a delegate to Congress, and was chairman of the committee, in 1783, to whom the treaty with Great Britain was referred. On their report, the treaty was unanimously ratified.

In 1784, he wrote an essay on coinage and currency for the United States, and to him we are indebted for the convenient denominations of our federal money, the dollar as a unit, and the system of decimals.

In May of this year, he was appointed, with Adams and Franklin, a minister to negotiate treaties of commerce with foreign nations. In company with his eldest daughter, he reached Paris in August. Dr. Franklin having obtained leave to return home, Mr. Jefferson was appointed to succeed him as minister at the French court, and he remained in France, until October, 1789. While there, he became popular among the literati, and his society was courted by the leading writers of the day.

During his absence the constitution had been formed, and under it Washington had been elected and inaugurated President of the United States. His visit home was under leave of absence, but Washington offered him a seat in his cabinet as secretary of state, and gave him his choice to remain in that capacity or return to France

He chose to remain, and he was one of the most efficient aids to the President during the stormy period of his first administration. He differed in opinion with Washington respecting the kindling revolution in France, but he agreed with him on the question of the neutrality of the United States. His bold avowal of democratic sentiments, and his expressed sympathies with the struggling populace of France in their aspirations for republicanism, made him the leader of the democratic party here, opposed to the federal administration of Washington;* and in 1793 he resigned his seat in the cabinet.

In 1796, he was the republican candidate for President, in opposition to John Adams. Mr. Adams succeeded, and Mr. Jefferson was elected Vice-President.† In 1800, he was again nominated for President, and received a majority of votes over Mr. Adams. Aaron Burr was on the ticket with him, and received an equal number of votes; but on the thirty-sixth balloting, two of Burr's friends withdrew, and Mr. Jefferson was elected.

Mr. Jefferson's administration continued eight years, he having been elected for a second term. The most prominent measures of his administration, were the purchase of Louisiana from France,‡ the embargo on the commerce and ocean-navigation of the United States;§ the non-

* In 1791, Washington asked his opinion respecting a national bank, a bill for which had been passed by Congress and approved by Washington. He gave his opinion in writing, and strongly objected to the measure as being unconstitutional.

† At that time, the candidate receiving the next highest number of votes to the one elected president, was vice president. The constitution, on that point, has since been altered. During the time he was vice president, he wrote a manual for the Senate, which is still the standard of parliamentary rule in Congress and other bodies.

‡ The United States agreed to pay fifteen millions of dollars to France for Louisiana (an area of more than a million of square miles), four millions of which France allowed to go toward the payment of indemnities for spoliations during peace.

§ The Embargo Act prohibited all American vessels from sailing for foreign ports; all foreign vessels from taking out cargoes; and all coasting vessels were required to give bonds to land their cargoes in the United States. These restric

intercourse and non-importation systems; the gun-boat experiment;* the suppression of Burr's expedition down the Mississippi river;† and the sending of an exploring company to the region of the Rocky mountains, and westward to the Pacific ocean.‡ Mr. Jefferson also introduced the practice of communicating with Congress by message, instead of by a personal address; a practice followed by all the Presidents since his time. The foreign relations of the United States during the whole time of his administration were in a very perplexing condition, yet he managed with so much firmness, that he kept other powers at bay, and highly exalted our Republic among the family of nations.

At the close of his second Presidential term, Mr. Jefferson retired to private life, and amid the quiet scenes of Monticello, he spent the remaining seventeen years of his being, in philosophical and agricultural pursuits. Through his instrumentality, a university was founded in 1818, at Charlottesville, near Monticello, of which he was rector until his death, and a liberal patron as far as his means would allow.

Toward the close of his life, his pecuniary affairs became embarrassed, and he was obliged to sell his library, which Congress purchased for thirty thousand dollars. A short time previous to his death, he received permis-

tive measures were intended so to affect the commerce of Great Britain, as to bring that government to a fair treaty of amity and commerce.

* Mr. Jefferson recommended the construction of a large number of gun-boats for the protection of American harbors. But they were unpopular with navy officers, and being liable to destruction by storms, the scheme, after a brief experiment, was abandoned.

† Aaron Burr organized a military expedition, ostensibly to act against the republic of Mexico; but the belief being generally entertained that it was really intended to dissever the Union, and form a separate government in the valley of the Mississippi, he was arrested, in 1807, on a charge of high treason. He was tried and acquitted.

‡ This expedition was under the direction of Captains Lewis and Clarke, and they made a toilsome overland journey from the Mississippi to the mouth of the Columbia River.

sion from the Legislature of Virginia, to dispose of his estate by lottery, to prevent its being sacrificed to pay his debts. He did not live to see it consummated.

In the spring of 1826, his bodily infirmities greatly increased, and in June he was confined wholly to his bed. About the first of July he seemed free from disease, and his friends had hopes of his recovery; but it was his own conviction that he should die, and he gave directions accordingly. On the third, he inquired the day of the month. On being told, he expressed an ardent desire to live until the next day, to breathe the air of the fiftieth anniversary of his country's independence. His wish was granted: and on the morning of the fourth, after having expressed his gratitude to his friends and servants for their care, he said with a distinct voice, "I resign myself to my God, and my child to my country."* These were his last words, and about noon on that glorious day he expired. It was a most remarkable coincidence that two of the committee (Mr. Adams and Mr. Jefferson) who drew up the Declaration of Independence; who signed it; who successively held the office of Chief Magistrate, should have died at nearly the same hour on the fiftieth anniversary of that solemn act.

He was a little over eighty-three years of age at the time of his death. Mr. Jefferson's manner was simple but dignified, and his conversational powers were of the rarest value. He was exceedingly kind and benevolent, an indulgent master to his servants, liberal and

---

* Mrs. Randolph, whom he tenderly loved. Just before he died, he handed her a morocco case, with a request that she would not open it until after his decease. It contained a poetical tribute to her virtues, and an epitaph for his tomb, if any should be placed upon it. He wished his monument to be a small granite obelisk with this inscription:—

"Here was buried
T H O M A S J E F F E R S O N,
Author of the Declaration of Independence,
Of the Statute of Virginia for Religious Freedom.
And Father of the University of Virginia"

friendly to his neighbors. He possessed remarkable equanimity of temper, and it is said he was never seen in a passion.* His friendship was lasting and ardent; and he was confiding and never distrustful.

In religion he was a freethinker; in morals, pure and unspotted; in politics, patriotic, honest, ardent and benevolent. Respecting his political character, there was (and still is) a great diversity of opinion, and we are not yet far enough removed from the theatre of his acts to judge of them dispassionately and justly. His life was devoted to his country; the result of his acts whatever it may be, is a legacy to mankind.

† During his presidency, Humboldt, the celebrated traveller, once visiting him, discovered in a newspaper upon his table, a vile and slanderous attack upon his character. "Why do you not hang the man?" asked Humboldt. "Put the paper in your pocket," said Jefferson, with a smile, "and on your return to your country, if any one doubts the freedom of our press, show it to him, and tell him where you found it."

"Monticello, Mr. Jefferson's Residence."

Benj Harrison

ENJAMIN HARRISON was born in Berkley, in Virginia, but the exact time of his birth is not certainly known. His ancestors were among the earlier settlers of that colony, having emigrated thither from England, in the year 1640. His paternal ancestor married in the family of the king's surveyor-genrall, and this gave him a oppurtunity to select the most fertile regions of the State for settlement and improvement. Thus he laid the foundation of that large estate which is still in the hands of the family.

184

The subject of this sketch was placed by his father in the college of William and Mary, with a view of giving him a thorough classical education. He was there at the time of his father's decease, which was sudden and awful;* and having had a dispute with one of the professors, he left the institution before the close of his term, and never returned to get his degree. Being the eldest of six sons, the management of the estate of his father devolved on him at his decease, and, although then a minor he performed his duties with great fidelity and skill.

Young Harrison, at a very early age, became a member of the Virginia House of Burgesses,[a] where his talents and sound judgment won for him the confidence and esteem of all parties. He was soon elected Speaker, and became one of the most influential men in that Assembly, where he occupied a seat during the greater part of his life. His great wealth, distinguished family connections, and personal worth, attracted the attention of the royal governor, who, desirous of retaining him on the side of the government, when the political agitations caused by the Stamp Act took place, offered him a seat in the executive council. But he had narrowly watched the gradual development of events, and he was convinced that a systematic scheme for enslaving the colonies was being matured by the home government. He therefore rejected the offer of the governor, boldly avowed his attachment to the republican cause, and joined with the patriotic burgesses of Virginia in their opposition to the oppressive acts of the British government.†

Mr. Harrison was one of the first seven delegates from

[a] 1764.

---

* This venerable man, and two of his four daughters, were instantly struck dead by lightning, during a violent thunder storm, in their mansion house at Berkley.

† Even before the Stamp Act was proposed, some of the measures of the British Parliament, affecting the interests of the American colonies, produced alarm, and the Virginia House of Assembly appointed a committee to draw up an address or petition to the king. Mr. Harrison was one of that committee.

Virginia to the Continental Congress of 1774, and he had the gratification of seeing Peyton Randolph, a very near relative, and his colleague from Virginia, elected president of that august body. Immediately after the return of the delegates to Virginia, a convention met in Richmond, and all the acts of the General Congress were sanctioned by them. They re-elected Mr. Harrison, with others, a delegate to the Congress of 1775, which met on the tenth of May of that year. During the autumn, he was appointed by Congress one of a committee to visit the army under Washington, at Cambridge near Boston and co-operate with the Commander-in-Chief in devising plans for future operations. Toward the close of 1775, he was appointed chairman of a committee to carry on foreign correspondence,* and in that capacity he labored with fidelity until the spring of 1777, when the necessity of such a committee no longer existed; a special agent or commissioner having been sent to Europe, and a new committee on foreign affairs organized, with different duties; and a secretary, who received a stipulated salary.

Mr. Harrison was constantly employed in active service, and was always among the first in advocating decisive and energetic measures. He was warmly in favor of independence, and when that great question was under discussion in committee of the whole, he was in the chair. He voted for the Declaration of Independence, on the fourth of July, 1776, and signed it on the second of August following. In 1777, his private affairs, and also public matters in his own State, demanded his presence there, and he resigned his seat in Congress and returned home.

* Congress deemed it essential to have a good understanding with the rival powers of Great Britain, and in order to have *some* communication with them (which could not be done by open diplomacy) this committee was established for the purpose, as expressed by the resolution constituting it, "to hold correspondence with the friends of America in Great Britain, Ireland, and *other parts of the world.*"

He was immediately elected a member of the House of Burgesses, and as soon as he took his seat, he was elevated to the Speaker's chair. That office he held until 1782, without interruption.

Having been appointed lieutenant of his native county, (which appointment constituted him commander of all the militia, with the title of colonel, and also presiding judge in all the civil courts of the county,) he was very active and efficient at the time the traitor Arnold invaded Virginia, and afterward when Cornwallis made incursions into it.

In 1782, Mr. Harrison was elected governor of the State, and he managed public affairs at that trying time, with great ability and firmness. He was governor two successive terms, and then retired to private life. But he was almost immediately elected a member of the House of Burgesses, and again resumed the Speaker's chair, by election.

In the year 1790, he was nominated for governor, but he declined on account of the then incumbent having filled the chair only two years; and he successfully promoted his re-election. Mr. Harrison was again elected governor in 1791, and the day after his election he invited a party of friends to dine with him. He had been suffering a good deal from gout in the stomach, but had nearly recovered. That night he experienced a relapse, and the next day death ended his sufferings. This event occurred in April, 1791.

Mr. Harrison was married in early life, to a niece of Mrs. Washington, Miss Elizabeth Bassett, who lived but one year after her husband's decease. They had a numerous offspring, but only seven lived to mature age. One of these was the lamented and venerated William Henry Harrison, late President of the United States.

Th.^s Nelson jr.

HOMAS NELSON was born at Yorktown, in Virginia, on the twenty-sixth of December, 1738. His father, William Nelson was a native of England, and emigrated to America about the beginning of the last century. By prudence and industry he accumulated a large fortune, and held rank among the first families of Virginia.

Thomas was the oldest son of his parents, and his father, in conformity to the fashion of the times among the opulent of that province, sent him to England at the age of fourteen years to be educated. He was placed in a

188

distinguished private school not far from London, and after completing a preparatory course of studies there, he went to Cambridge and was entered a member of Trinity College. He there enjoyed the private instructions of the celebrated Dr. Proteus, afterward the Bishop of London. He remained there, a close and diligent student until 1761, when he returned to America.

Mr. Nelson watched with much interest the movements of the British Parliament, during and after the time of the administration of Mr. Grenville,* and his sympathies were keenly alive in favor of the Americans and their cause. His first appearance in public life, was in 1774, when he was elected a member of the House of Burgesses of Virginia, and there he took sides with the patriots. It was during that session, that the resolutions reprobating the "Boston Port Bill" caused Lord Dunmore, the royal governor of Virginia, to dissolve the Assembly. Eighty-nine of the members, among whom was Mr. Nelson, met the next day at a neighboring tavern, and formed an association far more efficient in throwing up the strong bulwarks of freedom, than was the regular Assembly. Mr Nelson was a member of the first general convention of Virginia, which met at Williamsburgh in August, 1774, and elected delegates to the first Continental Congress. In the spring of 1775, he was elected a member of another general convention, and there he displayed such boldness of spirit, that he was looked upon as an efficient leader in the patriotic movements of the day. Much to the alarm of his friends, he proposed in that convention, the bold and almost treasonable measure of organizing the militia of the State for the defence of

---

* George Grenville, the Prime Minister of England in 1765, was the author of the Stamp Act. He is represented as an honest, but short-sighted politician, and the Stamp Act was doubtless more an error of his head than of his heart. He saw an empty treasury, with large demands upon it waiting to be satisfied, and he thought to replenish it by taxing the American colonies.

the chartered rights of the people. Patrick Henry, Richard Henry Lee, and others, warmly seconded the proposition, and it was adopted by the convention.* This act told Governor Dunmore and his royal master, in language that could not be mistaken, that Virginia was determined to exercise with freedom all the privileges guarantied to her by the British Constitution.†

In August 1774, the Virginia convention elected Mr. Nelson a delegate to the General Congress, and he took his seat in September. There he was very active, and gave such entire satisfaction to his constituents that he was unanimously re-elected for 1776. Although he seldom took part in the debates, he was assiduous and efficient in committee duty. He was a zealous supporter of the proposition for independence, and voted for and signed the declaration thereof.

In the spring of 1777, Mr. Nelson was seized with an alarming illness, which confined its attack chiefly to his head, and nearly deprived him, for a time, of his powers of memory. His friends urged him to withdraw from Congress for the purpose of recruiting his health, but he was loath to desert his post. He was, however, compelled to leave Philadelphia, and he returned to Virginia to recruit, with the hope and expectation of speedily resuming his seat in Congress. But his convalescence was slow; and when the convention met, he resigned his seat and retired to private life. But he was not suffered long to

---

* Mr. Nelson was appointed to the command of one regiment, Patrick Henry of another, and Richard Henry Lee of another, each holding the rank of colonel.

† It was not long before the wisdom of those military movements became apparent, for the royal governor of Virginia, as well as those of some of the other colonies, attempted to secure the powder and other munitions of war in the public magazines, under a secret order from the British ministry. This movement clearly divulged the premeditated design of disarming the people, and reducing them to slavery. The interesting movements in Virginia which immediately preceded the abdication of the royal governor, and his escape on board a British ship-of-war, cannot be detailed within our brief space, and we must refer the reader to the published history of the times.

remain there, for the appearance of a British fleet off the coast of Virginia, and the contemplated attack of the enemy upon the almost defenceless seaboard, called him into the field at the head of the militia of the State.* The alarm soon subsided, for the fleet of Lord Howe, instead of landing a force upon Virginia, sailed up the Chesapeake bay for the purpose of making an attack, by land, upon Philadelphia.

About this time, the financial embarrassments of Congress caused that body to make an appeal to the young men of the Union, of wealth and character, to aid in recruiting the army, and otherwise assisting their country. Mr. Nelson entered heartily into the measure, and by the free use of his influence and purse, he raised a volunteer corps, who placed him at their head, and proceeded to join Washington at Philadelphia.† Their services were not called into requisition, and they returned home, bearing the honor of a vote of thanks from Congress. The physical activity which this expedition produced, had an excellent effect upon General Nelson's health, and in 1779, he consented to be again elected a delegate to the Continental Congress. He took his seat in February, but a second attack of his old complaint obliged him to leave it in April, and return home. In May, the predatory operations of the enemy upon the coast, in burning Portsmouth, and threatening Norfolk and other places, caused General Nelson again to resume the services of the field. He collected a large force and

---

* Mr. Nelson's popularity at that time in Virginia was almost unbounded. The governor and council appointed him Brigadier General and Commander-in-Chief of the military forces of the State.

† The sudden call of the militia from their homes left many families in embarrassed circumstances, for a great part of the agricultural operations were suspended. General Nelson used the extent of his means in ameliorating the condition of their families, by having his own numerous servants till their land. He also distributed his money liberally among them, and thus more than a hundred families were kept from absolute want.

proceeded to Yorktown, but the fleet of the enemy soon afterward returned to New-York.

In 1781, Virginia became the chief theatre of warlike operations. The traitor Arnold, and General Phillips, with a small flotilla ravaged the coasts and ascended the rivers on predatory excursions; and Cornwallis, from southern fields of strife, marched victoriously over the lower counties of the State. About this time, the term of Mr. Jefferson's official duties as Governor of the State expired, and General Nelson was elected his successor. This, however, did not drive him from the field, but as both governor and commander-in-chief of the militia of the State,* he placed himself at the head of a considerable force, and formed a junction with La Fayette, who had been sent there to check the northward progress of Cornwallis. By great personal exertions and a liberal use of his own funds,† he succeeded in keeping his force together until the capture of Cornwallis at Yorktown. He headed a body of militia in the siege of that place, and although he owned a fine mansion in' the town, he did not hesitate to bombard it.‡ In this as in

* The active Colonel Tarleton, of the British army, made every effort to effect the capture of the legislature of Virginia. He succeeded in getting some into his custody, and so irregular became their meetings, in consequence of being frequently obliged to disperse and flee for personal safety, that they passed an act which placed the government of the State in the hands of the governor and his council. The council, too, being scattered, General Nelson had the whole responsibility laid upon his shoulders, and in the exercise of his individual powers he was compelled, by the exigencies of the times, to do some things that were not strictly legal; but the legislature subsequently legalized all his acts.

† Mr. Nelson made many and great pecuniary sacrifices for his country. When, in 1780, the French fleet was hourly expected, Congress felt it highly necessary that provision should be made for them. But its credit was prostrate, and its calls upon the States were tardily responded to. Virginia proposed to raise two millions of dollars, and Mr. Nelson at once opened a subscription list. But many wealthy men told Mr. Nelson that they would not contribute a penny on the security of the Commonwealth, but they would lend him all he wanted. He at once added his personal security.

‡ During the siege he observed that while the Americans poured their shot and shells thick and fast into every part of the town, they seemed carefully to avoid

everything else, his patriotism was conspicuous, and General Washington in his official account of the siege, made honorable mention of the great services of Governor Nelson and his militia.

Within a month after the battle of Yorktown, Governor Nelson, finding his health declining, resigned his office and retired to private life. It was at this period, while endeavoring to recruit his health by quiet and repose, that he was charged with mal-practice, while governor, as alluded to in a preceding note. A full investigation took place, and the legislature, as before mentioned, legalized his acts, and they also acquitted him of all the charges preferred. He never again appeared in public life, but spent the remainder of his days alternately at his mansion in Yorktown, and his estate at Offly. His health gradually declined until 1789, when, on the fourth day of January, his useful life closed. He was in the fifty third year of his age.

firing in the direction of his house, Governor Nelson inquired why his house was spared, and was informed that it was out of personal regard for him. He at once begged them not to make any difference on that account, and at once a well directed fire was opened upon it. At that moment a number of British officers occupied it, and were at dinner enjoying a feast, and making merry with wine. The shots of the Americans entered the house, and killing two of the officers, effectually ended the conviviality of the party.

13

Francis Lightfoot Lee

RANCIS LIGHTFOOT LEE, a younger brother of Richard Henry Lee, was born
in Westmoreland county, Virginia, on
the fourteenth day of October, 1734.
He was too young when his father died
to be sent abroad to be educated, but
was favored with every advantage in the way of learning which the colony afforded. He was placed at an
early age under the care of the Reverend Doctor
Craig, a Scotch clergyman of eminent piety and learning. His excellent tutor not only educated his head but

194

his heart, and laid the foundation of character, upon which the noble superstructure, which his useful life ex hibited, was reared.

On the return of Richard Henry Lee from England, whither he had been to acquire a thorough education, Francis, who was then just stepping from youth into manhood, was deeply impressed with his various acquirements and polished manners, and adopted him as a model for imitation. He leaned upon his brother's judgment in all matters, and the sentiments which moved the one impelled the other to action. And when his brother with his sweet voice and persuasive manner, endeavored, by popular harangues, to arouse his friends and neighbors to a sense of the impending danger, which act after act of British oppression shadowed forth, Francis caught his spirit; and when he was old enough to engage in the strife of politics, he was a full-fledged patriot, and with a "pure heart and clean hands" he espoused the cause of freedom.

In 1765, Mr. Lee was elected a member of the Virginia House of Burgesses, for Loudon county, while his brother was member of the same House, for Westmoreland county. By annual election, he continued a member of the Virginia Assembly for Loudon, until 1772, when he married the daughter of Colonel John Taylor, of Richmond, and moved to that city. He was at once elected a member for Richmond, and continued to represent that county until 1775, when the Virginia Convention elected him a delegate to the Continental Congress. During his whole term of service in the General Assembly of his State, he always acted in concert with the patriotic burgesses. Mr. Lee was not a fluent speaker, and seldom engaged in debate; but his sound judgment, unwavering principles, and persevering industry, made him a useful member of any legislative assembly. He sympathized with his brother in his yearnings for independence, and it was with great joy, that he voted for and signed the instrument which declared his country free.

Mr. Lee continued in Congress, until 1.79, and was the member, for Virginia, of the committee which framed the Articles of Confederation. Early in the spring of 1779, he retired from Congress and returned home, with the intention of withdrawing wholly from public life, to enjoy those sweets of domestic quiet which he so ardently loved. But his fellow citizens were unwilling to dispense with his valuable services, and elected him a member of the Virginia Senate. He, however, remained there but for a brief season, and then bade adieu to public employments. He could never again be induced to leave his domestic pleasures; and he passed the remainder of his days in agricultural pursuits, and the enjoyments to be derived from reading and study, and the cheerful intercourse with friends. Possessed of ample wealth, he used it like a philosopher and a Christian in dispensing its blessings for the benefit of his country and his fellow men.

In April, 1797, he was prostrated by an attack of pleurisy, which terminated his life in the course of a few days. He was in the sixty-third year of his age. His wife was attacked by the same disease, and died a few days after the decease of her husband.

Carter Braxton

ARTER BRAXTON was born at Newington, in King and Queen's county, Virginia, on the tenth of September, 1736. His father, George Braxton, was a wealthy farmer, and highly esteemed among the planters of Virginia. His mother was the daughter of Robert Carter, who, for a time, was president of the royal council for that State. They both died while Carter and his brother George were quite young.

Carter Braxton was educated at the college of William and Mary, and at the age of nineteen years, on leaving that institution, he was married to Miss Judith Robinson the daughter of a wealthy planter in Middlesex county. His own large fortune was considerably augmented by this marriage, and he was considered one of the wealthiest men in his native county.*

In 1757, Mr. Braxton went to England, for the purpose of self-improvement and personal gratification. He remained there until 1760, when he returned to America, and soon afterward married the daughter of Mr. Corbin, the royal receiver-general of the customs of Virginia.† Notwithstanding the social position, and patrician connections of Mr. Braxton, which would seem naturally to have attached him to the aristocracy, he was among the earliest in Virginia who raised the voice of patriotism. In 1765 he was a member of the House of Burgesses. How much earlier he appeared in public life is not certainly known. He was present when Patrick Henry's

---

* His wife died at the time of the birth of her second child, when she was not quite twenty-one years of age.

† Mr. Braxton had a large family by his second wife. She was the mother of sixteen children.

resolutions respecting the Stamp Act, were introduced, and was one of those who, fired by the wonderful eloquence of the orator on that occasion, boldly voted in support of them.*

Mr. Braxton was a member of the Virginia Convention in 1769, when Lord Botetourt, one of the best disposed royal governors that ever ruled in Virginia, suddenly dissolved it, in consequence of some acts therein which he deemed treasonable. Mr. Braxton was one of the members who immediately retired to a private room and signed a non-importation agreement. Lord Botetourt died toward the close of 1770, and was succeeded by Lord Dunmore, a man of very defective judgment and unyielding disposition, whose unpopular management greatly increased the spirit of opposition to royal misrule in Virginia. During the interval between the death of Botetourt and the arrival of Dunmore, Mr. Braxton held the office of high sheriff of the county where he resided, but he refused to hold it under the new governor. He was one of the eighty-nine members of the Assembly who, on the dissolution thereof by Governor Dunmore, in the summer of 1774, recommended a general convention of the people of Virginia, to meet at Williamsburg. They did so, and elected delegates to the Continental Congress, which met at Philadelphia on the fourth of the month following. Mr. Braxton was a member of that convention.

When, in 1777, the attempt of Lord Dunmore to take

* The eloquence of Henry on that occasion, fell like successive thunderbolts on the ears of the timid Assembly. "It was in the midst of the magnificent debate on those resolutions," says Mr. Wirt, "while he was descanting on the tyranny of the obnoxious Act, that he exclaimed, in a voice of thunder, and with the look of a God; 'Cæsar had his Brutus, Charles the First his Cromwell—and George the Third'—'Treason!' cried the Speaker—'treason, treason,' echoed from every part of the House. It was one of those trying moments which are decisive of character. Henry faltered not for an instant; but rising to a loftier altitude, and fixing on the Speaker an eye of the most determined fire, he finished the sentence with the firmest emphasis—'and George the Third-may profit by their example. If that be treason make the most of it.' "

the ammunition from the public magazines on board the Fowey ship-of-war, then lying off Williamsburg, excited the people to the highest pitch, and threatened open rebellion and armed resistance,* Mr. Braxton, by a wise and prudent course, succeeded in quelling the disturbance, and in bringing about such an arrangement as quite satis fied the people, and probably saved the town from de struction.†

Mr. Braxton was an active member of the last House of Burgesses that convened under royal authority in Virginia, and he was a member of the committee of that Assembly to whom was referred the difficulty that existed between it and Governor Dunmore. It was while this committee was in conference, that the tumult above alluded to, and the abdication of the governor, took place, and this, of course, rendered further action quite unnecessary; for the governor refused to return to his palace, and the legislature, of course, would not go on board the vessel to meet him. By this abdication all power reverted to the people, and a Provincial Government was at once formed by a convention of the inhabitants, in which movement Mr. Braxton took a conspicuous part, and was chosen a representative in the newly formed Assembly.

In December, 1775, he was chosen a delegate to the Continental Congress to fill the vacancy occasioned by the death of Peyton Randolph. He took an active part in favor of independence, and voted for and signed the

---

* Patrick Henry put himself at the head of a military company, and marched toward Williamsburg, to demand from Lord Dunmore the return of the powder His company rapidly augmented in numbers as he approached the town, and he entered it at the head of an overwhelming force. The governor, finding resistance vain, finally agreed to pay for the powder, and was then allowed quietly to retire with his family on board the ship-of-war in the river.

† The captain of the Fowey had declared his intention to fire upon and destroy the town, if the governor should experience any personal violence, and he placed the broadside of his vessel parallel with the shore, and shotted his guns for the purpose.

Declaration. He remained in Congress during only one session, and then resumed his seat in the Virginia Legislature, where he continued with but little interruption, until 1785. In 1786, he was appointed a member of the council of the State, and held that station until 1791. He was elected to the same office in 1794, where he continued until within four days of his death. This event, which was occasioned by paralysis, occurred on the tenth day of October, 1797, when he was in the sixty-first year of his age.

Mr. Braxton was not a brilliant man, but he was a talented and very useful one. He possessed a highly cultivated mind, and an imagination of peculiar warmth and vigor, yet the crowning attribute of his character, was sound judgment and remarkable prudence and forethought. These, in a movement like the American Revolution, were essential elements in the characters of those who were the prominent actors, and well was it for them and for posterity, that a large proportion of not only the Signers to the Declaration of Independence, but those who were called to act in the councils of the nation, possessed these requisites *to* a remarkable degree. While fiery spirits were needed to arouse, and bold, energetic men were necessary to control and guide, the success of that rebellion, so far as human ken can penetrate, depended upon the calm judgment and well directed prudence of a great body of the patriots.

Of this class Mr. Braxton was a prominent one. His oratory, though not brilliant, was graceful and flowing, and it was persuasive in the highest degree. He always fixed the attention of his auditors and seldom failed to convince and lead them. In public, as well as in private life, his virtue and morality were above reproach, and as a public benefactor, his death was widely lamented

Wm Hooper

ILLIAM HOOPER was born in Boston, Massachusetts, on the seventeenth day of June, 1742. His father was a Scotchman and a graduate of the University of Edinburgh. Soon after leaving that institution, he emigrated to America, and fixed his residence at Boston, where he was married. William was his first born, and he paid particular attention to his preparation for a collegiate course. He was placed under the charge of Mr. Lovell, then one of the most eminent instructors in the colony of Massachusetts Bay

201

Having completed his preparatory studies, William was entered a pupil at Harvard University, where he remained a close and industrious student for three years, and in 1760 he graduated with distinguished honors.

His father designed him for the clerical profession, but as he evinced a decided preference for the bar, he was placed as a student in the office of the celebrated James Otis. On the completion of his studies, perceiving that the profession was quite full of practicians in Massachusetts, he went to North Carolina, where many of his Scotch relations resided, and began business in that province in 1767.

Mr. Hooper formed a circle of very polished acquaintances there, and he soon became highly esteemed among the literary men of the province. He rose rapidly in his profession, and in a very short time he stood at the head of the bar in that region. He was greatly esteemed by the officers of the government, and his success in the management of several causes, in which the government was his client, gave him much influence.

When, in 1770–'71, an insurrectionary movement was set on foot by a party of the people termed the "Regula tors,"*Mr. Hooper took sides with the government, and

---

* This movement of the "Regulators" has been viewed in quite opposing lights; one party regarding them as only a knot of low-minded malcontents, who had everything to gain and nothing to lose, and who hoped by getting up an excite. ment, to secure something for themselves in the general scramble. This was the phase in which they appeared to Mr. Hooper, and thus regarding them, he felt it his duty to oppose them and maintain good order in the State. Others viewed them as patriots, impelled to action by a strong sense of wrong and injustice, the author of which was Governor Tryon, whose oppressive and cruel acts, even his partisans could not deny. From all the lights we have upon the subject, we cannot but view the movement as a truly patriotic one, and kindred to those which subsequently took place in Massachusetts and Virginia, when Boston harbor was made a teapot, and Patrick Henry drove the royal governor Dunmore from the Province of Virginia. Governor Tryon was a tyrant of the darkest hue, for he commingled, with his oppressions, acts of the grossest immorality and wanton cruelty. Although the "Regulators" were men moving in the common walks of life, and doubtless many vagabonds enrolled themselves among them), yet the rules

advised and assisted Governor Tryon in all his measures to suppress the rebellion. For this, he was branded as a royalist, and even when he openly advocated the cause of the patriots, he was for a time viewed with some suspicion lest his professions were unreal. But those who knew him best, knew well how strongly and purely burned that flame of patriotism which his zealous instructor, Mr. Otis, had lighted in his bosom; and his consistent course in public life, attested his sincerity.

Mr. Hooper began his legislative labors in 1773, when he was elected a member of the Provincial Assembly of North Carolina, for the town of Wilmington. The next year he was returned a member for the county of Hanover; and from his first entrance into public life, he sympathised with the oppressed. This sympathy led him early to oppose the court party in the state, and so vigorous was his opposition that he was soon designated by the royalists as the leader of their enemies, and became very obnoxious to them. The proposition of Massachusetts for a General Congress was hailed with joy in North Carolina, and a convention of the people was called in the summer of 1774, to take the matter into consideration. The convention met in Newbern, and after passing resolutions approving of the call, they appointed William Hooper their first delegate to the Continental Congress. Although younger than a large majority of the members, he was placed upon two of the most important committees in that body, whose business it was to arrange and propose measures for action—a duty which required talents and judgment of the highest order.

Mr. Hooper was again elected to Congress in 1775, and was chairman of the committee which drew up an

of government they adopted, the professions they made and the practices they exhibited, all bear the impress of genuine patriotism; and we cannot but regard the blood shed on the occasion by the infamous Tryon, as the blood of the earl martyrs of our Revolution.

address to the Assembly of the island of Jamaica. This address was from his pen, and was a clear and able exposition of the existing difficulties between Great Britain and her American Colonies. He was again returned a member in 1776,* and was in his seat in time to vote for the Declaration of Independence. He affixed his signature to it, on the second of August following. He was actively engaged in Congress until March, 1777, when the derangment of his private affairs, and the safety of his family, caused him to ask for and obtain leave of absence, and he returned home.

Like all the others who signed the Declaration of Independence, Mr. Hooper was peculiarly obnoxious to the British, and on all occasions, they used every means in their power to possess his person, harass his family, and destroy his estate. When the storm of the Revolution subsided, and the sun-light of peace beamed forth, he resumed the practice of his profession, and did not again appear in public life until 1786, when he was appointed by Congress one of the judges of the federal court established to adjudicate in the matter of a dispute about territorial jurisdiction, between Massachusetts and New York. The cause was finally settled by commissioners, and not brought before that court at all.

Mr. Hooper now withdrew from public life, for he felt that a fatal disease was upon him. He died at Hillsborough, in October, 1790, aged forty-eight years.

* He was at home for some time during the spring of that year, attending two different Conventions that met in North Carolina, one at Hillsborough, the seat of the Provincial Congress, the other at Halifax. The Convention at the former place put forth an address to the people of Great Britain. This address was written by Mr. Hooper; and we take occasion here to remark, that as early as the twentieth of May, 1775, a convention of the Committees of Safety of North Carolina met at Charlotte Court House, in Mecklenburg county, and by a series of resolutions, declared themselves free and independent of the British Crown; to the support of which they pledged their lives, their fortunes, and their sacred honor. For an account of this Macklenburg Convention we refer the reader to a work of the writer, entitled "1776, or the War of Independence," page 155.

Joseph Hewes

HE parents of JOSEPH HEWES were na tives of Connecticut, and belonged to the Society of Friends, or Quakers. Immediately after their marriage they moved to New Jersey, and purchased a small farm at Kingston, within a short distance of Princeton. It was there that Joseph was born, in the year 1730. He was educated at the college in Princeton, and at the close of his studies he was apprenticed to a merchant in Philadelphia to qualify him for a commercial life. On the termination of his apprenticeship, his father furnished him with a little money capital, to which he added the less fleeting capital of a good reputation, and he commenced mercantile business on his own account. His business education had been thorough, and he pursued the labors of commerce with such skill and success, that in a few years he amassed an ample fortune.

At the age of thirty years, Mr. Hewes moved to North Carolina, and settled in Edenton, which became his home for life. He entered into business there, and his uprightness and honorable dealings soon won for him the profound esteem of the people. While yet a comparative stranger among them, they evinced their appreciation of his character, by electing him a member of the legislature of North Carolina, in 1763, and so faithfully did he discharge his duties, that they re-elected him several consecutive years.

Mr. Hewes was among the earliest of the decided patriots of North Carolina, and used his influence in bringing about a Convention of the people of the State, to second the call of Massachusetts for a General Congress. The convention that met in the summer of 1774, elected him one of the delegates for that State, in the Continental Congress that met at Philadelphia in September following. He took his seat on the fourteenth of the month, and was immediately placed upon the committee appointed to draw up a Declaration of Rights. During that session he was actively engaged in maturing a plan for a general non-importation agreement throughout the Colonies, and he voted for and signed it. In this act his devoted patriotism was manifest, for it struck a deadly blow at the business in which he was engaged. It was a great sacrifice for him to make, yet he cheerfully laid it upon the altar of Freedom.

Mr. Hewes was again elected a delegate to Congress in

1775, and took his seat at the opening, on the tenth of May. He seldom engaged in debate, but as an unwearied committee-man, he performed signal service there. He was at the head of the naval committee, and was in effect the first Secretary of the Navy of the United States. He was also a member of the "Secret Committee," to which we have before alluded in these memoirs.

Mr. Hewes was a member of Congress for 1776, and North Carolina having early taken a decided stand in favor of independence, his own views upon this question were fully sustained by his instructions, and he voted for, and signed the Declaration thereof. As soon, thereafter as the business of the session would admit, he returned home, for the troubles there demanded his presence, and his private affairs needed his attention to save his fortune from being scattered to the winds. He remained at home until July, 1779, when he resumed his seat in Congress. But his constitution, naturally weak, could not support the arduous labors of his station, and his health failed so rapidly, that he was obliged to resign his seat. He left it on the twenty-ninth of October; 1779, and being too unwell to travel, he remained in Philadelphia. But he only lived eleven days after he left his seat in Congress. He died on the tenth of November following, in the fiftieth year of his age. He was the first and only one of all the signers of the Declaration, who died at the seat of Government, while attending to public duty, and his remains were followed to the grave by Congress in a body and a large concourse of the citizens of Philadelphia,

John Penn

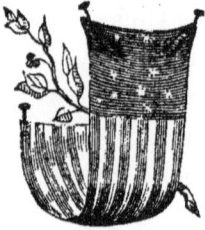

OHN PENN was born in the county of Carolina, Virginia, on the seventeenth of May, 1741. His father, Moses Penn, seemed to be utterly neglectful of the intellectual cultivation of his son; and, although he possessed the means of giving him a good English education, he allowed him no other opportunity, than that which two or three years' tuition in a common county school in his neighborhood afforded. Mr. Penn died when his son was about eighteen years of age, and left him the sole possessor of a competent, though not large estate.

It has been justly remarked, that the comparative obscurity in which the youth of Penn was passed, was, under the circumstances, a fortunate thing for him, for he had formed no associates with the gay and thoughtless, which, on his becoming sole master of an estate, would have led him into scenes of vice and dissipation, that might have proved his ruin. His mind, likewise, was possessed of much vigor, and he was naturally inclined to pursue an honorable and virtuous course.

Young Penn was a relative of the celebrated Edmund Pendleton, and resided near him. That gentleman kindly gave him the free use of his extensive library, and this opportunity for acquiring knowledge was industriously improved. He resolved to qualify himself for the profession of the law, and strong in his faith that he should be successful, he entered upon a course of legal study, guided and instructed only by his own judgment and good common sense. He succeeded admirably, and at the age of twenty-one years, he was admitted to the bar, in his native county. His profession soon developed a native eloquence before inert and unsuspected, and by it, in connection with close application to business, he rapidly soared to eminence. His eloquence was of that sweet persuasive kind, which excites all the tender emotions of the soul, and possesses a controlling power at times irresistible.

In 1774 Mr. Penn moved to North Carolina, and commenced the practice of his profession there. So soon did his eminent abilities and decided patriotism become known there, that in 1775 he was elected a delegate from that state to the Continental Congress, and he took his seat in that body, in October of that year. He remained there three successive years, and faithfully discharged the duties of his high station. Acting in accordance with the instruction of his state convention, and the dictates of his own judgment and feelings, he voted for the Declaration of Independence, and joyfully placed his sign manual to the parchment.

When, in 1780, Cornwallis commenced his victorious march northward from Camden, in South Carolina,* the the western portion of North Carolina, which lay in his path, was almost defenceless. Mr. Penn was a resident of that portion of the State, and the legislature, unable to act efficiently in its collective capacity, conferred upon him almost absolute dictatorial powers, and allowed him to take such measures for the defence of the state, as the

---

* After the defeat of the Americans under General Gates, at Sanders' Creak, near Camden, Lord Cornwallis left Colonel Ferguson to keep the Americans in South Carolina at bay, and at once proceeded northward with the intention of invading Virginia. He had made arrangements for General Leslie to reinforce him in that State, by landing somewhere upon the shore of the Chesapeake. But while pursuing his march northward, and grently harassed by bands of patriots, who had been set in motion by the active energies of Penn, he heard of the defeat and death of Colonel Ferguson at King's Mountain, and he hastened back to South Carolina and thus almost defenceless Virginia was saved from a destructive invasion.

14

exigency of the case required. This was as extraordinary evidence of great public confidence, but in no particular did he abuse the power thus conferred. He performed his duties with admirable fidelity and skill and received the thanks of the Legislature, and the general benedictions of the people.

Mr. Penn retired from public life in 1781, and resumed the practice of his profession. But he was again called out in 1784, when Robert Morris, the Treasurer of the Confederation, appointed him a Sub-Treasurer, or receiver of taxes for North Carolina. It was an office of honor and great trust, but unpopular in the extreme. Still he was willing to serve his country in any honorable capacity where he could be useful, but he soon found that he would do but little that could in anywise conduce to the public weal, and after holding the office a few weeks, he resigned it, and resumed his private business. He did not again appear in public life, and in September, 1788, he died in the forty-seventh year of his age.

The life of John Penn furnishes another example of the high attainments which may crown him who, though surrounded by adverse circumstances, by persevering industry cultivates mind and heart, and aims at an exalted mark of distinction. If young men would, like him, resolve to rise above the hindrance of adverse circumstances and push boldly on toward some honorable goal, they would seldom fail to reach it, and the race would be found to be far easier than they imagined it to be, when girding for its trial.

Edward Rutledge

DWARD RUTLEDGE was of Irish descent. His father, Doctor John Rutledge, emigrated from Ireland to America, in 1735, and settled at Charleston, South Carolina. He there commenced practice as a physician, in which he was very successful, and in the course of a few years, he married a young lady by the name of Hert, who brought him, as a marriage dowry, an ample fortune. When she was twenty-seven years of age, Dr. Rutledge died, and left her with a family of seven children, of whom Edward, the subject of this memoir, was the youngest. He was born at Charleston, in November, 1749.

After receiving a good English and classical education, young Rutledge commenced the study of law with his elder brother, John, who was then a distinguished member of the Charleston bar. As a finishing stroke in his legal education, preparatory to his admission to the bar, he was sent to England at the age of twenty, and entered as a student at the Inner Temple, London,* where he had an opportunity of witnessing the forensic eloquence of those master spirits of the times, Mansfield, Wedderburn, Thurlow, Dunning, Chatham and Camden. He returned to Charleston about the close of 1772, was admitted to the bar, and commenced practice early in 1773.

Mr. Rutledge, though young, had watched with much interest the political movements of the day, and when old enough to act as well as think, he took a decisive stand on the side of the patriots. This, together with the distinguished talents which he manifested on his first appearance at the bar, drew toward him the attention of the public mind, when the Massachusetts Circular aroused the people to vigorous action. Although then only twenty-five years of age, the convention of South Carolina elected him a delegate to the first General Congress, and he was present at the opening, on the fifth of September, 1774. There he was active and fearless, and receiving the entire approbation of his constituents, he was re-elected in 1775, and 1776: and when, preparatory to

---

* A number of Inns of Court, or sort of colleges for teaching the law were established in London at various times. The Temple (of which there were three Societies, namely, the Inner, the Middle, and the Outer) was originally founded, and the Temple Church built, by the Knights Templar, in the reign of Henry II. 1185. The Inner and Middle Temple were made Inns of Law in the reign of Edward III., about 1340; the Outer, not until the reign of Elizabeth, about 1560 *See Stowe's Survey.*

the consideration of the subject of absolute independence, Congress, by resolution, recommended the several colonies to form permanent governments, Mr. Rutledge was associated with Richard Henry Lee and John Adams, in preparing the prefatory preamble to the recommendation. He was warmly in favor of independence, and fearlessly voted for the Declaration, notwithstanding there were large numbers of people in his State opposed to it, some through timidity, some through self-interest, and some through decided attachment to the royal cause.

When, during the summer of 1776, Lord Howe, came commissioned to prosecute the war or negotiate for peace, Mr. Rutledge was appointed one of a committee with Dr. Franklin and John Adams, to meet him in conference upon Staten Island. The commissioners were instructed not to enter upon negotiations for peace, except in the capacity of representatives of free states, and having independence as a basis. As Lord Howe could not thus receive them, or listen to such proposals, the conference, as was anticipated, failed to produce any important results.

Partly on account of ill health, and partly because of the disturbed condition of his State, he withdrew from Congress in 1777, but was returned again in 1779. In the interval he was actively engaged at home in measures for the defence of the State, and to repel invasion.

Mr. Rutledge took up arms and was placed at the head of a corps of artillery. In 1780, while Charleston was invested by the enemy, he was active in affording succor to General Lincoln, then within the besieged city. In one of these operations, in attempting to throw troops into the city, he was taken prisoner, and was afterward sent captive to St. Augustine in Florida.* He remained

---

* After the fall of Charleston, and the capture of Lincoln and the American army. Cornwallis became fearful of the influence of many citizens, and finally

a prisoner nearly a year, and was then exchanged and set at liberty. It was a gloomy time for the patriots, and the stoutest hearts began to quail. The bulk of the southern army, under Lincoln, had been made prisoners. But still hope did not quite expire, and the successes of Greene, and the victories of Marion and Sumpter, reanimated the fainting hearts of the republicans.

After the British evacuated Charleston in 1781, Mr. Rutledge retired, and resumed the practice of his profession; and for about seventeen years, his time was alternately employed in the duties of his business and service in the Legislature of his State. In the latter capacity he uniformly opposed every proposition for extending the evils of slavery.*

In 1794, Mr. Rutledge was elected to the United States Senate, to supply the vacancy caused by the resignation of Charles Cotesworth Pinckney; and in 1798, he was elected Governor of his native State. But he did not live to serve out his official term. He had suffered much from hereditary gout, and on returning to Charleston after the adjournment of the Legislature, which sat at Columbia, he caught a severe cold, that brought on a paroxysm of his disease and terminated his life on the twenty-third day of January, in the year 1800. He was in the sixtieth year of his age.

adopted a most cowardly measure. By his order, the Lieutenant Governor, (Gadsden,) most of the civil and military officers, and some others of the friends of the republicans, of character, were taken out of their beds and houses by armed parties, and collected at the Exchange, when they were conveyed on board a guard-ship, and transported to St. Augustine. Mr. Rutledge was one of the number. His mother did not escape the persecutions of their masters. Cornwallis also feared her talents and influence, and compelled her to leave her country residence and move into the city, where she would be more directly under the vigilant eye of his minions.

* As a means of relief to those who, during the war, had lost a great many slaves, and were pressed for payment by those of whom they were purchased on credit, it was proposed to import a sufficient number, either from the West Indies, or from Africa direct, to make up the defeciency. All such evil propositions met no favor from Edward Rutledge.

HOMAS HAYWARD was born in St. Lukes parish, South Carolina, in the year 1746. His father, Colonel Dame Hayward was one of the wealthiest planters in the Province, and fully appreciating the advantages of education, he placed his son Thomas in the best classical school in that region. He was a thoughtful and industrious student; and so readily did he master the Latin, that he read with fluency the works of the Roman historians and poets, in that language.

215

As soon as young Hayward had completed his preparatory studies, he entered as a student, the law office of
Mr. Parsons, a barrister of considerable eminence in
South Carolina, at that time. Having accomplished his
task well, his father sent him to England at the age of
about twenty years, to finish his legal education there. He
entered one of the Inns of court at the Temple, and there
he prosecuted his studies with as much zeal as if poverty
had been his inheritance, and the bread of his future existence depended upon his personal exertion when he
should enter the profession. This zeal brought him in-
valuable treasures in the form of a well-stored mind, and
he left that intellectual retreat, a polished lawyer.

While in England, Mr. Hayward, became deeply impressed with the injustice of the prevailing feeling there,
that a *colonial* British subject was quite inferior (and
should be treated as such) to the native born English-
man. Such was the sentiment of society, and upon this
sentiment, the government seemed to act by appointing
to office in the colonies few but natives of the British
Islands; and in its carelessness of the rights and privileges of the colonists, as if they were not equally protected by the broad ægis of the British Constitution. These
things, even at that early age, alienated his affection from
the mother country, and he returned to his native land
with mortified feelings, and a heartfelt desire to free it
from the bondage of trans-atlantic rule.

Before returning to America, Mr. Hayward visited
several of the states of Europe, and instead of being
dazzled by the pomp and trappings of royalty and its
minions, he looked upon them all as the costly and blood-
stained fruit of wrong and oppression; and he saw in the
toiling, down-trodden millions of the producers, such a
contrast to the happy laborers of his own dear land, that
he felt an affection for his country of the tenderest nature

and his patriotism took deep root, even while he stood before the throne of royal rulers.

Soon after his return, Mr. Hayward entered upon the practice of his profession. He married a most amiable and accomplished young lady, named Matthews; and with a sedateness and energy of purpose, rare at his age, he commenced his career of usefulness. He was among the earliest in South Carolina who resisted the oppressive measures of the Home Government, and from the passage of the Stamp Act, until the battle of Lexington, he consistently and zealously promoted the patriot cause, ever repudiating the degrading terms of conciliation—absolute submission—which the British Government demanded. The openness and manly frankness with which he es poused the patriot cause, made him a leader in the revolutionary movements in that Province, and he was placed in the first General Assembly, that organized after the abdication of the colonial governor. He was also appointed a member of the first "Committee of Safety" there.

In 1775, Mr. Hayward was chosen a delegate to the General Congress. He at first modestly declined the honor, but being waited upon personally by a deputation of the people, he complied, and took his seat early in 1776. He warmly supported Mr. Lee's motion for absolution from British rule, when brought forward in June of that year, and he joyfully voted for and signed the Declaration of Independence. He remained in Congress until 1778, when he accepted the appointment of Judge of the criminal and civil courts of South Carolina. This acceptance and his previous offence in signing the Declaration, made him very obnoxious to the enemy, and great efforts were made, through the treacherous tories, to get possession of his person.*

* The position he held was one of great danger and trial, and nothing but the promptings of pure patriotism could have kept him there, for his pecuniary means

Mr. Hayward held a military commission while he was Judge, and he was in active service, with Edward Rutledge, in the skirmish with the enemy at Beaufort, in 1780. In that skirmish he received a gun-shot wound, which scarred him for life. When, soon after, Charleston was captured by Sir Henry Clinton and Admiral Arbuthnot, Mr. Hayward was taken prisoner, and it was generally believed that he would be excluded from the terms of capitulation, as an arch traitor. This, however, was not the case, and he was sent, with Mr. Rutledge and others, to St. Augustine, in Florida, where he remained nearly a year.*

On his return to South Carolina, Judge Hayward resumed his seat upon the bench, and was actively engaged in his judicial duties until 1798. He was a member of the convention of his state, which framed its constitution, in 1790. Having again married an amiable lady, by the name of Savage, he coveted the retirement and happiness of domestic life, from which he had been so long an exile, and in 1799, he withdrew entirely from public life, and in the bosom of his family he bore the honor, which a nation's gratitude conferred, and there calmly awaited the summons for another world. His death took place in March, 1809, when he was sixty-three years of age.

were such, that he might have lived at ease in the retiracy of private life. At the time he was appointed Judge, the enemy were in force at Charleston and vicinity. But this had no effect upon him, for he tied, and caused to he executed, virtually within sight of the British lines, several persons who were found guilty of treason

* While confined prisoner there, a detachment of British soldiers were sent to his plantation, and carried off all his slaves. They were sent to Jamaica, and sold there to the sugar planters. He recovered some of them afterward, but about one hundred and thirty, valued at fifty thousand dollars, were a total loss. In addition to this loss of property, he met with another, in the meanwhile, a thousand times more afflictive and irreparable—that of the affectionate wife of his bosom.

HOMAS LYNCH, JUNIOR, was born in
Prince George's parish, upon the
North Santee river, South Carolina,
on the fifth day of August, 1749.
He was a descendant of an ancient
Austrian family, natives of the town
of Lintz. A branch of the family
moved to England, and settled in the county of Kent.
Thence they went to Connaught in Ireland, and it
was from that place that the great-grandfather of
our subject emigrated to America and settled in South
Carolina, a short time after its first settlement. He pur

219

chased large tracts of land, and when they fell into the possession of the father of Thomas Lynch, junior, they possessed great value, and gave him a splendid fortune. He was a man of great influence, and having early espoused the cause of the colonists, he was elected a delegate to the first Continental Congress which met in Philadelphia, in 1774. He continued a member of that body until his death.

Thomas Lynch, junior, was sent to England, to be educated, at the age of thirteen years. He had previously received a good academical education, at Georgetown, in South Carolina. In England he was placed in Eton School, that seminary of preparation for higher instruction, in which, for a long period, many eminent men were educated. After completing his preparatory studies there, he entered the University of Cambridge, where he took his degree, and he left the institution bearing the highest respect of the tutors, because of his studious and virtuous career while there.

On leaving Cambridge, young Lynch entered upon the study of the law in one of the inns of the Temple, where, by close application, he became a finished lawyer at the close of his studies. He there became acquainted with some of the leading politicians of the day, and acquired a pretty thorough knowledge of the movements of the government. And when he heard the murmur of discontent come from his native land, and listened to the haughty tone of British statesmen, when speaking of the colonies, he felt an irrepressible desire to return home. He obtained permission of his father, and reached South Carolina in 1772. He soon afterward married a beautiful young lady, named Shubrick, between whom and himself, a mutual attachment had existed from childhood. This tender relation and the possession of an ample fortune, were calculated to wed him to he ease and enjoyments of domestic life, but young Lynch had caught the spirit of his patriotic father, and he stood up, like a strong young oak, to breast the storm of the Revolution, then gathering black on every side.

Mr. Lynch's first appearance in public life, was at a town meeting called in Charleston in 1773, to consider the injuries Great Britain was inflicting on her colonies. He addressed the numerous assemblage with a patriotic eloquence that won their hearts, and the people at once looked upon him as an efficient instrument in working out the freedom of his country. They elected him by acclamation to many civil offices of trust, and when the first provincial regiment was raised in South Carolina, in 1775, a captain's commission was offered to Mr. Lynch, which he accepted.[*] In company with Captain, afterward General C. C. Pinckney, he made a recruiting excursion into North Carolina, to raise the company he was to command. In this service he was greatly exposed to the inclemencies of the weather, and his health received a shock from which it never recovered. He raised his company and joined his regiment, but a few days afterward, intelligence reached him of the sudden and severe illness of his father from paralysis, at Philadelphia, and he asked permission to attend him. But Colonel Gadsden, absolutely refused to grant the request, on the ground that no private consideration should interfere with public duty. But his filial yearnings were speedily gratified, for his father resigned his seat in Congress, and his son was immediately elected by the Provincial Assembly to fil it. He joyfully accepted it, and hastened to Philadelphia, where he took his seat in Congress, in 1776. He supported the propo-

---

[*] His father, then in Congress at Philadelphia, was desirous that he should enter the service with higher rank than captain, but young Lynch expressed his opinion that the commission was quite as exalted as his experience would warrant him to receive

sition for Independence, and was one of the signers to the glorious Declaration thereof.

Mr. Lynch did not long remain in Congress, for the declining health of both himself and his father caused him to resign his seat and return home. They travelled slowly until they reached Annapolis, where his father had another paralytic stroke, which terminated his life. With a sad heart and debilitated frame, the bereaved son returned home. But the canker of disease was preying upon his vitals, and by the advice of physicians, he resolved to go to the south of Europe, with the faint hope, that restored health might be the result. It being perilous at that time to go in an American vessel, he sailed for the West Indies toward the close of 1779, with the expectation of finding a neutral vessel there, in which to embark for Europe. His affectionate wife accompanied him, but they never reached their destination. The vessel was supposed to have foundered at sea, and all on board perished, for it was never heard of afterward.

Thus, at the early age of thirty years, terminated the life of one of that sacred band who pledged life, fortune and honor, in defence of American freedom. Like a brilliant meteor, he beamed with splendor for a short period, and suddenly vanished forever

RTHUR MIDDLETON was born at Middleton Place, the residence of his father, in South Carolina, in 1743. His father, Henry Middleton, was of English descent, and a wealthy planter, and he gave his son every opportunity for mental and moral culture which the Province afforded, until he arrived at a proper age to be sent to England for a thorough education. This, as we have before observed, was a prevailing custom among the men

of wealth in the southern provinces, previous to the Revolution, and their sons consequently became political and
social leaders, on account of their superior education.

Arthur Middleton was sent to England, when he was
about twelve years of age, and was placed in a school at
Hackney.* At fourteen he was transferred to a school
in Westminster, where he remained four years, and then
entered the University at Cambridge. While there, he
shunned the society of the gay and dissipated, and became
a very close and thoughtful student. He remained at
Cambridge four years, and at the age of twenty-two, he
graduated with distinguished honors. He carried with
him, from that institution, the sincere respect and esteem
of professors and students.

Young Middleton remained in England some time
after leaving Cambridge, for the twofold purpose of self-
improvement and of forming acquaintances with the
branch of his family that remained there. He then
went to the continent, and for two years he travelled and
made observations of men, and manners, and things, in
southern Europe. He passed several months at Rome
where his highly–cultivated mind became thoroughly
schooled in the theory of the fine arts, and made him
ouite proficient as a painter.

Mr. Middleton returned to South Carolina, in 1768,
and very soon afterward married an accomplished young
lady, named Izard. About a year after this event, he
took his young wife and made a second tour on the continent of Europe, and spent some time in England. They
returned in 1773, and, by the indulgence of his father,
he took the family seat for his residence. There in the
possession of wealth and every domestic enjoyment, he
had a bright prospect of worldly happiness. But even

* Several of the Southern members of Congress received their education at this
school, preparatory to their entering the college a; Cambridge

then the dark clouds of the Revolution were gathering, and in less than two years the storm burst upon the South, as well as all along the Atlantic sea-board, with great fury. Men could not remain neutral, for there was no middle course, and Arthur Middleton, as well as his father, laid their lives and fortunes upon the altar of pa triotism. When the decision was made and the die was cast, Mr. Middleton laid aside domestic ease and entered at once upon active life. He was a member of one of the committees of safety of South Carolina, appointed by the Provincial Congress in 1775. In that body he was firm and unyielding in principle, and when, soon afterward, Lord William Campbell was appointed governor, and it was discovered that he was acting with duplicity, Mr. Middleton laid aside all private feeling, and recommended his immediate arrest.* This proposition was too bold to meet the views of the more timid majority of the committee, and the governor was allowed to flee from the State.†

In the winter of 1776, Mr. Middleton was one of a committee appointed to form a government for South Carolina; and early in the spring of that year he was elected by the Provincial Legislature, a delegate to the General Congress, at Philadelphia. There he was an active promoter of the measures tending toward a severance of the Colonies from Great Britain, and voted for and signed the Declaration of Independence. By this pa-

* Lord William Campbell was nearly related to Mr. Middleton's wife, and the greatest intimacy existed between the families. But private feelings and close ties of relationship had no weight in the scale against Mr. Middleton's convictions of duty, and he was among the first to recommend meetings to destroy the power of the governor.

† Had the proposition of Mr. Middleton been carried into effect, much blood. shed might have been saved in South Carolina, for Lord Campbell, after his flight joined Sir Henry Clinton, and representing the tory interest as very powerful in that State, induced that commander, in connection with the fleet of Sir Peter Parker, to ravage the coast and make an attack upon Charleston. In that engagement Lord Campbell was slain.

15

triotic act, he placed himself in a position to lose life and property, should the contest prove unsuccessful, but these considerations had no weight with him.

Mr. Middleton continued a member of Congress until the close of 1777, when he returned to South Carolina. In 1778, the Assembly adopted a State Constitution, and Arthur Middleton was elected first governor under it. Doubting the legality of the proceedings of the Assembly in framing the constitution, he declined the acceptance of the appointment.

When, in 1779, South Carolina was invaded by the British, Mr. Middleton's property was exposed to their ravages. Yet he heeded not the destruction that was wrought, but joining Governor Rutledge in his attempts to defend the State, he left his estate entirely unprotected and only wrote to his wife to remove with the family a a day's journey from the scene of strife. In this invasion a large portion of his immense estate was sacrificed. The following year, after the surrender of Charleston to the British, he was one of the many influential men who were taken prisoners and sent to St. Augustine in Florida. There he remained about one year, and was then sent, as an exchanged prisoner, to Philadelphia. He was at once elected by the Assembly of South Carolina, a representative in Congress, and he remained there until November, 1782, when he returned to his family.

He was a representative in his State Legislature until near the close of 1787, when disease removed him from his sphere of usefulness. By exposure he contracted an intermittent fever, which he neglected until it was too late to check its ravages upon his constitution. He died on the first day of January, 1788. He left his wife a widow with eight children. She lived until 1814, and had the satisfaction of seeing her offspring among the honored of the land.

UTTON GWINNETT was born in England, in 1732. The pecuniary means of his parents were limited, yet they managed to give him a good common education. He was apprenticed to a merchant in Bristol, and after completing his term of service, he married, and commenced business on his own account. Allured by the promises of wealth and distinction in America, he resolved to emigrate hither, and he arrived at Charleston, in South Carolina, in the year 1770. There he commenced mercantile business, and after pursuing it for two years, he sold out his stock, moved to Georgia, and purchased large tracts of land on St. Catharine's Island in that province. He purchased a number of slaves, and devoted himself to agricultural pursuits.

Mr. Gwinnett favored the opposition of the Colonies to British oppression, to some degree, yet he was one of those cautious, doubting men at that time, who viewed the success of the colonies in an open rupture with the home government, as highly problematical. Therefore, when, in 1774, Georgia was solicited to unite her voice with the other colonies in a General Congress, Mr. Gwinnett looked upon the proposition with disfavor, as one fraught with danger and many evils. But falling in with Doctor Lyman Hall, and a few other decided patriots, his judgment became gradually convinced that some powerful movement was necessary, and at length he came out before the people, as one of the warmest advocates of unbending resistance to the British Crown. His culti

227

vated mind and superior talents rendered him very popular with the people as soon as he espoused their cause, and every honor in their gift was speedily bestowed upon him.

It was in the beginning of 1775, that Mr. Gwinnett openly espoused the cause of the patriots, and the parish of St. John elected him a delegate to the Continental Congress.* In February, 1776, he was again elected a delegate to that body by the General Assembly of Georgia, and under their instructions, and in accordance with his own strong inclinations, he voted for the Declaration of Independence, and signed it on the second of August following. He remained in Congress until 1777, when he was elected a member of the Convention of his State to form a Constitution, in accordance with the recommendation of Congress after the Declaration of Independence was made, and the grand outlines of that instrument are attributed to Mr. Gwinnett.

Soon after the State Convention adjourned, Mr. Bullock, the president of the council, died, and Mr. Gwinnett was elected to that station, then the highest office in the gift of the people. The civil honors, so rapidly and lavishly bestowed upon him, excited his ambition, and while he was a representative in Congress, he aspired to the possession of military honors also. He offered himself as a candidate for the office of Brigadier General, and his competitor was Colonel M'Intosh, a man highly esteemed for his manly bearing and courageous disposition. Mr. Gwinnett was defeated, and with mistaken views he looked

---

* At the early stage of the controversy with Great Britain, Georgia, sparsely populated, seemed quite inactive, except in the district known as the parish of St. John. There all the patriotism of the province seemed to have been concentrated. The General Assembly having refused to send delegates to the Congress of 1774, that parish separated from the province, and appointed a representative in the Continental Congress. The leaven, however, soon spread and George gave her vote, in 1776, for independence.

upon his rival as a personal enemy.* A decided aliena
tion of their former friendship took place, and the breach
was constantly widened by the continued irritations which
Mr. Gwinnett experienced at the hands of Colonel M'Intosh and his friends. At length he was so excited by the
conduct of his opposers, and goaded by the thoughts of
having his fair fame tarnished in the eyes of the community, from whom he had received his laurels, that he listened to the suggestions of false honor, and challenged
Colonel M'Intosh to single combat. They met with pis-
tols, and at the first fire both were wounded, Mr. Gwinnett
mortally; and in the prime of life, at the early age of forty-
five, his life terminated. He could well have said, in the
language of the lamented Hamilton, when fatally wounded
in a duel by Aaron Burr: "I have lived like a man, but
I die like a fool."

Mr. Gwinnett left a wife and several children, but they
did not long survive him.

---

* As we have elsewhere remarked in the course of these memoirs, native born
Englishmen were in the habit of regarding the colonists as inferior to themselves,
and they were apt to assume a bearing toward them highly offensive. In some
degree Mr. Gwinnett was obnoxious to this charge, and he looked upon his rapid
elevation in public life, as an acknowledgment of his superiority. These feelings were too thinly covered not to be seen by the people when he was president
of the council, and it soon engendered among the natives a jealousy that was
fully reciprocated by him. This was doubtless the prime cause of all the difficulties which surrounded him toward the close of his life, and brought him to his
tragical death.

Lyman Hall

YMAN HALL was born in Connecticut in the year 1721. His father
was possessed of a competent fortune, and he gave his son an opportunity for acquiring a good education.
He placed him in Yale College, at
the age of sixteen years, whence he graduated after four
years' study. He chose the practice of medicine as a
profession, and he entered upon the necessary studies
with great ardor, and pursued them with perseverance

230

As soon as Mr. Hall had completed his professional studies, and was admitted to practice, with the title of M. D., he married and emigrated to South Carolina, in 1752. He first settled at Dorchester, but during the year he moved to Sunbury, in the district of Medway in Georgia, whither about forty New England families, then in South Carolina, accompanied him. He was very successful in the practice of his profession, and by his superior intelligence, probity, and consistency of character, he won the unbounded esteem and confidence of his fellow citizens.

Doctor Hall was a close observer of the "signs of the times," and he was among the earliest of the southern patriots who lifted up their voices against British oppression and misrule. The community in which he lived was strongly imbued with the same feeling, for the people brought with them from New England the cherished principles of the Pilgrim Fathers—principles that would not brook attempts to enslave, or even to destroy a single prerogative of the colonies. The older settlers of Georgia, many of whom were direct from Europe, had these principles of freedom inwoven with their character in a much less degree, and therefore the parish of St. John, wherein Doctor Hall resided, seemed, at the first cry of liberty, to have all the patriotism of the province centred there.

Early in 1774 Doctor Hall and a few kindred spirits, endeavored, by calling public meetings, to arouse the people of the province to make common cause with their brethren of the North, but these efforts seemed almost futile. Finally, a general meeting of all favorable to republicanism was called at Savannah, in July, 1774, but the measures adopted there, were temporizing and noncommittal in a great degree, and Doctor Hall almost despaired of success in persuading Georgia to send delegates to the General Congress, called to meet at Philadelphia in September.* He returned to his constituents with a heavy heart, and his report filled them with disgust at the pusillanimity of the other representatives there. Fired with zeal for the cause, and deeply sympathizing with their brother patriots of New England, the people of the parish of St. John resolved to act, in the matter, independent of the rest of the colony, and in March, 1775, they elected Doctor Hall a delegate to the General Congress, and he appeared there with his credentials on the thirteenth of May, following.† Notwithstanding he was not an accredited delegate of a colony, Congress, by a unanimous vote, admitted him to a seat.‡

During the summer, Georgia became sufficiently aroused to come out as a colony in favor of the republican cause, and at a convention of the people held in Savannah, in July, five delegates to Congress were elected, of whom Doctor Hall was one. He presented his new credentials in May, 1776, and he took part in the debates which ensued on the motion of Mr. Lee for Independence. Doctor Hall warmly supported it, and voted for it on the fourth of July. He signed the Declaration on the second of August, and soon afterward returned home for a season.

Doctor Hall was a member of Congress nearly all the while until 1780, when the invasion of his state, by the

* Another convection of representatives of the people of the province met at Savannah, about six months after, but the extent of their proceedings was to petition Great Britain to redress the wrongs of the colonies, a petition which the patriots of the north knew to be as powerless to stay the oppressions of the Crown, as a barrier of down against a tornado.

† The people of the parish of St. John, convinced that the rest of the province was too apathetic to act, appealed to the Committee of Safety of South Carolina, to allow them to join with them in their non-importation agreements, and other commercial regulations. Owing to some difference of opinion they were not successful in their application. They therefore united among themselves, established a non-importation association, and proceeded to elect a delegate to Congress.

‡ As they sometimes voted by colonies, Congress was somewhat embarrassed in the case of Mr. Hall, but his own wisdom obviated the difficulty. He proposed to debate, and listen to others, but not to vota when Congress voted by colonies.

British, called him home to look after the safety of his family. He arrived there in time to remove them, but was obliged to leave his property entirely exposed to the fury of the foe. He went north, and while the British had possession of the state, and revived royal authority in government there, his property was confiscated.

He returned to Georgia, in 1782, just before the enemy evacuated Savannah.* The next year he was elected governor of the State. He held the office one term, and then retired from public life, and sought happiness in the domestic circle. But that was soon invaded by the arch-destroyer. His only son was cut down in the flower of his youth, and the father did not long survive him. He died in the year 1784, in the sixty-third year of his age, greatly beloved and widely lamented.†

---

* After the capture of Cornwallis and his army at Yorktown, in 1781, the war virtually ceased. Armies were still on duty, and arrangements were made for regular campaigns the ensuing season; but unimportant skirmishes in the Southern States made up the bulk of actual hostilities from that time until the proclamation of peace. Georgia was the only rendezvous of the remnant of the British at the South, in the beginning of the year 1782. In June of that year, General Wayne arrived there with a portion of the Pennsylvania line, and the enemy retreated from all their outposts into Savannah. The State was thus evacuated, and republican authority was re-established. Wayne was attacked within five miles of Savannah, on the twenty-fourth of June, by a party of British and Indians, and in that skirmish Colonel John Laurens was killed. This was the last battle of the Revolution. Cessation of hostilities was proclaimed, and in July the British force evacuated Savannah, and the last hostile foot left the soil of Georgia.

† During the present session (1848) of the Legislature of Georgia, the sum of fifteen hundred dollars was appropriated for the purpose of erecting a lead monument to the memory of Lyman Hall, and George Walton, two delegates from Georgia, who signed the Declaration of Independence. Their remains are to be removed to Augusta where the monument is to be reared.

Geo Walton.

EORGE WALTON was descended from parentage quite obscure, and the glory that halos his name derives not a gleam from ancestral distinction—it is all his own. He was born in the county of Frederick, in Virginia, in the year. 1740. His early education was extremely limited, and at the age of fourteen years he was apprenticed to a carpenter. He was possessed of an inquiring mind, and an ardent thirst for knowledge, but his master's authority hung like a mill-stone about the neck of his aspirations. He was an ignorant man, and looked upon a studious boy as an idle one, considering the time spent in reading as wasted. With this feeling, he would allow young Walton no time to read by day, nor lights to study by night; but the ardent youth overcame these difficulties, and by using torch-wood for light, he spent his evenings in study. Persevering in this course, he ended his apprenticeship with a well-stored mind. He then moved into the province of Georgia, and commenced the study of law in the office of Mr. Young, an eminent barrister in that colony.

Mr. Walton commenced the practice of law in the year 1774, a time when the colonies were in a blaze respecting the various acts of the British Parliament which invaded colonial rights. But Georgia was either very apathetic or very timid, for the people, although induced by active patriots to meet together in convention at Savannah, did not so far approve of the call for a General Congress, as to appoint delegates thereto, and Georgia was the only colony unrepresented there.

Soon after commencing the practice of his profession, Mr. Walton became acquainted with some of the leading patriots in that province, among whom was Dr. Hall; and they found in him an apt pupil in the school of patriotism, His law tutor was an ardent patriot also, and these influences, combined with his own natural bias, made him espouse the republican cause with hearty zeal. He boldly opposed the movements of the loyalists, and soon called down upon his head the denunciations of the ruling powers. 'He labored assiduously to have the whole province take the road toward freedom, which the parish of St. John had chosen, yet his labor seemed almost fruitless. But at length the fruits of the zeal of himself and others began to appear, and in the winter of 1776, the Assembly of Georgia declared for the patriot cause, and in February appointed five delegates to the Continental Congress. Of these delegates, Mr. Walton was one.

The royal governor was so incensed at this daring and treasonable act of the Assembly that he threatened to use military force against them. But they utterly disregarded his authority, organized a new government, and elected Archibald Bullock president of the Executive Council.

The Congress was in session at Baltimore when he arrived, having adjourned there from Philadelphia because of the expected attack upon that city by the British under Lord Cornwallis. The confidence which that body reposed in him was manifested three days after his arrival, by his appointment upon a committee with Robert Morris and George Clymer, to repair to Philadelphia and act as circumstances might require. This was a post of great trust and danger, and the powers delegated to the committee were almost unlimited; in their keeping and disposition nearly the whole of the finances of Congress were intrusted. This service was performed with the utmost fidelity.

Mr. Walton was favorable to the proposition for independence, and he used all his influence to bring about that result. He voted for and signed the Declaration of Independence, and the fortune and honor he there pledged, were freely devoted to its support. He remained in Congress until near the close of 1778, when he returned home, having been appointed by the legislature colonel of a regiment in his State, then threatened by an invasion of the enemy from the sea. Colonel Walton hastened to join his regiment, and was there in time to enter the battalion of General Howe,* at Savannah, when Colonel Campbell,

---

* This was General Robert Howe, of the American army. There were three commanding officers by the name of Howe engaged in our Revolutionary war; General Robert Howe, just named; General Sir William Howe, of the British army; and his brother, Lord Howe, Admiral in its navy. At the time in question, General Robert Howe had about eight hundred men under his command. and

from New York, landed there and besieged it. In that engagement he received a severe shot wound in his thigh, and he fell from his horse. In this condition he was taken prisoner, but was soon afterward exchanged.*

In October, 1779, the Legislature of Georgia appointed Mr. Walton governor of the State. He did not hold that office long, for in January, 1780, he was again elected to a seat in Congress for two years, but in October following he withdrew from that body, and was again elected governor of his State, which office he then held a full term. Near the close of the term, he was appointed by the Legislature, Chief Justice of the State, and he retained that office until his death. In 1798, he was elected a member of the Senate of the United States, where he remained one year and then retired to private life, except so far as his duties upon the bench required him to act in public. His useful life was terminated in Augusta, Georgia, on the second day of February, 1804, when he was in the sixty-fourth year of his age.

Mr. Walton had but one child, a son, who was a great solace to the declining years of his father.† Judge Walton was universally beloved by those who knew him intimately, and the carpenter's apprentice became the most exalted citizen of the Commonwealth in which he resided. Even at this late day, the remembrance of his services and exalted character, is fresh in the hearts of the people.

would doubtless have maintained a successful defence of Savannah, had it not been for a treacherous negro, who pointed out to the enemy a path across a morass that defended the Americans in the rear. By this treachery the Americans were attacked front and rear, and were obliged to surrender themselves prisoners of war.

* He then held the active position of major, with the rank of colonel, yet being a member of Congress and guilty of the great offence of having signed the Declaration of Independence, a brigadier general was demanded in exchange for him. He was finally exchanged for a naval captain.

† When General Jackson was governor of West Florida, Judge Walton's son held the office of Secretary of State, and was regarded as one of the most estimable men in that territory.

LTHOUGH ROBERT R. LIVINGSTON was not one of those who signed the Declaration of Independence, yet his name should ever be inseparably connected with theirs, for he was one of the committee of the immortal Congress of 1776, to whom was intrusted the momentous task of framing that revered document. With such considerations, we have deemed it our duty to append the memoir of that great man, to the biographies of his colleagues in the National Council whence emanated that Declaratory Act which gave birth and freedom to a great nation.

Robert R. Livingston was of noble lineage—noble, not only by royal patent, but in high and virtuous deeds.* He was born in the city of New York, in the year 1747, and was educated at King's (now Columbia) College. He graduated with honor in 1764, at the age of seventeen years, and then entered upon the study of the law, in New York, under Mr. Smith, a barrister of considerable eminence there, and subsequently Chief Justice of Canada. He was also an historian of New York.

Not long after obtaining his license as attorney and counsellor, Mr. Livingston was appointed Recorder of the city of New York. At that time (1771), the excitement in the colonies against the home government was strong and general, and he warmly espoused the patriot cause. His father was also an unswerving patriot, and because of adhesion to the "rebels" they were both ejected from office.

* James Livingston, about the middle of the sixteenth century, was appointed Regent of Scotland, during the minority of James I. A grand-daughter of this Livingston married Donald, king of the Hebrides. Several members of the family had distinct titles; one was Earl of Newburgh, another Earl of Linlithgow, another Earl of Callander, and another Earl of Livingstone. The latter was the common ancestor of the branch of the family that emigrated to America. He was hereditary governor of Linlithgow Castle, in which Mary, Queen of Scots, was born, and his daughter was one of the four ladies who attended Mary to France, as her companions. The grandson of Lord Livingston, who was an eminent divine, emigrated to Rotterdam, in 1663, in consequence of the religious persecusions in Scotland, and he was one of the commissioners in the negotiations for that peace, which eventuated in the transfer of the colony of New York from the states of Holland to England. His son Robert emigrated to America, in 1678, and in 1686 he obtained a patent for the Manor of Livingston, upon the Hudson river, in Columbia County, New York. He was afterward chiefly instrumental, in a conference with King William and others, in causing the expedition which was fitted out against the pirates that infested the American coast. Captain Kidd was appointed the agent in the enterprise, but through the connivance as is supposed, of Governor Fletcher, of New York, he became a greater pirate himself than those he came to subdue. Robert R. Livingston, the subject of this sketch, was un great-grandson of Robert, the first proprietor of the Livingston manor.

In 1775, Mr. Livingston was elected a member of the Continental Congress, assembled in Philadelphia, where his activity and zeal were such that he was re-elected for 1776.* He took part in the debates which occurred on the motion of Richard Hency Lee, of Virginia, declaring the United Colonies free and independent; and he was placed upon the committee, which Congress appointed to draw up a Declaration of Independence, in conformity with the spirit of the revolution, and was present when it was adopted.

The name of Mr. Livingston was not affixed to the Declaration of Independence, but in regard to the reasons why his signature was withheld, his biographers are silent. We venture the opinion that he regarded as correct the doctrine that the representative is bound to act in accordance with the expressed will of his constituents. At the time the Declaration was acted upon and adopted, the Provincial Assembly of New York still withheld all sanction of so strong a measure, and hence it is probable that Mr. Livingston did not think proper to take the responsibility of concurring in such an important measure, without the sanction of his constituents. That sanction, however, *was* given on the twelfth of July by a vote of the Assembly then in session at White Plains, in which they approved of the action of Philip Livingston and others who were afterward signers. The question does not in the least affect the character of Mr. Livingston, for his patriotism was undoubted, and his subsequent career attests the firm confidence of his countrymen.

When, after the Declaration was adopted, Congress re-

* General Richard Montgomery married a sister of Mr. Livingston, and, toward the close of 1775, he commanded an expedition against Quebec. In endeavoring to scale the heights of Abraham near that city, he was mortally wounded by a cannon shot. His remains were taken to the city of New York, in 1818, and deposited beneath a monument placed under the portico of St. Paul's Church, in that city.

commended the several states to form constitutions for their governments respectively, Mr. Livingston was elected a member of the convention of New York, assembled for that purpose. He served alternately in Congress and in the legislature of his native state from 1775 till 1781, when, under the Articles of Confederation, he was appointed Secretary for Foreign Affairs, which station he filled, with great industry and fidelity, until 1783. On retiring from the office he received the thanks of Congress. He was that year appointed Chancellor of the State of New York, and was the first who held the office under the new constitution of the State.

Mr. Livingston was a member of the convention of New York which assembled at Poughkeepsie, in 1788, to take into consideration the newly formed Federal Constitution, and he was then one of its warmest advocates in procuring its ratification by that body.

In April, 1789, Washington, the first President of the United States, was inaugurated in the city of New York. It was one of the most august occasions the world has ever witnessed, and Chancellor Livingston had the exalted honor of administering the oath of office to that great leader, and of witnessing before high heaven his solemn pledge to support the constitution.

In 1801, Chancellor Livingston was appointed by President Jefferson, minister to the court of France, at the head of which was then the young conqueror of Italy, Napoleon Bonaparte, First Consul of the French Republic. He at once won the esteem and confidence of that great captain, and successfully negotiated with his ministers for the purchase of Louisiana, then in possession of France.

The treaty was signed in April, 1802, by Mr. Livingston and Mr. Monroe, on the part of the United States, and by the Count de Marbois in behalf of France.

16

When it was signed, Mr. Livingston arose from his seat and with solemn and prophetic voice said, "We have lived long, but this is the noblest work of our whole lives. The treaty which we have just signed has not been obtained by art or dictated by force; equally advantageous to both contracting parties, it will change vast solitudes into flourishing districts. From this day the United States take their place among the powers of the first rank; the English lose all exclusive influence in the affairs of America." Napoleon, too, spoke prophetically. "This accession of territory," said he, "strengthens for ever the power of the United States; and I have given to England a maritime rival, that will sooner or later humble her pride."

While in Europe, Chancellor Livingston indulged and cultivated his taste for literature and the Fine Arts; and he sent to the American Academy of Fine Arts, which was established in New York, in 1801, a very fine collection of antique busts and statues (now in possession of its rival and successor, the National Academy of Design) and some admirable paintings. Science, too, claimed his attention, and the aid and encouragement which he rendered Robert Fulton in his steamboat experiments, by which they were made successful, form an imperishable monument of honor to his memory.* Agriculture was his

* Chancellor Livingston was the only man of influence who seemed to appreciate the character of Fulton's genius, and sympathize with him in his efforts to render steam subservient to purposes of navigation. He warmly entered into all his plans, fully comprehended his theories, and was convinced at the outset of the practicability of the project. He had himself made many advances in the same road with Mr. Fulton, before he became acquainted with him. He applied to the Legislature of New York, in 1798, for a special act, giving him the exclusive right to navigate the waters of the Hudson river with boats "propelled by fire or steam" for twenty years. Dr. Samuel Mitchell, then in the House of Aseembly introduced a bill accordingly, and it brought down upon him an avalanche of ridicule; and the debates which arose upon it were amusing in the extreme. It is said that when any of the younger members wished to indulge in a little fun they would call up Dr. Mitchell's "hot water bill," and bandy their jokes without stint. Many

study and delight, and to him the farmers of this country are indebted for the introduction of gypsum or plaster, for manure, and the clover grass.

Chancellor Livingston continued actively engaged in public life until a year or so before his death, which occurred at his country-seat at Clermont, on the twenty-sixth day of February, 1813, when he was in the sixty-sixth year of his age. He was a prominent actor in scenes which present features of the most remarkable kind, as influencing the destinies of the world. His pen, like his oratory, was chaste and classical; and the latter, because of its purity and ease, obtained for him from the lips of Doctor Franklin, the title of the "Cicero of America." And to all of his eminent virtues and attainments he added that of a sincere and devoted Christian, the crowning attribute in the character of a good and great man.

of the older members declared that the project of propelling vessels by steam was too preposterous to be seriously thought of, and was unworthy of being dignified by legislative action. But an act granting the privilege was finally Passed; yet the experiments of Mr. Livingston were not sufficiently successful to warrant him to build a boat of any considerable size. For a while he abandoned the scheme, and it was not until after his return from France, whither Mr. Jefferson sent him as minister, that he resumed his experiments. He became acquainted with Mr. Fulton in Paris, and on his return to the United States, they united their interests and their talents, and produced a boat, in 1807, which was propelled by steam from New York to Albany, at the rate of five miles an hour.

The first trip which this boat made was one of intense interest to Fulton and his warm-hearted colleague, Chancellor Livingston. A few doubting friends ventured on board, and when the boat left the wharf, they almost wished themselves again on shore, for they felt the jeers of the crowd that huzzaed for "Fulton's folly" as the vessel moved out into the stream. On she went some distance up the river and stopped! 'Just as I expected,' was the feeling of all, and the expression of many. But Fulton's confidence was not shaken; he discovered the cause and the boat moved on. They reached the Taappan Sea, glided through Haverstraw Bay, and at length entered the great amphitheatre of the Highlands at Caldwell's. Onward moved the mysterious vessel. West Point was passed, magnificent Newburgh Bay was entered, the green fields of Dutchess and Columbia, and the towering peaks of the Catskills were passed, and Albany was reached. The victory was complete—Science vindicated the claims of Genius, and a new creation of the western world began. Now the fruits of that victory are seen world wide, and the achievements of Fulton and Livingston on that day are now honored as having given an almost omnipotent sceptre to civilization.

THE

DECLARATION OF INDEPENDENCE,

HISTORICALLY CONSIDERED.

AN aspiration for political independence was not a prevailing sentiment among the people of the Anglo-American colonies, until about the commencement of the year 1776. It had indeed been a favorite idea with a very few of the early leaders in the political movements antecedent to, and productive of, the War of the Revolution; yet manifest expediency, and a lingering hope of obtaining justice from the mother country, and through it reconciliation, caused them to confine the audible expression of this sentiment to the private circle of tried friendship. Samuel Adams, Richard Henry Lee, Patrick Henry, Timothy Dwight,* and a few others had indeed breathed the subject in the ears of their countrymen, but the idea met with little favor, even among the most ardent patriots.

* "In the month of July, 1775," says Timothy Dwight, "I urged, in conversation, with several gentlemen of great respectability, firm whigs, and my intimate friends, the importance and even the necessity of a declaration of independence *on the* part of the colonies, and alleged for this measure, the very same arguments which afterward were generally considered as decisive; but found them disposed to give me and my arguments, a hostile and contemptuous, instead of a cordial reception. Yet, at his time, all the resentment and enthusiasm awakened by the odious measures of Parliament, by the peculiarly obnoxious conduct of the British agents in this country, and by the recent battles of Lexington and Breed's Hill, were at the highest pitch. These gentlemen may be considered as representatives of the great body of the thinking men in this country. A few may, perhaps, be excepted, but none of these durst at that time openly declare their opinions to the public. For myself, I regarded the die as cast, and the hopes of reconciliation as vanished; and believed that the colonists would never be able to defend themselves unless they renounced their dependence on Great Britain."—*Dwight's Travels in New England,* vol. i., p. 159.

There were some who, from the first, seemed to have a presentiment that reconciliation was out of the question. Among these was Patrick Henry. As early as 1773, he uttered the following prediction. Speaking of Great Britain, he said, "She *will* drive us to extremities; no accommodation *will* take place; hostilities *will* soon commence; and a desperate and bloody touch it will be." This, Mr. Wirt asserts, was said in the presence of Colonel Samuel Overton, who at once asked Mr. Henry if he thought the Colonies sufficiently strong to oppose successfully, the fleets and armies of Great Britain? "I will be candid with you," replied Mr. Henry, "I doubt whether we *shall* be able, *alone,* to cope with so powerful a nation; but," continued he, rising from his chair with great animation, "where is France!—where is Spain!—where is Holland—the natural enemies of Great Britain? Where will they be all this while? Do you suppose they will stand by, idle and indifferent spectators to the contest? Will Louis XVI. be asleep all this time? Believe me, *no!* When Louis XVI. shall be satisfied by our serious opposition, and our *Declaration of Independence,* that all prospect of a reconciliation is gone, then, and not till then, will he furnish us with arms, ammunition and clothing; and not with them only, but he will send his fleets and armies to fight our battles for us; he will form a treaty with us, offensive and defensive, against our unnatural mother. Spain and Holland will join the confederation! Our independence will be established! and we shall take our stand among the nations of the earth!" How literally these predictions were soon fulfilled, the pen of History has already recorded.

But the pride of political birth-right, as a child of Great Britain, kept actively alive a loyal spirit; and a separation from the British empire was a proposition too startling to be readily embraced, or even favorably received, by the great mass of the people, who regarded "Old England" with filial reverence. Great Britain, the revered parent, and America, the dutiful child, had long been bound together by interest, by sameness of habits, manners, religion, laws and government. The recollection of their original consanguinity had always been cherished with an amiable sensibility, or a kind of mechanic enthusiasm that promoted mutual felicity when they met on each other's shores, or in distant lands saluted each other with the same language.*

When intelligence reached America that the King had declared the colonists *rebels*—that thousands of German troops had been engaged by Parliament to come hither to assist in the work of subjugating a people struggling for right and justice—and that the British government was collecting all its mighty energies, for the purpose of striking a blow of such intensity as to scatter into fragments every vestige of the rightful claims of the colonists, to enjoy the prerogatives granted to them by Magna Charta, a deep and solemn conviction seized the minds of the people, that the last ray of hope of reconciliation had faded away, and that unbending resistance or absolute slavery was the only alternative left them. The bonds of filial affection were rudely severed by the unnatural parent, and the deserted and outlawed children were driven by necessity to seek shelter beneath a palladium of their own construction.

During the winter of 1776, the ablest persons in America were busy in the preparation of pamphlets and essays for gazettes, all filled with arguments to prove the necessity of a close union of the colonies to meet the threatened blow, and the paramount necessity of making the rallying cry "Independence or Slavery."

* Mrs. Warren's "Rise and Progress of the American Revolution."—vol. .i p 303.

Among the former, one entitled *Common Sense,* written by Thomas Paine, produced a powerful effect upon the people, and awakened in the hearts of thousands a longing for independence, where before, loyalty to the British crown was a cherished principle. In all the colonies, men of the highest rank and influence boldly avowed their sentiments in favor of independence. Nor was the pen alone the asserter and vindicator of this sentiment, but in various ways, distinguished men presented the subject in all its bearings before the people. The course of William Henry Drayton, Chief Justice of South Carolina, may be cited as one of many ways in which, not only personal influence, but official station,was brought to bear upon the minds and hearts of the people, in favor of independence. In his charge to the grand jurors, in April, 1776, he proceeded to vindicate the course that had been pursued by the colonies in forming new governments, and then added, "I think it my duty to declare, in the awful seat of justice, and before Almighty God, that in my opinion, the Americans can have no safety, but by divine favor, their own virtues, and their being so prudent, as not to leave it in the power of British rulers to injure them. Indeed, the ruinous and deadly injuries received on our side, and the jealousies entertained, and which in the nature of things must daily increase against us, on the other, demonstrate to a mind the least given to reflection, that true reconcilement can never exist between Great Britain and America the latter being subject to the former. . . . . The Almighty created America to be independent of Great Britain: let us beware of the impiety of being backward to act as instruments in the Almighty hand, now extended to accomplish his purpose, and by the completion of which, alone, America, in the nature of human affairs, can be secure against the crafty and insidious designs of her enemies, who think her favor and prosperity already by far too great. In a word, our piety and political safety are so blended, that to refuse our labor in this divine work, is to refuse to be a great, a free, a pious and a happy people."*

When the minds of the people seemed to be sufficiently prepared to receive the novel idea of independence of the British Crown, the colonial assemblies began to move in the matter. North Carolina was the first to take the bold, progressive step. On the twenty-second of April, 1776, the convention of North Carolina empowered their delegates in the General Congress "to concur with those in the other colonies in declaring independence."

On the tenth of May, the general assembly of Massachusetts requested the people of that colony, at the then approaching election of new representatives, to give them instructions on the subject of independence.† On the twenty-third of May, the people of Boston, pursuant to this request, instructed their representatives to use their best endeavors to have their delegates in Congress "advised, that in case Congress should think it necessary, for the safety of the united colonies, to declare themselves independent of Great Britain, the inhabitants of that colony, with their lives, and the *remnants* of their fortunes, would most cheerfully support them in the measure."

On the seventeenth of May, the convention of Virginia unanimously resolved, "that the delegates appointed to represent this colony in the General Congress, be instructed to propose to that respectable body to declare the-united colonies free and independent states, absolved

---

* In the charge, from which we make this extract, Chief Justice Drayton ably descanted upon the various oppressive acts of the British Government, and drew admirable parallels between the causes which led to the revolution in England in 1688, and those which caused the revolution in America then in progress. He placed James II. on one side, and George III. on the other, and showed clearly that the acts of the latter were more *criminal* than those of the former.

† Bradford, vol. ii., p. 104

from all allegiance to, or dependence upon, the Crown or Parliament of Great Britain; and to support whatever measures may be thought proper and necessary by the Congress for forming foreign alliances, and a confederation of the colonies, at such time, and in such manner, as to them may seem best—provided, that the power of forming governments for, and the regulation of the internal concern of each colony, be left to the respective colonial legislatures."*

The assembly of Rhode Island, during its session in May, directed the oath of allegiance, thereafter, to be taken to the *colony,* instead of to the King of Great Britain. They also instructed their delegates to join with the other colonies "upon the most proper measures for promoting and confirming the strictest union and confederation, between the colonies, for exerting their whole strength and force to annoy the common enemy, and to secure to the said colonies their rights and liberties, both civil and religious; whether by entering into *treaties* with any prince, state, or potentate; or by such other prudent and effectual *ways* and *means* as should be devised and agreed upon; and in conjunction with the delegates from the united colonies, to enter upon, and attempt, all such measures, taking the greatest care to secure to this colony, in the most perfect manner, its present forms, and all the power of government, so far as relates to its internal police, and conduct of affairs, civil and religious."†

On the eighth of June, the delegates from New York wrote to the convention of that colony, asking their advice on the question of independence, then agitated in Con gross. The convention did not feel themselves authorized

---

*After the adoption of this resolution, the convention proceeded to the establishment of a regular independent government, a course which Congress shortly afterward recommended to all the states.

Records of the assembly of Rhode Island.

to advise their delegates to declare that colony independent, but recommended, by resolution, that the people, who were about to elect new representatives, should give instructions on the subject.*

On the fourteenth of June, a special assembly was called in Connecticut, and a resolution was adopted, by a unanimous vote, instructing the delegates of that colony, in the General Congress, to "give their assent to a declaration of independence, and to unite in measures for forming foreign alliances, and promoting a plan of union among the colonies."†

On the fifteenth of June, the representatives of New Hampshire unanimously instructed their delegates to join the other colonies in this question.‡

On the twenty-first of the same month, new delegates to the Continental Congress were elected by the convention of New Jersey, and they were instructed, "in case they judged it necessary and expedient for supporting the just rights of America, to join in declaring the united colonies independent, and entering into a confederation for union and defence."

The assembly of Pennsylvania, held in June, removed the restrictions laid upon their delegates by instructions in November preceding; but they neither instructed them, nor gave them leave, to concur with the other colonies in a declaration of independence. The convention of Maryland positively forbade, by a resolution passed about the last of May, their delegates voting for independence. Georgia and Delaware left their representatives free to act without any instructions or restrictions,

*Records of the convention of New York.

† The convention of that special session issued a proclamation, in which it was recommended "to all persons of every rank and denomination to furnish themselves, with all possible expedition, with good sufficient fire-arms, and other was like accoutrements."

† Pitkin, vol. i., p. 363.

In the meanwhile, the General Congress was busy in preparing the way for a declaration of absolute independence of the British Crown. On the tenth of May, 1776, that body adopted a resolution recommending to the assemblies and colonies, where no sufficient government had been established, "to adopt such government as should, in the opinion of the representatives of the people, best conduce to the happiness and safety of their constituents in particular, and America in general." In the preamble to this resolution, Congress declared it to be "irreconcilable to reason and good conscience for the colonists to take the oaths required for the support of the government under the Crown of Great Britain." They also declared it necessary that all royal power should be suppressed, and "all the powers of government exerted under the authority of the people of the colonies, for the preservation of internal peace, virtue, and good order, as well as for the defence of their lives, liberties, and properties, against the hostile invasions and cruel depredations of their enemies." This was a bold and vigorous stride toward a declaration of independence.

While a majority of the members of the Congress were yearning, with anxious and irrepressible zeal, for the consummation of an event which they felt must inevitably occur—and all eyes were turned with earnest gaze upon that august assembly as the organ that should proclaim "liberty to the land, and to the inhabitants thereof," there seemed to be no one courageous enough to step forth and take the awful responsibility of lifting the knife that should sever the cord that bound the American colonies to the British throne. It was very properly apprehended, that the person who should first propose to declare the colonies independent, would be specially marked by the royal government as an arch rebel, and that no effort would be spared to quench his spirit or bring his person to the scaffold. In that dark hour of hesitation and fearful dread, Richard Henry Lee, of Virginia, assumed the perilous responsibility of presenting to Congress a proposition to dissolve all political connection with Great Britain. The assembly of Virginia, as we have already seen, had instructed its delegates to *propose* a declaration of independence; and, as soon as the instructions arrived, the Virginia delegation appointed Mr. Lee to move a re-solution conformably to it. Accordingly, on the seventh of June, Mr. Lee moved the resolution, (among others,) "That these united colonies are, and of right ought to be, free and independent states; and that all political connec-tion between them and the state of Great Britain is, and ought to be, totally dissolved."* The consideration of the resolutions was deferred until the next morning.

On the eighth, Congress discussed the resolutions in committee of the whole house, and finally deferred the farther consideration of them until Monday, the tenth. On that day it was *"Resolved,* That the consideration of the *first resolution* [motion for independence] *be postponed* to the first Monday in July next, and, in the meanwhile, that no time be lost, *in case the Congress agree thereto,* a committee be appointed to prepare a declaration, to the effect of the first resolution, which is in these words, to wit: 'That these united colonies are, and of right ought to be, free and independent states; that they are absolved

---

*Congress being of opinion that the member who made the first motion on the subject of independence would certainly be exposed to personal and imminent danger, directed its Secretary to omit the name of the mover. Accordingly, in the journal of Friday, June 7th, it is thus stated: "Certain resolutions respecting independence being *moved* and seconded, it was resolved, that the consideration of them be deferred until to-morrow morning; and that the members be enjoined to attend punctually at ten o'clock, in order to take the same into their considera-tion." The name, neither of him who moved the resolutions, nor of him who seconded them, was mentioned. Richard Henry Lee was the mover, and John Adams seconded them.—See *Life of Richard Henry Lee, by his grandson,* vol. i., p. 170.

from all allegiance to the British Crown; and that all political connection between them and the state of Great Britain is, and cught to be, totally dissolved.'"

Richard Henry Lee, and John Adams, were the chief speakers in favor of the resolutions, during the debates which occurred from the seventh to the tenth of June inclusive; and they left no argument unused that was calculated to convince the hesitating, confirm the wavering, or persuade and encourage the timid and fearful. Lee, in particular, was incessant in his labors; and his sweet, persuasive eloquence, with all its wonted allurements, was constantly employed. His first speech on the resolution fixed the earnest attention of the Congress, and the concluding sentences, as recorded by Botta, were replete with eloquent force: "Why then, sir," he exclaimed, "do we longer delay? Why still deliberate? Let this happy day give birth to an American republic! Let her arise, not to devastate and conquer, but to re-establish the reign of peace and law. The eyes of Europe are fixed upon us; she demands of us a living example of freedom, that may exhibit a contrast, in the felicity of the citizen, to the ever-increasing tyranny which desolates her polluted shores. She invites us to prepare an asylum, where the unhappy may find solace, and the persecuted repose. She entreats us to cultivate a propitious soil, where that genuine plant, which first sprang and grew in England, but is now withered by the blasts of Scottish tyranny, may revive and flourish, sheltering under its salubrious and interminable shade all the unfortunate of the human race. If we are not this day wanting in our duty to our country, the names of the American legislators of '76 will be placed by posterity at the side of those of Theseus, of Lycurgus, of Romulus, of Numa, of the three Williams of Nassau, and of all those whose memory has been, and forever will be, dear to virtuous men and good citizens."

The resolution to postpone the further consideration of the subject, and to appoint a committee to prepare a declaration of independence, was adopted, and the next day (the eleventh) a committee of five was formed, consisting of Thomas Jefferson, of Virginia, John Adams, of Massachusetts, Benjamin Franklin, of Pennsylvania, Roger Sherman, of Connecticut, and Robert R. Livingston, of New York. On the evening of the tenth, Mr. Lee received intelligence, by express, from Virginia, that his lady was seriously ill, and he was compelled to ask leave of absence for a short time. He left Philadelphia the next morning before the committee was formed, and this circumstance deprived him of the honor of being a member of it, and of acting as chairman, which position usual legislative courtesy would have assigned him. Mr. Jefferson was appointed chairman of the committee, and his colleagues assigned to him the task of preparing a draft of the declaration to be presented to Congress. It was unanimously adopted by the committee after a few verbal alterations by Mr. Adams and Doctor Franklin, and on the first of July, according to the resolution of the tenth of June, Congress resumed the consideration of Mr. Lee's resolution, and the committee reported the draft of a declaration of independence. The following is a copy of the original draft, before any amendments were made in Committee of the Whole.* The passages omitted by

---

*On the eighth of July, four days after the Declaration, as amended, was adopted, Mr. Jefferson wrote the following letter, and sent it, with the original draft, to Mr. Lee:—

PHILADELPHIA, July 8, 1776.

DEAR SIR,—For news, I refer you to your brother who writes on that head. I enclose you a copy of the Declaration of Independence, as agreed to by the House, and als as originally framed; you will judge whether it is the better or the worse for the critics. I shall return to Virginia after the 11th of August. I wish my successor may be Certain to come before that time: in that case, I shall hope to see you, and not Wythe, in convention, that the business of government, which is of everlasting concern, may receive your aid. Adieu, and believe me to be,   Your friend and servant,

To Richard Henry Lee, Esq.   THOMAS JEFFERSON.

Congress, are printed in Italics, and the substitutions are given at the bottom of each page.

A Declaration by the Representatives of the UNITED STATES OF AMERICA, *in general Congress assembled.*

When, in the course of human events, it becomes necessary for one people to dissolve the political bands which have connected them with another, and to assume, among the powers of the earth, the separate and equal station to which the laws of nature and of nature's God entitle them, a decent respect to the opinions of mankind requires that they should declare the causes which impel them to the separation.

We hold these truths to be self-evident: that all men are created equal; that they are endowed by their Creator with *inherent and inalienable** rights; that among these are life, liberty, and the pursuit of happiness; that to secure these rights, governments are instituted among men, deriving their just powers from the consent of the governed; that whenever any form of government becomes destructive of these ends, it is the right of the people to alter or *to* abolish it, and to institute new government, laying its foundation on such principles, and organizing its powers in such form, as to them shall seem most likely to effect their safety and happiness. Prudence indeed, will dictate, that governments, long established should not be changed for light and transient causes. And, accordingly, all experience hath shown, that mankind are more disposed to suffer, while evils are sufferable, than to right themselves by abolishing the forms to which they are accustomed. But when a long train of abuses and usurpations, *begun at a distant period,* and pursuing invariably the same object, evinces a design to reduce

*Certain unalienable.

them under absolute despotism, it is their right, it is their duty, to throw off such government, and to provide new guards for their future security. Such has been the patient sufferance of these colonies; and such is now the necessity which constrains them to *expunge** their former systems of government. The history of the present king of Great Britain, is a history of *unremitting* † injuries and usurpations; *among which appears no solitary fact to contradict the uniform tenor of the rest; but* all *have,‡* in direct object, the establishment of an absolute tyranny over these states. To prove this, let facts be submitted to a candid world; *for the truth of which we pledge a faith yet unsullied by falsehood.*

He has refused his assent to laws the most wholesome and necessary for the public good.

He has forbidden his governors to pass laws of immediate and pressing importance, unless suspended in their operation till his assent should be obtained; and when so suspended, he has *neglected utterly§* to attend to them.

He has refused to pass other laws for the accommodation of large districts of people, unless those people would relinquish the right of representation in the legislature; a right inestimable to them, and formidable to tyrants only.

He has called together legislative bodies at places unusual, uncomfortable, and distant from the repository of their public records, for the sole purpose of fatiguing them into compliance with his measures.

He has dissolved representative houses repeatedly *and continually,* for opposing with manly firmness his invasions on the rights of the people.

He has refused, for a long time after such dissolutions, to cause others to be elected, whereby the legislative powers, incapable of annihilation, have returned to the

---

* Alter.   † Repeated,   ‡ Having.   § Utterly neglacted.

people at large for their exercise, the state remaining in the mean time exposed to all the dangers of invasion from without and convulsions within.

He has endeavored to prevent the population of these states: for that purpose obstructing the laws for naturalization of foreigners; refusing to pass others to encourage their migrations hither; and raising the conditions of new appropriations of lands.

He has suffered the administration of justice totally to cease in some of these states,* refusing his assent to laws for establishing judiciary powers.

He has made *our* judges dependent on his will alone, for the tenure of their offices and the amount and payment of their salaries.

He has erected a multitude of new offices *by a self-assumed power,* and sent hither swarms of officers to harass our people and eat out their substance.

He has kept among us, in times of peace, standing armies *and ships of war,* without the consent of our legislatures.

He has affected to render the military independent of, and superior to, the civil power.

He has combined with others to subject us to a jurisdiction foreign to our constitutions, and unacknowledged by our laws; giving his assent to their acts of pretended legislation:

For quartering large bodies of armed troops among us;

For protecting them, by a mock trial, from punishment for any murders which they should commit on the inhabitants of these states;

For cutting off our trade with all parts of the world

For imposing taxes on us without our consent;

For depriving us† of the benefits of trial by jury;

* He has obstructed the administration of Justice, by.
  In many cases.

17

For transporting us beyond the seas to be tried for pretended offences.

For abolishing the free system of English laws in a neighboring province, establishing therein an arbitrary government, and enlarging its boundaries, so as to render it at once an example and fit instrument for introducing the same absolute rule into these *states;* *

For taking away our charters, abolishing our most valuable laws, and altering fundamentally the forms of our governments;

For suspending our own legislatures, and declaring themselves invested with power to legislate for us in all cases whatsoever.

He has abdicated government here, *withdrawing his governors, and*† declaring us out of his *allegiance and* protection, and waging war against us.

He has plundered our seas, ravaged our coasts, burnt our towns, and destroyed the lives of our people.

He is at this time transporting large armies of foreign mercenaries to complete the works of death, desolation, and tyranny, already begun with circumstances of cruelty and perfidy,‡ unworthy the head of a civilized nation.

He has endeavored to bring on the inhabitants of our frontiers the merciless Indian savages, whose known rule of warfare is an undistinguished destruction of all ages, sexes and conditions *of existence; he has excited treasonable insurrections of our fellow citizens with the allurements of forfeiture and confiscation of our property.*

He has constrained *others,*‖ taken captive on the high seas, to bear arms against their country, to become the executioners of their friends and brethren, or to fall themselves by their hands.

He has waged civil war against human nature itself, vio-

---

* Colonies.   † By.
‡ Scarcely paralleled in the most barbarous ages, and totally
‖ Our fellow citizen.

*lating its most sacred rights of life and liberty in the per-
sons of a distant people, who never offended him, captivating and carrying them into slavery in another hemisphere,
or to incur miserable death in their transportation thither.
This piratical warfare, the opprobium of infidel powers, is
the warfare of the* Christian *king of Great Britain. Determined to keep open a market where* MEN *should be bought
and sold, he has prostituted his negative for suppressing
every legislative attempt to prohibit or to restrain this ex-
ecrable commerce. And that this assemblage of horrors
might want no fact of distinguished dye, he is now exciting
those very people to rise in arms among us, and to purchase
that liberty of which he has deprived them, by murdering
the people upon whom he obtruded them: thus paying off
former crimes committed against the* liberties *of one people
with crimes which he urges them to commit against the
lives of another.*

In every stage of these oppressions, we have petitioned
for redress in the most humble terms: our repeated petitions have been answered only by repeated injury. A
prince whose character is thus marked by every act which
may define a tyrant, is unfit to be the ruler of a people
who mean to be free. Future ages will scarce believe that
the hardiness of one man adventured within the short compass of twelve years only, to build a foundation, so broad
and undisguised, for tyranny over a people, fostered and
fixed in principles of freedom.*

Nor have we been wanting in attentions to our British
brethren. We have warned them, from time to time, of
attempts by their legislature to extend *a†* jurisdiction over
these our states.‡ We have reminded them of the circumstances of our emigration and settlement here; *no one of
which could warrant sc strange a pretension; that these*

---

* Free people.   † An unwarrantable.   ‡ Us.

were effected at the expense of our own blood and treasure, unassisted by the wealth or the strength of Great Britain: that in constituting indeed our several forms of government, we had adopted one common king, thereby laying a foundation for perpetual league and amity with them; but that to their parliament was no part of our constitution, nor ever in idea, if history may be credited; and we* appealed to their native justice and magnanimity *as well as to*† the ties of our common kindred, to disavow these usurpations which *were likely to*‡ interrupt our connexions and correspondence. They too have been deaf to the voice of justice and of consanguinity; *and when occasions have been given them, by the regular course of their laws, of removing from their councils the disturbers of our harmony, they have by their free election, re-established them in power. At this very time too, they are permitting their chief magistrate to send over, not only soldiers of our common blood, but* [*Scotch and*] *foreign mercenaries to invade and destroy us. These facts have given the last stab to agonizing affection; and manly spirit bids us to renounce for ever these unfeeling brethren. We must endeavor to forget our former love for them;* we must, therefore, acquiesce in the necessity which denounces our separation, and hold them, as we hold the rest of mankind, enemies in war; in peace, friends.

We might have been a free and great people together; but a communication of grandeur and of freedom, it seems is below their dignity. Be it so, since they will have it The road to happiness and to glory is open to us too; we will climb it apart from them, and acquiesce in the necessity which denounces our eternal separation.

We, therefore, the representatives of the United States of America in general Congress assembled, appealing to the Supreme Judge of the world for the rectitude of our

---

* Have.   † And we have conjured them by.   ‡ Would inevitably

intentions, do, in the name, and by the authority of the good people of these *states, reject and renounce all allegiance and subjection to the kings of Great Britain, and others who may hereafter claim by, through, or under them; we utterly dissolve all political connection which may heretofore have subsisted between us and the Parliament or people of Great Britain; and, finally, we do assert the colonies to be free and independent states,** and that, as free and independent states, they have full power to levy war, conclude peace, contract alliances, establish commerce, and to do all other acts and things which independent states may of right do. And, for the support of this declaration,† we mutually pledge to each other our lives, our fortunes, and our sacred honor."

The foregoing draft of a Declaration of Independence was debated, paragraph after paragraph, from the twenty-eighth of June (the day it was reported), until the fourth of July; and many alterations, omissions, and amendments, it has been seen, were made. In the meanwhile, the friends of the measure were fearful that a unanimous vote of all the colonies could not be obtained, inasmuch as Maryland and Pennsylvania refused to sanction the measure. The delegates from the former colony were unanimously in favor of it, while those of the latter were divided in opinion.

In consequence of the action in the Assembly of Pennsylvania, it was deemed important that the sense of the people upon the momentous question before Congress should be taken, and accordingly a convention was called to meet at Philadelphia on the twenty-fourth of June, consisting of committees from each county. The members of that convention, acting as the representatives of the

---

* Colonies, solemnly publish and declare, that these United Colonies are, and of right ought to be, free and independent states; that they are absolved from all allegiance to the British crown, and that all political connection between them and the state of Great Britain, is, and ought to be, totally dissolved.

† With a firm reliance on the protection of Divine Providence.

people of Pennsylvania passed a resolution in which they expressed "their willingness to concur in a vote of Congress, declaring the united colonies free and independent states." This resolution left the Pennsylvania delegates free to act according to the dictates of their own judgments and consciences.

As we have already observed, in the biography of Charles Carroll and others of the delegates from Maryland, the convention of that colony, as late as the latter part of May, instructed their delegates not to vote for independence; but through the indefatigable labors and great influence of Chase, Carroll, Paca, and others, another convention was held in that colony; and on the twenty-eighth of June they recalled their former instructions and empowered their delegates "to concur with the other colonies in a declaration of independence, in forming a union among the colonies, in making foreign alliances, and in adopting such measures as should be judged necessary for securing the liberties of America.*

On the day upon which the committee reported the Declaration, it was referred to a committee of the whole House, and all the colonies assented to it except Pennsylvania and Delaware. Four of the seven delegates from the former voted against it, and the two delegates from Delaware, who were present, were divided—Thomas M'Kean in favor of it, and George Read opposed to it. It came up for final decision on the fourth of July. Robert Morris and John Dickinson, of Pennsylvania, were absent. The former was in favor, the latter was against, the resolution. Of the five who were present, Doctor Franklin, James Wilson, and John Morton, were in favor of it, and Willing and Humphreys were opposed to it; so the vote of Pennsylvania was secured. To obtain the vote of Delaware,

* Pitkin vol i., p. 364

Mr. M'Kean after the vote on the first of July, sent an express after Mr. Rodney, the other delegate from that colony, then eighty miles distant. He arrived in time to cast his vote on the fourth, and thus made a majority for Delaware. Thus a *unanimous* vote of the colonies was given in favor of declaring the United Colonies FREE AND INDEPENDENT STATES, "having full power to levy war, conclude peace, contract alliances, establish commerce, and to do all other acts and things which independent states may of right do." From that day the word *colony* is not known in our history.*

Several of the amendments and alterations of the original draft of the Declaration of Independence, were merely verbal ones, but there were others involving matters of serious import. It has been said that the paragraph commencing with the words "He has waged a cruel war against human nature itself," &c., was not palatable to those delegates who were slave-holders, and that it was stricken out lest it should be a cause for them to cast a negative vote on the question. But there is not the least shadow of evidence to prove that such selfish motives guided any one in that august assembly. On the contrary, it was a high and holy regard for truth and justice, which caused that eloquent paragraph to be stricken out. The Congress in that Declaration was enumerating those aggressions against the rights and privileges of the colonies, justly chargeable upon George III. as an individual, having been done by his personal sanction, or by his delegated representatives. Such being the case, it was manifestly unjust, indeed not strictly true, to charge him with the evils concomitant to slavery and the slave-trade.

* On the ninth of September ensuing, Congress adopted the following resolution: "That in all continental commissions where heretofore the words *"United Colonies"* have been used, the style be altered in future to the *"United States."* In 1777, the red ground of the American flag was altered to thirteen red and white stripes, as an emblem of the thirteen states united in a war for liberty.

This trade was begun and carried on, long before the reign of even the first George; and it is not known that George the Third ever gave his assent to anything relating to slavery, except to abolish it and declare the trade a piracy.*

The Declaration as amended, and adopted by Congress, and which was sent forth to the world as the voice of the people of the thirteen United States, was as follows:

"When, in the course of human events, it becomes necessary for one people, to dissolve the political bands which have connected them with another, and to assume, among the powers of the earth, the separate and equal station to which the laws of nature and of nature's God entitle them, a decent respect to the opinions of mankind requires that they should declare the causes which impel them to the separation.

We hold these truths to be self-evident—that all men are created equal; that they are endowed by their Creator, with certain unalienable rights; that among these are life, liberty, and the pursuit of happiness. That to secure these rights, governments are instituted among men. deriving their just powers from the consent of the governed; that whenever any form of government becomes destructive of these ends, it is the right of the people to alter or abolish it, and to institute a new government, laying its foundation on such principles, and organizing its powers in such form, as to them shall seem most likely to effect their safety and happiness. Prudence, indeed, will dictate that governments long established, should not be changed for light and transient causes; and, accordingly, all experience hath shown, that

* By a resolution of the Congress of the United States, the slave-trade has been declared a piracy, and the maritime nations of Europe were by that resolution Invited to so consider it by the law of nations. Mr. Jefferson was, doubtless, the first man in modern times who denounced the traffic as a "piratical warfare."- See *Life of Richard Henry Lce,* vol. i., p. 176.

mankind are more disposed to suffer, while evils are sufferable, than to right themselves, by abolishing the forms
to which they are accustomed. But when a long train of
abuses and usurpations, pursuing invariably the same
object, evinces a design to reduce them under absolute
despotism, it is their right, it is their duty, to throw off
such government, and to provide new guards for their
future security. Such has been the patient sufferance of
these colonies; and such is now the necessity which constrains them to alter their former systems of government.
The history of the present king of Great Britain is a history of repeated injuries and usurpations, all having in
direct object the eatablishment of an absolute tyranny
over these states. To prove this, let facts be submitted to
a candid world.

He has refused his assent to laws the most wholesome
and necessary for the public good.

He has forbidden his governors to pass laws of immediate and pressing importance, unless suspended in their
operations till his assent should be obtained; and, when so
suspended, he has utterly neglected to attend to them.

He has refused to pass other laws for the accommodation of large districts of people, unless those people would
relinquish the right of representation in the legislature—a
right inestimable to them, and formidable to tyrants only.

He has called together legislative bodies at places unusual, uncomfortable, and distant from the repository of
their public records, for the sole purpose of fatiguing
them into compliance with his measures.

He has dissolved representative houses, repeatedly, for
opposing with manly firmness his invasions on the rights
of the people.

He has refused, for a long time after such dissolutions,
to cause others to be elected; whereby the legislative
powers, incapable of annihilation, have returned to the

people at large for their exercise; the state remaining, in the meantime, exposed to all the dangers of invasion from without and convulsions within.

He has endeavored to prevent the population of these states; for that purpose obstructing the laws for the naturalization of foreigners; refusing to pass others to encourage their migration hither, and raising the conditions of new appropriations of lands.

He has obstructed the administration of justice, by refusing his assent to laws for establishing judiciary powers.

He has made judges dependent on his will alone for the tenure of their offices, and the amount and payment of their salaries.

He has erected a multitude of new offices, and sent hither swarms of officers, to harass our people and eat out their substance.

He has kept among us, in times of peace, standing armies, without the consent of our legislatures.

He has affected to render the military independent of, and superior to, the civil power.

He has combined with others to subject us to a jurisdiction foreign to our constitutions, and unacknowledged by our laws; giving his assent to their acts of pretended legislation:

For quartering large bodies of armed troops among us:

For protecting them, by a mock trial, from punishment for any murders which they should commit on the inhabitants of these states:

For cutting off our trade with all parts of the world:

For imposing taxes on us without our consent:

For depriving us, in many cases, of the benefits of trial by jury:

For transporting us beyond seas, to be tried for pretended offences:

For abaishing the free system of English laws in a neighboring province, establishing therein an arbitrary government, and enlarging its boundaries, so as to render it at once an example and fit instrument for introducing the same absolute rule into these colonies:

For taking away our charters, abolishing our most valuable laws, and altering, fundamentally, the forms of our governments:

For suspending our own legislatures, and declaring themselves invested with power to legislate for us in all cases whatsoever.

He has abdicated government here, by declaring us out of his protection, and waging war against us.

He has plundered our seas, ravaged our coasts, burnt our towns, and destroyed the lives of our people.

He is, at this time, transporting large armies of foreign mercenaries, to complete the works of death, desolation, and tyranny, already begun with circumstances of cruelty and perfidy scarcely paralleled in the most barbarous ages, and totally unworthy the head of a civilized nation.

He has constrained our fellow-citizens, taken captive on the high seas, to bear arms against their country, to become the executioners of their friends and brethren, or to fall themselves by their hands.

He has excited domestic insurrections among us, and has endeavored to bring on the inhabitants of our frontiers the merciless Indian savages, whose known rule of warfare is an undistinguished destruction, of all ages, sexes, and conditions.

In every stage of these oppressions we have petitioned for redress in the most humble terms: our repeated petitions have been answered only by repeated injury. A prince whose character is thus marked by every act which may define a tyrant, is unfit to be the ruler of a free people.

Nor have we been wanting in attentions to our British brethren. We have warned them, from time to time, of attempts by their legislature to extend an unwarrantable jurisdiction over us. We have reminded them of the circumstances of our emigration and settlement here. We have appealed to their native justice and magnanimity and we have conjured them by the ties of our common kindred, to disavow these usurpations which would inevitably interrupt our connections and correspondence. They, too, have been deaf to the voice of justice and of consanguinity. We must, therefore, acquiesce in the necessity which denounces our separation, and hold them as we hold the rest of mankind—enemies in war—in peace, friends.

We, therefore, the representatives of the United States of America, in general Congress assembled, appealing to the Supreme Judge of the world, for the rectitude of our intentions, do, in the name, and by the authority of the good people of these colonies, solemnly publish and declare that these united colonies are, and of right ought to be, free and independent states: that they are absolved from all allegiance to the British crown, and that all political connection between them and the state of Great Britain is, and ought to be, totally dissolved; and that, as free and independent states, they have full power to levy war, conclude peace, contract alliances, establish commerce, and to do all other acts and things which independent states may of right do. And for the support of this Declaration, with a firm reliance on the protection of Divine Providence, we mutually pledge to each other our lives, our fortunes, and our sacred honor."

This Declaration was signed, on the day of its adoption, by John Hancock, the President of Congress, only; and, with his name alone, it was sent forth to the world. It was ordered to be entered at length upon the journal; and it was also ordered to be engrossed upon parchment for the delegates to sign it. This solemn act was done on the second day of August following, by fifty-four delegates, and two others signed it subsequently, (they not being present at that time,) making the whole number of the signers, *fifty-six.* *

The Declaration was received with public demonstrations of approbation throughout the whole land. Processions were formed; cannons were fired; bells were rung; orations were pronounced; and everything which delight could suggest was exhibited. Everywhere, the hearts of the patriots were gladdened,† and, although long years of trial, and misery, and bloody strife, appeared before them, they felt that by this act half the work was accomplished, for, as "union is strength," they were then strong.‡

Having thus briefly glanced at the events immediately connected with the conception, preparation and adoption of the Declaration of Independence, we now propose to examine, and prove the truth, of the various specific charges made therein against the King of Great Britain. It must be borne in mind that the royal governors— the King's deputies—acting as his representatives, were regarded, in these charges, as the King himself; and, whenever they were guilty of a sin of omission or com-

---

* It is said that after the Declaration was signed, a deep solemnity rested upon all present, and profound silence pervaded the assembly. It was at length broken by Dr. Franklin, who remarked, "Gentlemen, we must now all *hang together,* or we shall most assuredly *hang separately."*

† Washington, then encamped upon York Island, received a copy of the Declaration on the ninth of July, and at six o'clock that evening the regiments of his army were paraded, and the document was read aloud in the hearing of them all It was greeted with the most hearty demonstrations of joy and applause.

‡ Samuel Adams, in a letter to Richard Henry Lee, dated at "Philadelphia, July 15th, 1776," said, "Our Declaration of Independence has given vigor to the spirits of the people. Had this decisive measure been taken nine months ago, it is my opinion that Canada would by this time have been in our hands. But what does it avail to find fault with what is past? Let us do better for the future."

mission, in the exercise of their authority, it was considered as the act of the Sovereign.

I. *He has refused his assent to laws the most wholesome and necessary for the public good.*

After the conclusion of a general peace in 1763, between Great Britain and the states of Europe with which she had been at war for seven long years, the conduct of the government toward its American colonies was very materially altered. Whether it arose from avarice, or from a jealousy of the *power* of the colonies so signally displayed during the war just closed, or a fear that a knowledge of that power would make the colonists aspire to political independence, it is not easy to determine. It is probable that these several causes combined engendered those acts of direct and indirect oppression, which finally impelled the colonies to open rebellion.

The growing commercial importance of the colonies, and their rapidly accumulating wealth and more rapid increase of population, required new laws to be enacted, from time to time, to meet the exigencies which these natural increments produced. The colonial assemblies made several enactments touching their commercial operations, the emission of a colonial currency, and colonial representation in the imperial parliament, all of which would have been highly beneficial to the colonies, and not at all prejudicial to the best interests of Great Britain. But the jealousies of weak or wicked ministers, excited by the still stronger jealousies of colonial governors, interposed between the King and his American subjects, and to these laws, so "wholesome and necessary for the public good," he refused his royal assent. When the excitements produced by the "Stamp Act" resulted in popular tumults, and public property was destroyed, and royal authority was defied, the home government, through Secretary Conway, informed the Americans that these things should be overlooked, provided the assemblies should, by appropriations, make full compensation for all losses thus sustained. This requisition the assemblies complied with; but in Massachusetts, where most of the indemnification was to be made, the legislature, in authorizing the payment thereof, granted free pardon to all concerned in the tumults, desiring thus to test the sincerity of the proposition of the Crown to forgive the offenders. This act was "wholesome and necessary for the public good," for it would have produced quiet, and a return of confidence in the promises of the King. But the King and his council disallowed the act—he "refused his assent."

II. *He has forbidden his governors to pass laws of immediats and pressing importance, unless suspended in their operation till his assent should be obtained; and, when so suspended, he has utterly neglected to attend to them.*

In 1764, the assembly of New York were desirous of taking measures to conciliate the Indian tribes, particularly the Six Nations, and to attach them firmly to the British colonies. To this measure Governor Colden lent his cheerful assent, privately; but representations having been made to the King, by an agent of Lord Bute, then travelling in the colonies, that the ulterior design was to add new strength to the physical power of the colonists for some future action inimical to their dependence upon Great Britain, the monarch sent instructions to all his governors to desist from such alliances, or to suspend their operations until his assent should be given. With this order, the matter rested, for then (as was doubtless his intention) he "utterly neglected to attend to them."

The assembly of Massachusetts, in 1770, passed a law

for taxing the commissioners of customs and other offi
cers of the Crown, the same as other citizens. Of this
they complained to the King, and he sent instructions to
Governor Hutchinson to assent to no tax bill of this
kind, without first obtaining the royal consent. These
instructions were in violation of the expressed power of
the charter of Massachusetts; and the assembly, by resolution, declared "that for the Governor to withhold his
assent to bills, merely by force of his instructions, is
vacating the charter, giving *instructions* the force of *law*
within the province." Neither the assembly nor the
Governor would yield, and no tax bill was passed that
session. The assembly was prorogued until September,
and then again until April, 1772; and all that while laws
of pressing importance were virtually annulled—the King
"utterly neglected to attend to them."

III. *He has refused to pass other laws for the accommodation of large districts of people unless those people would
relinquish the right of representation in the legislature,
a right inestimable to them and formidable to tyrants
only.*

In the spring of 1774, Parliament passed a bill, by
which the free system of English government in Canada,
or, as it was called, the "province of Quebec," was radically changed. Instead of the popular representative *sys*
tem by a colonial assembly, as obtained in the other Anglo
American colonies, the government was vested in a Legislative council, having all power, except that of levying
taxes. The members of the council were appointed by
the crown, the tenure of their office depending upon the
will of the King. Thus the people were deprived of
the representative privilege. A large majority of the inhabitants were French Roman Catholics, and as the same
act established that religion in the province, they consid

ered this a sufficient equivalent for the political privilege that had been taken away from them. But "large districts" of people of English descent bordering on Nova Scotia, felt this act to be a grievous burden, for they had ever been taught that the right of representation was the dearest prerogative conferred by the Magna Charta of Great Britain. They therefore sent strong remonstrances to parliament, and humble petitions to the King, to restore them this right. But not only were their remonstrances and petitions unheeded, but their efforts to procure the passage of laws by the Legislative Council touching their commercial regulations with Nova Scotia, were fruitless, and they were plainly told by Governor Carleton (under instructions from the Secretary for Foreign Affairs) that no such laws should be passed until they should cease their clamors for representation, and quietly submit to the administration of the new laws. But, like their more southern neighbors, they could not consent to sacrifice a principle, even upon the stern demands of hard necessity, and they were obliged to forego the advantages which asked-for enactments would have given. The right which they claimed, was a right guarantied by the British constitution, and was "inestimable to them." But as the right was "formidable to tyrants," and as the King, by his sanction of the destruction of free English laws in Canada had dared to become such, they were obliged to submit, or else "relinquish the right of representation in the Legislature."

About the same time, a bill was passed "For the better regulating the government in the province of Massachusetts Bay." This bill provided for an alteration in the constitution of that province, as it stood upon the charter of William III. to do away with the popular elections which decided everything in that colony; to take away the executive power out of the hands of the growing do

18

mocratic party; and to vest the nominations of the council, of the judges, and of magistrates of all kinds, including sheriffs, in the Crown, and in some cases in the King's governor. This act deprived the people of free "representation in the legislature;" and when in the exercise of their rights, and on the refusal of the Governor to issue warrants for the election of members of Assembly, in accordance with the provisions of their charter before altered, they called a convention, their expressed wishes, for the passage of "laws for the accommodation of large districts of people" were entirely disregarded. They were refused the passage of necessary laws, unless they would quietly "relinquish the right of representation in the legislature,—a right inestimable to them, and formidable to tyrants only."

IV. *He has called together legislative bodies at places unusual, uncomfortable, and distant from the repository of their public records, for the sole purpose of fatiguing them into compliance with his measures.*

The inhabitants of Boston became the special objects of ministerial vengeance, after the news of the destruction of tea in that harbor reached England. That event occurred on the evening of the sixteenth of December, 1773, and in February following the matter was laid before Parliament. It was at once determined to punish severely the people of that refractory town; and accordingly Lord North, then prime minister, presented a bill which provided for the total annihilation of the trade and commerce of Boston, and the removal of the courts, officers of customs, &c., therefrom. This was the famous Boston Port Bill," and it went into effect on the first of June following.

General Gage, who had been appointed governor of the province arrived at Boston about the last of May, and at once proceeded, according to his instructions to remove the courts, &c., from that town. He also adjourned the assembly, on the thirty-first of May, to meet on the seventh of June, at Salem. But he retained all the public records in Boston, so that if the members of the assembly had been so disposed they could not have referred to them. Military power ruled there—two regiments of British troops being encamped upon the Commons. The patriotic assembly, although "distant from the repository of the public records," and in a place extremely "uncomfortable," were *not* "fatigued into compliance with his measures," but, in spite of the Governor, they elected delegates to a general Congress. They adopted various other measures for the public good, and then adjourned.

V. *He has dissolved representative houses repeatedly, for opposing with manly firmness his invasions on the rights of the people.*

In January, 1768, the assembly of Massachusetts addressed a circular to all the other colonies, asking their co-operation with them in asserting and maintaining the principle that Great Britain had no right to tax the colonies without their consent. This was a bold measure, and more than all others displeased the British ministry. As soon as intelligence of this proceeding reached the ministry, Lord Hillsborough, the secretary for foreign affairs, was directed to send a letter to Bernard, the Governor of Massachusetts, in which it was declared, that "his majesty considers this step as evidently tending to create unwarrantable combinations, to excite unjustifiable opposition to the constitutional authority of parliament;" and then he added, "It is the King's pleasure, that as soon as the general court is again assembled, at the time prescribed by the charter, you require of the house of representatives, in his majesty's name, to reseind the resolutions which gave birth to the circular letter from the speaker, and to declare their disapprobation of, and dissent to, that rash and hasty proceeding. If the new assembly should refuse to comply with his majesty's reasonable expectations, it is the King's pleasure that you should immediately dissolve them."

In accordance with his instructions, Governor Bernard required the assembly to rescind the resolutions. To this requisition, the house replied: "If the votes of this house are to be controlled by the direction of a minister, we have left us but a vain semblance of liberty. We have now only to inform you that this house have voted not to rescind, and, that on a division on the question, there were ninety-two yeas and seventeen nays." The Governor at once proceeded to dissolve the assembly; but before the act was accomplished, that body had prepared a list of serious accusations against him, and a petition to the King for his removal. Counter circulars were sent to the several colonies, warning them to beware imitating the factious and rebellious conduct of Massachusetts; but they entirely failed to produce the intended effect, and the assemblies in several of the colonies were dissolved by the respective governors.

In 1769, the assemblies of Virginia and North Carolina were dissolved by their governors, for adopting resolutions boldly denying the right of the King and parliament to tax the colonies—to remove offenders out of the country for trial—and other acts which infringed upon the sacred rights of the people.

In 1774, when the various colonial assemblies entertained the proposition for a general congress, they were nearly all dissolved by the respective governors, to prevent the adoption of the scheme and the election of delegates to that national council. But the people assembled in popular conventions, assumed legislative power, and elected their delegates to a General Congress, in spite of the efforts of royal minions to restrain them. These dissolutions of "representative houses repeatedly" only tended to inflame the minds of the people and widen the breach between them and their rulers.

VI. *He has refused, for a long time after such dissolutions, to cause others to be elected; whereby the legislative powers, incapable of annihilation, have returned to the people at large for their exercise, the state remaining, in the meantime, exposed to all the dangers of invasion from without and convulsions within.*

Soon after the repeal of the Stamp Act, in 1767, the colonists were again alarmed at the expressed intention of ministers to enforce a new clause in the Mutiny Act. This act granted power to every officer, upon obtaining a warrant from a justice, to break into any house by day or by night, in search of deserters. The new clause alluded to provided that the troops sent out from England should be furnished with quarters, beer, salt and vinegar, at the expense of the colonies. The people justly regarded this as disguised taxation, and opposed it as a violation of the same principles as those upon which the Stamp Act trampled. Besides, the soldiers were insolent and overbearing toward the citizens; they were known to be quartered here for the purpose of abridging and subduing the independent actions of the people, and the supplies demanded were to be drawn from the very men whom they came to injure and oppress.

The Assembly of New York refused to make the required provisions for the troops, and in consequence of this disobedience of royal orders, its legislative functions were entirely suspended. The Assembly was prohibited from making any bill, order, resolution or vote, except for adjourning, or choosing a speaker, until the requirements

were complied with. Consequently "the legislative powers, incapable of annihilation, returned to the people at
large for their exercise, the state remaining, in the meantime, exposed to all the dangers of invasion from without
and convulsions within." Thus matters stood for several
months.

The Assembly of Massachusetts, also, after its dissolution
by the governor in July, 1768, was not permitted to meet
again until the last Wednesday of May, 1769, and then
they found the state house surrounded by a military guard,
with cannon pointed directly at the place wherein they
met for deliberation. Thus restricted in the free exercise of their functions as legislators, the power they had
possessed "returned to the people," because it was annulled in them by restraining their freedom of action.

VII. *He has endeavored to prevent the population of
these states—for that purpose, obstructing the laws for
the naturalization of foreigners, refusing to pass others
to encourage their migration hither, and raising the conditions of new appropriations of lands.*

John, Earl of Bute, was the pupil and favorite com-
panion of George III. while he was yet Prince of Wales,
and when, on the sudden death of his grandfather, George
Il., he became King, he looked to this nobleman for council
and advice. He was one of his first cabinet, and so completely did he influence the mind of the King, at the beginning of his reign, that those who wished for place or pre-
ferment, first made their suits to the Earl of Bute.

Among other measures advised by Bute, was the employment of men, in secret service, in different parts of the
realm, to keep the King advised of all that in any way
effected the power, stability and glory of the crown.

An agent of this kind was sent by Bute to America

and the glowing account which he gave of the rapid growth of the colonists in wealth and number, after the peace of 1763, and the great influx of German immigrants, caused Bute to advise his royal master to look well to those things, lest a spirit of independence should grow side by side with the increase of power, which would finally refuse to acknowledge a distant sovereignty, and defy the authority of the British crown. Some of the colonial governors within whose jurisdiction immigrants had been most freely settled, encouraged this idea, for they found the German people, in general, strongly imbued with principles of political freedom. Added to this innate characteristic, they remembered the German battle-fields where George II., in his efforts to maintain the Electorate of Hanover, had been the cause of the offering of whole hecatombs of their countrymen upon the altar of the Moloch, W a r.

George III. therefore, at the instigation of Bute, took measures to arrest any influence which this' Germanic leaven might exert, and he cast obstacles in the way of further immigration to any extent. He also became jealous of the tendency to immigration to the more salubrious states, especially Roman Catholic Maryland, which the French of Canada exhibited, fearing their ancient animosities might, by contact with the English colonies, weaken the loyalty of the latter.

The colonists on the other hand, joyfully hailed the approach of the German immigrants, and extended the right hand of fellowship to their now peaceful French brethren. Both interest and policy dictated this course toward the immigrant, and the colonial assemblies adopted various measures to encourage their migration hither. Unwilling to excite alarm among the colonists the King endeavored to thwart the operation of these measures by instructing his governors to refuse their assent to many of those enact ments until the royal consent should be obtained. Such refusals were made under various pretences, and there was so much delay in the administration of the naturalization laws, through which alone foreigners could hold lands in fee, and enjoy other privileges, that immigration in a measure ceased. The easy condition too, upon which lands on the frontiers were conveyed to foreigners, were so changed, that little inducement was held out to them to leave their native country; and the bright prospect of the valley of the Ohio peopled and cultivated, which appeared at the peace of '63, faded away, and the gloom of the interminable forest alone met the eye. So much did these obstructions check immigration, that when the war of the Revolution broke out, the current had quite ceased to flow hitherward. Bute, however, was right in his conjecture about the independent spirit which the German immigrants would evince, if occasion should offer, for when the Revolution broke forth, almost the entire German population, numbering about two hundred thousand, took side with the patriots.

VIII. *He has obstructed the administration of justice, by refusing his assent to laws for establishing judiciary powers.*

Under the act already referred to, "For the better regulation of the government of Massachusetts Bay," adopted in March, 1774, the judiciary powers were taken out of the hands of the people. The judges were appointed by the Crown, were subject to its will, and depended upon it for the emoluments of office. These emoluments, too, were paid to them out of moneys extracted from the people of the colonies by the "Commissioners of Customs," in the form of duties; and, therefore, the judges were more obnoxious to the hate and contempt of the colonists. They were also, by this act, deprived, in most cases, of the benefits of trial by jury, and the lives and property of the people were placed in the custody of the myrmidons of royalty. The "administration of justice" was effectually obstructed, and the very rights which the people of England so manfully asserted, and successfully defended in the revolution of 1688, were trampled under foot. In other colonies, too, the administration of justice was so obstructed by the interference of the royal govern ors, that it had but the semblance of existence left. The people tried every honorable means, by petitions to the King, addresses to the parliament, and votes in legislative assemblies and in popular conventions, to have laws passed, either in the provincial legislature, or in the supreme national council, for "establishing judiciary powers;" but their efforts were ineffectual. Power stood in the place of right, and exercised authority; and under the goadings of a system of wrong and oppression, the people resorted to arms to "right themselves by abolishing the forms," and in prostrating the power of a monarchy become odious though the mal-administration of weak or wicked ministers,

IX. *He has made judges dependent on his will alone for the tenure of their offices, aud the amount and payment of their salaries.*

In 1773, an act was passed by the British Parliament on motion of Lord North, to make the governors and judges quite independent of those they governed, by paying thcir salaries directly from the National Treasury, instead of making them dependent upon the appropriations of the Colonial Assemblies for that purpose. This measure, making the public servants in the colonies wholly dependent upon the Crown for support, and independent of the people, was calculated to make them pliant instruments in the hands of their masters—ready at all times to do the bidding of the King and his council. The various Colonial Assemblies strongly protested against the measure; and out of the excitement and just alarm which followed, that mighty lever of the revolution, the system of Committees of Correspondence, was brought forth and vigorously applied.

Early in 1774, the Massachusetts Assembly required the judges in that colony to state explicitly whether they intended to receive their salaries from the Crown. Chief Justice Oliver declared that to be his intention, and the Assembly proceeded at once to impeach him. By a vote of ninety-six to nine, he was declared to be obnoxious to the people of the colony, and a petition to the Governor for his removal *was* adopted. The Governor refused compliance with this expressed will of the people, and this was presumptive evidence that the Governor, too, intended to receive his salary from the Crown. This matter produced much irritation, and just cause for bitter complaint on the part of the colonists. The Governor assuming the right to keep a judge in his seat, contrary to the wishes of the people, and the Crown paying his salary, made him dependent upon the will of the King alone for the tenure of his office, and the amount and payment of his emoluments."

X. *He has erected a multitude of new offices, and sent hither swarms of officers to harass our people, and eat out their substance.*

The passage of the Stamp Act, in 1765, called for the establishment of a new officer in every sea-port town, who was entitled Stamp Master. It was his business to dispose of the stamps and collect the revenue accruing from the same.

In 1766, an act was passed for imposing rates and duties, payable in the colonies. This act called for the creation of collectors of the customs, and "swarms of offi cers" were brought into being.

In 1767 an act was adopted "to enable his majesty to put the customs, and other duties in America, under the management of commissioners," &c., and a board of commissioners was at once erected. The members *were* paid high salaries, besides having many perquisites—all of which were paid by the colonists.

In 1765 Admiralty and Vice-Admiralty courts were established on a new model, and an increase in the numher of officers was made; and thus, by act after act, each receiving the royal signature, were "sent hither swarms of officers to harass our people and eat out their substance."

XI. *He has kept among us, in times of peace, standing armies, without the consent of our legislatures.*

After the "Peace of Paris." in 1764, when, by treaty, the "Seven Years' War" was ended, and quiet was for a time restored in both Europe and America, Great Britain, instead of withdrawing her regular troops from America, left quite a large number here, and required the colonists to contribute to their support. On the surface of things, there appeared no reason for this "standing army in time of peace;" but there can be little doubt, as we have before said, that growing jealousy of the power and independent feeling of the colonists, and an already conceived design to tax the colonies without their consent, were the true cause of the presence of armed men among a peaceful people. They were doubtless intended to *suppress democracy and republican independence, and to enforce every revenue law, however arbitrary and unjust soever it might be.* The colonists felt this, and hence the presence of the British troops was always a cause for irritation, and unappeased discontent. And, finally, when the people of Massachusetts began openly to resist the encroachments of British power, a large standing army was quartered in its capital, for no other purpose than to awe them into submission to a tyrant's will.

XII. *He has affected to render the military independent of, and superior to, the civil power.*

In the spring of 1774, General Gage, who was the commander-in-chief of all the British forces in America, was appointed Governor of Massachusetts; and the first civil duty he was called upon to perform was to carry into effect the provisions of the Boston Port Bill. To sustain and enforce this harsh measure, he introduced two regiments of troops into Boston; and soon afterward they were reinforced by several regiments from Halifax, Quebec, New York, and Ireland. By an order of the King, the authority of the commander-in-chief, and under him, the brigadier-generals, was rendered supreme in all civil governments in America. This, be it remembered, was in a time of peace; and thus an uncontrolled military power was vested in officers not known as civil functionaries to the constitution of any colony. The military was rendered "independent of, and superior to, the civil power."

XIII. *He has combined with others to subject us to a jurisdiction foreign to our constitution, and unacknowledged by our laws, giving his assent to their acts of pretended legislation.*

One of the most prominent acts, obnoxious to this serious charge, was the establishment by act of Parliament, under the sanction of the King, of a Board of Trade in the colonies, independent of colonial legislation; and the creation of resident commissioners of customs, to enforce strictly the revenue laws. This act was passed in July, 1767; and when the news of its adoption

reached America, it produced a perfect tornado of indignation throughout the Colonies. The people perceived clearly that they were now not only to be subjected to the annoyance of unqualified assertions that Parliament had "a right to bind the colonies in all cases
whatsoever," but that they were to be subject to the actual
control of persons appointed to carry out these principles
avowed by the British Ministry.

The establishment of this Board of Trade in the
colonies, unto whom was given power to regulate the
customs and secure the revenue—the modeling of the
admiralty courts upon a basis which quite excluded trial
by jury therein—and the supremacy given to the military
power in 1774, as alluded to in the next preceding
charge—are all evidences that prove the truth and justice of this charge.

The Commissioners of Customs arrived in May, 1768,
and at Boston they entered vigorously upon their duties;
and the riots which ensued on the seizure by them of
a vessel belonging to John Hancock, attest the deep
feeling of resistance in the hearts of the people to a
"jurisdiction foreign to their constitution, and unacknowledged by *their* laws."

The powers which the Commissioners possessed, in
connexion with the Board of Trade, in the appointment
of an indefinite number of subordinates, and in controlling legislative action, were dangerous to the liberties
of the people; for they claimed the right of adjudicating
in all matters connected with the customs. The jurisdiction, too, of the newly-modeled Courts of Admiralty,
where, in many cases, a trial by jury was denied, was
"foreign to *their* constitution, and unacknowledged by
their laws."

When, in 1774, the charter of Massachusetts was
altered, the character of the colonial council was

changed. Before that time, the members of the council, (answering to our senate,) were chosen by the general assembly, but, in the alteration, it was provided that after the first of August of that year they should be chosen by the King, to consist of not more than thirty-six, nor less than twelve; and to hold their office during his pleasure. To the Governor was given almost unlimited power, and the people were subjected to "a jurisdiction foreign to their constitution," and the assent of the King was given to the acts of "pretended legisla–tion," made by these crown-chosen senators.

XIV. *For quartering large bodies of armed troops among us.*

In 1767, the patriotic movements of the colonists so alarmed the British ministry, that they determined to repress the republican feeling by force, if necessary. For this purpose, Lord Hillsborough sent a secret letter to General Gage, then in Halifax, telling him that it was the King's pleasure that he should send one regiment, or more, to Boston to assist the civil magistrate and the officers of revenue. About the same time, Governor Bernard, of Massachusetts, requested General Gage to send some troops to Boston. Seven hundred were accordingly sent; and on the first of October, 1774, they landed, under cover of the cannon of armed ships in the harbor. The people refused to provide quarters for them, and they were quartered in the State House.

This unwise movement, which greatly exasperated the people, was repeated the next year, not only at Boston, but in New York, Philadelphia, Charleston, and other sea-port towns. At the beginning of 1775, Parliament voted a supply of ten thousand men for the American service, and a large number of them landed at Boston in the spring of that year, accompanied by Generals Howe.

Clinton, and Burgoyne. The tragedies of Lexington and Concord soon followed; and in June, the blood of American patriots was profusely spilt upon Bunker Hill by the "large bodies of armed troops quartered among us."

XV. *For protecting them, by a mock trial, from punishment for any murders which they should commit on the inhabitants of these states.*

In 1768, a dispute occurred between some soldiers and citizens of Annapolis, in Maryland, and two of the latter were killed by the former. As they were marines, belonging to an armed vessel lying near, they were arraigned before the court of admiralty for murder, on the complaint of some of the citizens. The whole affair assumed the character of a solemn farce, so far as justice was concerned; and, as might have been expected, the miscreants were acquitted.

In 1771, a band of patriots, called the "Regulators," in North Carolina, became so formidable, and were so efficacious in stirring the people to rebellion, that Governor Tryon of that state, determined to destroy or disperse them. Having learned that they had gathered in considerable force upon the Alamance river, he proceeded thither with quite a large body of regulars and militia. They met near the banks of that stream, and a parley ensued. The "Regulators," asking only for redress of grievances, sought to negotiate, but Tryon peremptorily ordered them to disperse. This they refused to do, and some of his men, thirsting for blood, fired upon them and killed several. These soldiers were afterward arraigned for murder, through the clamorous demands of the people; but, after a mock trial had been acted, they were acquitted, and thus they were "protected from punishment for any murders which they should commit on the inhabitants of these states."

XVI. *For cutting off our trade with all parts of the world.*

The narrow, restrictive policy of Great Britain, begun as early as the middle of the seventeenth century, had a tendency to repress, rather than to encourage, the commerce of the colonies. Instead of allowing them free commercial intercourse with other nations, the home government did all in its power to compel the colonists to trade exclusively with Great Britain.* In 1764, the British Minister, under a pretence of preventing *illegal* traffic between the British colonies and foreign American possessions, made the naval commanders revenue officers—directed them to take the usual custom-house oaths—and to conform to the custom-house regulations. By this means a profitable trade with the Spanish and French colonies in America, which the colonists had long uninterruptedly enjoyed, (although in violation of the old Navigation Act,) was destroyed. This trade was advantageous to Great Britain as well as to the colonies; but as the enforcement of these laws was a part of the system of "reforming the American governments,"† began by Bute, the advantages to England were overlooked. Under this act, many seizures of vessels were made; and the Americans were so distressed and harassed, that they were obliged to abandon the trade.

Other measures, having a tendency to narrow the commerce of the colonies to a direct trade with Great Britain,

---

* The Navigation Act, first adopted in 1651, and extended in 1660, declared that no merchandise of the English plantations should be imported into England in any other than English vessels. There were also restrictive laws respecting the manufactures of the colonies, and their domestic commerce. For the benefit of English manufacturers, the colonists were forbidden to export, or introduce from one colony into another, hats and woollens of domestic manufacture; and hatters were forbidden to have, at one time, more than two apprentices. They were not allowed to import sugar, rum, and molasses, without paying an exorbitant duty, and forbade the erection of certain iron works.

† See Gordon, vol i., p. 108.

were adopted; and finally, in 1775, among the acts projected by Lord North for *punishing* the colonies, was one
for effectually stopping the commerce of New England
with Great Britain, Ireland, and the West Indies, and
also fishing on the Banks of Newfoundland. This
restrictive act, first applied to the New England colonies, was afterward extended to all the others, and thus,
as far as parliamentary enactments could effect it, "trade
with all parts of the world" was cut off.

XVII. *For imposing taxes on us without our consent.*

George Grenville, an honest but short-sighted statesman, became the Prime Minister, or "First Lord of the
Treasury," of Great Britain, in 1764. He found the
treasury drained empty by the vampire appetite of war,
and his first care was to devise means to replenish it.
Believing that the Crown had an unquestionable right to
tax its colonies, and perceiving the capacity of the
Americans to pay a tax if levied, he turned his attention
to a project for replenishing the treasury, by establishing
new duties upon all foreign goods imported by the
Americans. They were already submitting to the taxes,
in the shape of duties, which the Navigation Act, and
the Sugar Act, imposed; and when this new scheme was
proposed to Parliament, the people were at once aroused
to a sense of their danger—they saw clearly the design
of the British Ministry to impose tax upon tax, as long as
forbearance would allow it. Action on the subject was
taken in the colonial assemblies, and one sentiment
seemed to prevail,—*a denial of the right of Great Britain
to tax its colonies without their consent.* The fundamental
principle of a free government, that *"Taxation   and
equitable representatian are inseparable,"* was boldly
proclaimed, and petitions and remonstrances from the

19

colonies were transmitted to the King and Parliament. But the King, instead of heeding these remonstrances, asserted his right to tax the colonies, in his speech to Parliament at the opening in January, 1765, and recommended the adoption of Grenville's measures. Emboldened by this, the Minister proposed his famous Stamp Act in February, and in March it became a law, and received the royal signature.

The ferment which this act produced in America, and the violent opposition it met with from Pitt, and other leading minds in Parliament, caused its repeal in March 1766. The Repeal Act, however, was accompanied by a Declaratory Act, which contained the germ of other oppressions. It affirmed that Parliament had power *to bind the colonies in all cases whatsoever.* Although it was thought expedient to repeal the Stamp Act, yet the Declaratory Act asserted the correctness of the doctrine it contained and exhibited practically.*

Again in 1767, another tax was imposed in the shape of duties upon glass, paper, painter's colors, and tea. Here again taxes were imposed upon us "without our consent." The act was strongly condemned throughout the colonies, and the British ministry perceiving a tendency toward open rebellion in America, repealed this act also, excepting the duty upon tea. Finally, in 1773, Lord North attempted to draw a revenue from America by imposing additional duties upon tea; but it was met by firm opposition, and the celebrated Boston Tea Riot ensued. We might cite other proofs of the truth of this charge, but these may suffice.

* As the Stamp Act was the first and chief cause which fully aroused the reconists to a sense of the danger of euslavement by the mother country, and awakened the first notes of universal alarm that led to a general union of the Anglo-Americans in defence of their inalienable rights, and resulted finally in the adoption of a Declaration of Independence, we have inserted It in detail in the Appendix to this work.

XVIII. *For depriving us, in many cases, of the benefits of trial by jury.*

When the British ministry perceived that their scheme for taxing the colonies without their consent, met with determined opposition, and the Commissioners of Customs, in 1768, were obliged to flee for personal safety from Boston to Castle William, they so modified the Courts of Admiralty in America, as to make them powerful aids to these Commissioners and a strong right arm of oppression. An act was passed, in which it was ordained "that whenever offences should be committed in the colonies against particular acts, imposing various duties and restrictions upon trade, the prosecutor might bring his action for penalties in the Courts of Admiralty" by which means the subject lost the advantage of being tried "by an honest, uninfluenced jury of the vicinage, and was subjected to the sad necessity of being judged by a single man, a creature of the crown, and according to the course of law, which exempted the prosecutor from the trouble of proving his accusation, and obliged the defender either to evince his innocence, or suffer."*

XIX. *For transporting us beyond seas to be tried for pretended offences.*

On the fifteenth of April, 1774, Lord North introduced a bill in Parliament, entitled "A bill for the impartial administration of justice in the cases of persons questioned for any acts done by them in the execution of the laws, or for the suppression of riots and tumults in the province of Massachusetts Bay, in New England." This bill provided that in case any person indicted for murder in that province, or any other capital offence, or any indictment for riot, resistance of the magistrate, or impeding the revenue

---

* Address of the first continental congress, to the people of Great Britain.

laws in the smallest degree, he might, at the option of the Governor, or, in his absence, of the Lieutenant Governor, be taken to another colony, *or transported to Great Britain,* for trial, a thousand leagues from his friends, and amidst his enemies.

The arguments used by Lord North in favor of the measure, had very little foundation in either truth or justice, and the bill met with violent opposition in parliament. The minister seemed to be actuated more by a spirit of retaliation, than by a conviction of the necessity of such a measure. "We must show the Americans," said he, "that we will no longer sit quietly under their insults; and also, that even when roused, our measures are not cruel or vindictive, but necessary and efficacious." Colonel Barre, who, from the first commencement of troubles with America, was the fast friend of the colonists, denounced the bill in unmeasured terms, as big with misery, and pregnant with danger to the British Empire. "This," said he, "is indeed the most extraordinary resolution that was ever heard in the Parliament of England. It offers new encouragement to military insolence, already so insupportable. By this law, the Americans are deprived of a right which belongs to every human creature, that of demanding justice before a tribunal composed of impartial judges. Even Captain Preston,* who, in their own city of Boston, had shed the blood of citizens, found among them a fair trial, and equitable judges." Alderman Sawbridge, another warm friend of the Americans, in Parliament, also denounced the bill, not only as unnecessary and ridiculous, but unjust and cruel. He asserted that witnesses against the crown could never be brought over to England; that the Act was meant to enslave the Americans; and he expressed the ardent hope

* See biography of John Adams.

that the Americans would not admit of the execution of any of these destructive bills,* but nobly refuse them all. "If they do not," said he, "they are the most abject slaves upon earth, and nothing the minister can do is base enough for them."

Notwithstanding the manifest inexpediency of such a measure, the already irritated feeling of the colonists, and the solemn warning of sound statesmen in both Houses of Parliament, the bill was passed by one hundred and twenty-seven to forty-four, in the Commons, and forty-nine to twelve in the House of Lords. The king signed the bill, and it was thus decreed that Americans might be "transported beyond the seas, to be tried for pretended offences" or real crime.

XX *For abolishing the free system of English laws in a neighboring province, establishing therein an arbitrary government, and enlarging its boundaries, so as to render it at once an example and fit instrument for introducing the same absolute rule into these colonies.*

After the adoption of the Boston Port Bill, the bill for changing the government of Massachusetts, and the bill providing for the transportation of accused persons to England for trial, the British ministry were evidently alarmed at the fury of the whirlwind they themselves had raised; and they doubtless had a presentiment of the coming rebellion which their own cruel measures had engendered and ripened. They therefore thought it prudent to take steps in time to secure such a footing in America as should enable them to breast successfully the gathering storm. Accordingly a bill was introduced in the House of Lords in May, 1774, "for making more ef-

---

* The Boston Port Bill; the bill for altering, or rather for abolishing, the constitution of Massachusetts; and the bill under consideration.

fectual provision for the government of the province of Quebec, in North America."

This bill proposed the establishment, in Canada, of a Legislative Council, invested with all powers, except that of levying taxes. It was provided that its members should be appointed by the crown, and continue in authority during its pleasure; that Canadian subjects, professing the Catholic faith, might be called to sit in the Council; that the Catholic clergy, with the exception of the regular orders, should be secured in their possessions and of their tithes, from all those who professed their religion; that the French laws, without jury, should be re-established, preserving, however, the English laws, with trial by jury, in criminal cases. It was also added, in order to furnish the ministers with a larger scope for their designs, that the limits of Canada should be extended, so as to embrace the territory situated between the lakes, and the Ohio and Mississippi rivers.*

This was a liberal concession to the people of Canada, nearly all of whom were French, and but a small portion of them Protestants.† The nobility and clergy had frequently complained of the curtailment of their privileges, and maintained that they were better off under the old French rule previous to 1763, than now. The measure proposed was well calculated to quiet all discontent in Canada, and make the people loyal. By such a result,

* Soon after the introduction of this bill, Thomas and John Penn, son and grandson of William Penn, put in a remonstrance against the boundary proposition, as it contemplated an encroachment upon their territory, they being the proprietaries of Pennsylvania, and the counties of New Castle, Kent, and Sussex, in Delaware. Burke, also, who was then the agent for New York, contended against the boundary proposition, because it encroached upon the boundary line of that Colony.

† General Carleton, then Governor of Canada, asserted, during his examination before Parliament, that there were then in that province only about three hundred and sixty Protestants, besides women and children; while there were one hundred and fifty thousand Roman Catholics.

a place would be secured in the immediate vicinity of the refractory Colonies, where troops and munitions of war might be landed, and an overwhelming force be concentrated, ready at a moment's warning to march into the territory of, and subdue, the rebellious Americans. This was doubtless the ulterior design of the ministry in offering these concessions, and the eagle vision of Colonel Barre plainly perceived it. In the debate on the bill, he remarked, "A very extraordinary indulgence is given to the inhabitants of this province, and one calculated to gain the hearts and affections of these people. To this I cannot object if it is to be applied to good purposes; but if you are about *to raise a Popish army to serve in the Colonies,* from this time all hope of peace in America will be destroyed."

The bill was so opposed to the religious and national prejudices of the great mass of the people of Great Britain, that it met with violent opposition both in and out of Parliament, yet it passed by a large majority, and on the twenty-first of June it became a law by receiving the royal signature.

XXI. *For taking away our charters, abolishing our most valuable Laws, and altering, fundamentally, the forms of our governments.*

While the Boston Port Bill was before the Lords, Lord North, on the twenty-eighth day of March, 1774, in a Committee of the whole Lower House, brought in a bill "for the better regulating of the government in the province of Massachusetts Bay." It provided for an alteration in the Constitution of that province as it stood upon the charter of William III. By this act the people of Massachusetts were, without a hearing, deprived of some of the most important rights and privileges secured to them by their charter rights which they had enjoyed from the first settlement of the colony. The members of the Council, heretofore chosen under the charter, by the General Assembly, were, after the first of August of that year, to be chosen by the King; to consist of not more than thirty-six, and not less than twelve; and to hold their office during his pleasure. After the first of July the governor was authorized to *appoint* and *remove,* without the consent of the Council, all judges of the inferior Courts of Common Pleas, Commissioners of Oyer and Terminer the Attorney General, Provosts, Marshals, Justices of the Peace, and other officers belonging to the Council and courts of justice; and was also empowered to *appoint* sheriffs without the consent of the Council, but not to *remove* them without their consent.

The ministers did not confine themselves to these fundamental alterations in the charter of that province, but materially altered or totally repealed the laws relating to town meetings, and the election of jurors; laws which had been in existence from the commencement of the government, and deemed a part of the constitution of the colony. The right of selecting jurors by the inhabitants and freeholders of the several towns, was taken from them, and all jurors were by this act, to be summoned and returned by the sheriffs.*

This bill was zealously opposed by the friends of America in the British House of Commons. Barre and Burke, the leaders of this party, opposed it with all their strength of mind and eloquence of speech. "What," said the latter, "can the Americans believe but that England wishes to despoil them of all liberty, of all franchises; and by the destruction of their charters to reduce them to a state of the most abject slavery? As the Americans are no less ardently attached to liberty than the English

* Pitkin's Political and Civil History of the United States, vol i. p. 266.

themselves, can it ever be hoped they will submit to such exorbitant usurpation: to such portentous resolutions?" Governor Pownall, too, lifted up the voice of warning, and plainly told the ministers that their measures would be resisted, not only by the will and sentiment of the whole people, but probably by force of arms. But a false security shut the ears of the British ministry against all of these portentous warnings, and the British legislators seemed to have lost all sense of right and equity. The bill was adopted by an overwhelming majority—two

mons, and ninety-two against twenty in the House of Lords. The King gave the bill his royal signature, and

charters, abolishing our most valuable laws, and altering fundamentally, the *forms* of our governments."

XXII. *For suspending our own legislatures, and declaring themselves invested with power to legislate for us in all cases whatsoever.*

By the act described in the next preceding charge, entitled "For the better regulation of government in the province of Massachusetts Bay," the colonial legislature was virtually and actually "suspended;" for, according to the charter under which the people had always lived and been governed, they recognised no legislature but one of their own free choice and election. By that act, the members of the council were chosen by the King, and a free legislature was in fact suspended, and a declaration virtually made that the King and Parliament were "invested with power to legislate for us in all cases whatsoever." In 1767 the powers of the Legislature of New York were suspended indefinitely, because the Assembly refused to furnish the soldiers, quartered among them, with certain articles mentioned in a clause in the Mutiny Act.

In the language of the Declaration of Independence, by such an act of suspension of legislative functions, those "powers, incapable of annihilation, returned to the people at large for their exercise;" but the King and his council, by both word and deed, claimed that those powers return-ed to, and were vested in, the Crown, and thus asserted the principle, that it in connexion with the Council, was invested with power to legislate for the colonies "in all cases whatsoever."

Lord Dunmore, after dissolving the Assembly of Vir-ginia about the beginning of 1775, assumed the same right, and issued proclamations to the people, calling upon them to perform certain duties, which had not been re-quired of them by their own representatives in the House of Burgesses.

XXIII. *He has abdicated government here, by declaring us out of his protection, and waging war against us.*

As early as the meeting of Parliament in 1774, the King, in his address from the throne, spoke of the colo-nies as in a state of almost open rebellion, and assured Parliament that he should employ vigorous efforts to sup-press the unfolding insurrection. Again, in February 1775, he sent a message to the Commons, declaring his American subjects to be in a state of open rebellion, and informing them that it would be necessary to augment the naval and military force in the colonies. Toward the close of 1775, he gave his assent to an agreement, with several German princes, to send armies to America to assist in crushing his rebellious subjects; and he sanc-tioned the barbarous acts of his governors, who sought to engage the Indian tribes in a warfare upon the colonists. In these measures, he personally declared us "out of his protection," and waged war against them.

Through his representatives, his governors of colonies

Lord Dunmore, Governor of Virginia, fearing the just resentment of the people, "abdicated government," by

New York, "abdicated government," when, for fear of the resentment of the patriots, he fled on board a Halifax

also took refuge on board a British ship of war. Lord William Campbell, Governor of South Carolina, also

colony, and carrying off with him the royal seals and the instructions to governors; and he "waged war" against

and Sir Henry Clinton, in besieging Charleston. In various ways, both personally and by representatives, did

"cruel war against us."

XXIV. *He has plundered our seas, ravaged our coasts, burnt our towns, and destroyed the lives of our people.*

In 1764, when the provisions of the Navigation Act were strictly enforced, and the commanders of vessels were invested with the power of custom-house officers to enforce the revenue laws under that act, a great many American vessels were seized, by which much distress was produced. Although this was done under the sanction of written law, yet it was nothing more, in the mode of enforcing the law, than "plundering our seas."

In April, 1775, the "lives of our people" were destroyed at Lexington and Concord, by an expedition sent out by Governor Gage, of Massachusetts. In June of that year, he "burnt our towns," and destroyed the "lives of our people," by his troops setting fire to Charlestown, and attacking and slaying our people upon

Breed's, and Bunker Hill; and shortly afterward, the unprotected town of Bristol, in Rhode Island, was cannonaded, because the people refused to comply with an order from the commander of the vessels that appeared before it, to supply him with three hundred sheep.

In the autumn of 1775, several royal cruisers ravaging the coasts of New England. Captain Wallace, with the man-of-war, Rose, and two others, pursued a vessel which took shelter in the port of Stonington, Connecticut. He entered the harbor, and opened a fire upon the town, which he kept up nearly a whole day. He killed two men, and carried off some vessels. This was the same Captain (Sir James) Wallace who afterward commanded the flying squadron of small vessels that made a predatory expedition up the Hudson river, and, in connection with Colonel Vaughan of the land force, burnt Esopus or Kingston, in Ulster county.

On the eighteenth of October, Captain Mowatt, with a few armed vessels, burnt the town of Falmouth, upon the north-eastern coast of Massachusetts; and he asserted that he had orders to destroy, by fire, all the sea-port towns from Boston to Halifax.

In December, 1775, Governor Dunmore, of Virginia, having been obliged to take refuge on board the Fowey, a British armed vessel at Norfolk, tried every means in his power to bring the people to subjection under him. Finally, the frigate Liverpool arrived, and the Governor felt quite strong in his resources, believing, that with the two vessels and the armed force of tories and blacks which he had collected on board, he should be able to regain his lost power. He sent a peremptory order to the inhabitants of Norfolk to supply the vessels with provisions. The order was of course disobeyed; and on the first of January, 1776, the two vessels opened a destructive cannonading upon the town. At the same time, some marines were landed, who set fire to the town, and reduced it to ashes.

In June, 1776, while the proposition of independence was before Congress, a naval armament under Admiral Sir Peter Parker, and a land force under Sir Henry Clinton, made a combined attack upon Charleston, South Carolina, and many Americans were killed. And after the Declaration of Independence went forth, the King's minions continued to "plunder our seas, ravage our coasts, and destroy the lives of our people."

XXV. *Hs is at this time transporting large armies of foreign mercenaries to complete the works of death, desolation, and tyranny, already begun, with circumstances of cruelty and perfidy scarcely paralleled in the most barbarous ages, and totally unworthy the head of a civilized nation.*

Toward the close of 1775, Lord North introduced a bill in Parliament, which provided for prohibiting all intercourse with the colonies, until they should submit, and for placing the whole country under martial law. This bill included a clause for appointing resident commissioners in America, who should have discretionary powers to grant pardons and effect indemnities, in case the Americans should come to terms. Having thus determined to place the country under martial law, and to procure the submission of the colonies by force of arms, the next important consideration was to procure the requisite force. The estimated number of men sufficient to carry out successfully the designs of the ministry, was twenty-eight thousand seamen, and a land force of fifty-five thousand men.

This was a large force to raise within the brief space which the exigency of the case required, for the peace establishment at home was small enough already, and the delay in procuring volunteers, or waiting for the return of troops from foreign stations, might prove fatal to their plans. Ministers therefore resolved to *hire soldiers of some of the German princes,* and they at once appointed a commissioner for the purpose. Early in 1776, a treaty was concluded, and the Landgrave of Hesse-Cassel agreed to furnish twelve thousand one hundred and four men; the Duke of Brunswick, four thousand and eighty-four; the Prince of Hesse, six hundred and sixty-eight; the Prince of Waldeck, six hundred and seventy; making in all, seventeen thousand five hundred and twenty-six. The masters of these mercenaries, perceiving the stern necessity which had driven the British government to this atrocious resort, in its endeavor to crush the spirit of freedom in its American colonies, extorted hard terms—terms which none but a desperate suitor for favor would have agreed to. It was stipulated that they *were* to receive *seven pounds, four shillings and four pence sterling for each man, besides being relieved from the burden of maintaining them.* In addition, the princes were to receive a certain stipend, amounting in all to one hundred and thirty-five thousand pounds sterling, or about *six hundred and seventy-five thousand dollars.* And Great Britain further agreed to guaranty the dominions of those princes against foreign attacks during the absence of their soldiers.

This hiring of the bone and sinew, and even the *lives,* of foreign troops—purchased assassins—to aid in enslaving its own children, whose only crime was an irrepressible aspiration for freedom, is the foulest blot upon the escutcheon of Great Britain, which its unholy warfare against us during the revolution produced. The best friends of Great Britain, in and out of Parliament, deeply deplored the measure; and the opposition in the National Legislature, with a sincere concern for the fair fame of their country did all in their power to prevent the transaction. But Parliament, as if madly bent on the entire destruction of British honor, and on pulling down the very pillars of the Constitution, seconded the views of Ministers, and adopted the measure by an overwhelming majority.

For this act, the King and his Ministers were obliged to hear many home truths from statesmen in both Houses of Parliament. Among others, the Earl of Coventry inveighed most heartily against the employment of foreign mercenaries to fight the battles of England; even in a *just* war. He maintained that the war in question was an unnatural and unrighteous one, and, as such, would not terminate favorably to the oppressor. "Look on the map of the globe," said he; view Great Britain and North America; compare their extent; consider their soil, rivers, climate, and increasing population of the latter; nothing but the most obstinate blindness and partiality can engender a serious opinion that such a country will long continue under subjection to this. The question is not, therefore, how we shall be able to realize a vain, delusive scheme of dominion, but how we shall make it the interest of the Americans to continue faithful allies and warm friends. Surely that can never be effected by fleets and armies. Instead of meditating conquest, and exhausting our strength in an ineffectual struggle, we should wisely, abandoning wild schemes of coercion, avail ourselves of the only substantial benefit we can ever expect, the profits of an extensive commerce, and the strong support of a firm and friendly alliance and compact for mutual defence and assistance."

What blood and treasure would have been spared had such statesmanlike views prevailed in the British Parliament. But national pride was wounded, and its festerings produced relentless hate, whose counsels had no whispers of justice or of honorable peace. "Large armies of foreign mercenaries, to complete the work of death, desolation and tyranny, already begun," were sent hither, and the odious Hessians (the general title given to those German troops) performed their first act in the bloody drama, in the Battle of Long Island, on the twenty-ninth of August, 1776.

XXVI. *He has constrained our fellow-citizens, taken captive on the high seas, to bear arms against their country, to become the executioners of their friends and brethren, or to fall themselves by their hands.*

About the last of December, 1775, the British Parliament passed an act for prohibiting all trade and commerce with the colonies, and authorizing the capture and condemnation, not only of all American vessels with their cargoes, but all other vessels found trading with the colonies, and the crews were to be treated, not as prisoners, but as slaves. By a clause in the act, it was made lawful for the commander of a British vessel to take the masters, crews, and *other persons,* found in the captured vessels, and to put them on board any other British armed vessel, enter their names on the books of the same, and, from the time of such entry, such persons were to be considered in the service of his majesty, to all intents and purposes, as though they had entered themselves voluntarily on board such vessel.* By this means, the Americans were compelled to fight *even against their own friends and countrymen*—"to become the executioners of their friends and brethren, or to fall by their hands." This barbarous act was loudly condemned on the floor of Parliament, as unworthy of a Christian people, a "refinement of cruelty unknown among savage nations," and paralleled only "among pirates, the outlaws and ene

* Pitkin, vol. 1., p 357.

mies of human society." But the act became law, and to the disgrace of Great Britain it was put in force.

It was the provisions of this odious act which laid the British government under the necessity of providing a force to carry out its designs in America, which its resources in men were inadequate to do; and ministers resorted to the foul measure of hiring German soldiers to fight their battles against their brethren here

XXVII. *He has excited domestic insurrectians among us, and has endeavored to bring on the inhabitants of our frontiers, the merciless Indian savages, whose known rule of warfare is an undistinguished destruction of all ages, sexes and conditions.*

Lord Dunmore, one of the most unpopular governors Virginia ever had, became involved in difficulties with the people, soon after his accession. Like too many of the native born Englishmen at that time, he regarded the colonists as inferior people, and instead of using conciliatory measures, which might have made his situation agreeable to himself, he maintained a haughty carriage and aristocratic reserve. These private matters would have been tolerated, had not his public acts partaken of the same spirit. He seemed to be exceedingly deficient in judgment, and by various acts of annoyance he greatly exasperated the people. At length they arose in arms in consequence of his removing the powder of the colonial magazine on board of a ship of war, and he was obliged to fly thither himself, with his family, for fear of personal injury. This was early in May, 1775, and during the summer and autumn he attempted to regain his lost power. All moderate attempts having failed, he resolved on a bolder and more cruel measure. He issued his proclamation, and authoritatively summoned to his standard all capable of bearing arms; and in that proclamation, as

20

well as through private emissaries, he offered freedom to
the slaves if they would take up arms against their masters. Thus he "excited domestic insurrection."

In the spring of 1775, this same Governor Dunmore
was an accomplice in, and an active promoter of, a scheme
to "bring on the inhabitants of our frontiers, the merciless Indian savages." The plan adopted was to organize
an active co-operation of all the various Indian tribes on
the frontier, with the Tories. John Connelly, a Pennsyl-
vanian, has the honor of originating the plot; and he found
in Governor Dunmore a zealous coadjutor and liberal
patron in the enterprise. Fort Pitt (now Pittsburgh)
was to be the place of rendezvous, and ample rewards
were offered to the chiefs of the Indians, as well as to the
militia captains, who should join their standard.

In order to connect the plan, give it wider scope,
secure more efficiency, and have higher sanction, a mes-
senger was sent to Governor Gage, at Boston, then
commander-in-chief of all the British forces in America.
Gage entered heartily into the atrocious scheme, and
gave Connelly a commission as Lieutenant-Colonel. He
also sent an emissary named John Stuart, to the nation
of the Cherokees on the borders of the Carolinas. General
Carleton, governor of Canada, sent Colonel Johnson to
the Indians of St. Francis, and others, belonging to the
Six Nations, and in every case heavy bribes were offered.
Too well did these emissaries succeed, for during the
summer hundreds of innocent old men, women, and
young children, were butchered in cold blood upon the
frontiers of Virginia and the Carolinas.

This charge was true, not only at the time it was made
in the Declaration of Independence, but on several subsa-
quent occasions it might with verity have been made.
When Burgoyne prepared to invade the States from
Canada, he, by express orders of ministers, put under

arms, and secured for the British service several tribes of Indians inhabiting the country between the Mohawk river and Lake Ontario. And just before going to attack Ticonderoga, he gave a great war feast to the Indians, and issued a proclamation calling upon the Americans to surrender or suffer the consequences of savage ferocity.

The American Congress, in its Declaration of Independence, after asserting that "The History of the present King of Great Britain is a history of repeated injuries and usurpations, all having, in direct object, the establishment of absolute tyranny over these states," and submitting the foregoing charges as proofs of the truth of their declaration, they asserted:—

First: *That in every stage of these oppressions, we have petitioned for redress in the most humble terms. Our repeated petitions have been answered only by repeated injury.*

For ten long years, "in every stage of these oppressions," did the colonists "petition for redress in the most humble terms." It was done by the Colonial Congress which assembled in 1765, in consequence of the passage of the Stamp Act. They put forth *a Declaration of Rights,* the thirteenth section of which asserted, "That it is the right of the British subject in these colonies to petition the King, or either House of Parliament." This right was denied by the colonial governors, claiming it exclusively for the assemblies in their legislative capacity. But acting upon their declared right, that Congress sent a most humble petition to the King, setting forth the grievances which the acts for taxing the colonies imposed upon the people, and beseeching him to lay the subject before the Parliament and obtain redress for them. But this petition was unheeded, as well as those of the popular provincial conventions, and "repeated injuries" were inflicted, in the form of new and oppressive acts for taxing the colonists without their consent.

The first Continental Congress, that convened in September, 1774, humbly petitioned the King, and set forth the various measures of his government which bore heavily upon their prosperity and curtailed their rights as British subjects. The General Congress that met in May, the next year, also sent another humble petition to the King, but both were "answered only by repeated injuries." Instead of listening to their loyal importunities for redress, he deprived them in many cases of "trial by jury;" he prepared to "transport them beyond seas, to be tried for pretended offences;" he "abolished the free system of English laws in a neighboring province;" he took away their charters, abolished their "most valuable laws," and "altered, fundamentally, the *forms*" of their government; he "plundered their seas, ravaged their coasts, burnt their towns, and destroyed the lives of their people;" and he transported "large armies of foreign mercenaries to complete the works of death, desolation, and tyranny, already begun, with circumstances of cruelty and perfidy scarcely paralleled in the most barbarous ages, and totally unworthy the head of a civilized nation."

Secondly: *We have not been wanting in attention to our British brethren.*

This assertion the journals of the Continental Congress, and the proceedings of the British Parliament, fully corroborate. The first address put forth by the Continental Congress, in 1774, *was to the people of Great Britain,* in which the most affectionate terms of brotherhood, expressive of the strongest feelings which the ties of consanguinity could produce, were used. They concluded their address by expressing a hope "that the magnanimity and justice of the British nation will furnish a parliament of such wisdom, independence, and public spirit, as may save the violated rights of the whole empire from the devices of wicked ministers and evil counsellors, whether in or out of office; and thereby restore that harmony, friendship, and fraternal affection, between all the inhabitants of his majesty's kingdoms and territories, so ardently wished for by every true and honest American."

The second Continental Congress, in 1775, sent an affectionate address to the people of Ireland, in which they thanked them for the friendly disposition which they had always shown toward Americans; expressed a strong sympathy for them, on account of the grievances which the inhabitants of that fertile island suffered at the hands of the same arbitrary rulers, and closed with a "hope that the patient abiding of the meek may not always be forgotten;" and that God would "grant that the iniquitous schemes for extirpating liberty from the British empire might be soon defeated."

But, not only were British rulers unmindful of their petitions and of their remonstrances; their "British brethren" also were deaf to the "voice of justice and consanguinity;" and the colonists were obliged to acquiesco in the necessity which denounced their separation; and they held them, as they held the rest of mankind, "ENE-MIES IN WAR—IN PEACE, FRIENDS,"

THE CONFEDERATION.

THE Declaration of the representatives of the united colonies of North America, in General Congress assembled, that "these colonies are, and of right ought to be, free and independent states," was but the initial act in the great work of founding a free republic out of a dismembered portion of one of the mightiest empires of the earth. It was an easy matter to *declare* the states free, but they well knew it would be a laborious task to *support* that declaration, and consummate the work thus begun. Already fleets were hovering upon our coasts, and armies traversed our provinces, with the dire purpose of quelling rebellion by fire and sword, and all the vast iniquities of war. At the very time the Declaration was made, a British squadron was near our coast, bearing thousands of hired mercenaries, some of them veterans from the vast armies of Frederick the Great, all eager to win the laurels of glory or the gold of plunder, in the exercise of their desolating profession. Combined with these foes from without, were the more dreaded foes within—those who, through principle or interest, adhered to the Crown. They consisted chiefly of the timid, the time-serving, the ambitious, and the indolent, who feared British power, courted its caresses, sought the preferments it could bestow, or loved ease better than freedom. This class was not small nor weak, but by its secret treacheries, or open resistance, it weakened the bond of the American union, and greatly strengthened the royal arm.

With such a great work before them—with such beset

ments in the way—by such dangers surrounded—it is no wonder that great doubt, and anxiety, and dread, pervaded the minds of the people, and caused American legislators to desire a more tangible bond of union than a Federal Congress, and a Federal Army. The various state governments were in utter confusion, and in their practical operations they harmonized in few things, except in making provisions for the army; and even this paramount claim was often so neglected by particular states as almost to paralyze the military movements. Royal governments in all the colonies had been overturned, and the people, in spontaneous assemblies, collected the best fragments together and formed provincial congresses, in which they vested local governmental powers. But these were perceived to be but broken reeds to depend upon in the great work of the revolution yet to be performed; and the statesmen of that dark hour, feeling the necessity of a central power, regarded a confederation of the several states, with Congress as a controlling head, a measure essential to the perpetuity, not only of their efforts to become free, but of their very existence.

As early as July, 1775, that far-sighted and clear-headed statesman, Doctor Franklin, submitted to the consideration of Congress a sketch of articles of confederation between the colonies, limiting the duration of their vitality to the time when reconciliation with Great Britain should take place; or in the event of the failure of that desirable result, to be perpetual. At that time, Congress seemed to have no fixed plans for the future— the teeming present, with all its vast and novel concerns, engrossed their whole attention; and Doctor Franklin's plan seems not to have been discussed at all in the National Council. But when a declaration of independence was proposed, that idea alone suggested the necessity of a confederation of the states to carry forward the work to a successful consummation. Congress, therefore, on the eleventh of June, 1776, resolved that a committee should be appointed to prepare, and properly digest, a form of confederation to be entered into by the several states. The committee appointed under the resolution consisted of one delegate from each state. John Dickinson, of Pennsylvania, (who was opposed to the Declaration of Independence, and would have voted against it, if he had been present,) was chosen chairman, and through him the committee reported a draft of articles of confederation, on the twelfth of July. Almost daily debates upon the subject ensued until the twentieth of August, when the report was laid aside, and was not taken up again for consideration until the seventh of April, 1777. In the meanwhile, the several states had adopted constitutions for their respective government, and Congress was practically acknowledged the supreme head in all matters appertaining to the war, public finances, &c. It emitted bills of credit, or paper money, appointed foreign ministers, and opened negotiations with foreign governments.

From the seventh of April, until the fifteenth of November following, the subject was debated two or three times a week, and several amendments were made. As the Confederation might be a permanent bond of Union, of course local interests were considered prospectively. If the union had been designed to be temporary, to meet the exigencies arising from the state of war in which the colonies then were, local questions could hardly have had weight enough to have elicited debate; but such was not the case, and of course the sagacious mer, who were then in Congress, looked beyond the present, and endeavored to legislate accordingly. From the seventh of October, until the fifteenth of November, the debates upon it were almost daily, and the conflicting interests of the several states were strongly brought into view by the different speakers. On that day, the following draft, containing all of the amendments, was laid before Congress, and after a spirited debate was adopted:—

TO ALL TO WHOM THESE PRESENTS SHALL COME, WE, THE UNDERSIGNED, DELEGATES OF THE STATES AFFIXED TO OUR NAMES, SEND GREETING.

WHEREAS the delegates of the United States of America in Congress assembled, did, on the fifteenth day of November, in the year of our Lord one thousand seven hundred and seventy-seven, and in the second year of the independence of America, agree to certain articles of confederation and perpetual union between the States of New Hampshire, Massachusetts Bay, Rhode Island, and Providence Plantations, Connecticut, New York, New Jersey, Pennsylvania, Delaware, Maryland, Virginia, North Carolina, South Carolina, and Georgia, in the words following, viz.:—

Articles of Confederation and perpetual Union between the States of New Hampshire, Massachusetts Bay, Rhode Island and Providence Plantations, Connecticut, New York, New Jersey, Pennsylvania, Delaware, Maryland, Virginia, North Carolina, South Carolina, and Georgia.

ARTICLE 1. The style of this confederacy shall be, "The United States of America."

ARTICLE 2. Each state retains its sovereignty, freedom, and independence, and every power, jurisdiction, and right, which is not by this confederation expressly delegated to the United States in Congress assembled.

ARTICLE 3. The said states hereby severally enter into a firm league of friendship with each other for their common defence, the security of their liberties, and their mu-

tual and general welfare; binding themselves to assist
each other against all force offered to, or attacks made
upon them, or any of them, on account of religion, sovereignty, trade. or any other pretence whatever.

ARTICLE 4 The better to secure and perpetuate mutual friendship, and intercourse among the people of the
different states in this Union, the free inhabitants of each
of these states, paupers, vagabonds, and fugitives from
justice excepted, shall be entitled to all privileges and immunities of free citizens in the several states; and the
people of each state shall have free ingress and regress
to and from any other state, and shall enjoy therein all the
privileges of trade and commerce subject to the same
duties, impositions, and restrictions, as the inhabitants
thereof respectively, provided that such restrictions shall
not extend so far as to prevent the removal of property
imported into any state to any other state, of which the
owner is an inhabitant; provided also, that no imposition,
duties, or restriction, shall be laid by any state on the
property of the United States or either of them.

If any person guilty of or charged with treason, felony,
or other high misdemeanor, in any state, shall flee from
justice, and be found in any of the United States, he shall
upon demand of the governor or executive power of the
state from which he fled, be delivered up and removed to
the state having jurisdiction of his offence.

Full faith and credit shall be given in each of these
states to the records, acts, and judicial proceedings of the
courts and magistrates of every other state.

ARTICLE 5. For the more convenient management of
the general interests of the United States, delegates shall
be annually appointed in such manner as the legislature
of each state shall direct, to meet in Congress on the first
Monday in November, in every year, with a power reserved to each state to recall its delegates or any of them

at any time within the year, and to send others in their stead for the remainder of the year.

No state shall be represented in Congress by less than two, nor by more than seven members; and no person shall be capable of being a delegate for more than three years in any term of six years; nor shall any person, being a delegate, be capable of holding any office under the United States, for which he, or another for his benefit receives any salary, fees, or emoluments of any kind.

Each state shall maintain its own delegates in a meeting of the states, and while they act as members of the committee of the states.

In determining questions in the United States in Congress assembled, each state shall have one vote.

Freedom of speech and debate in Congress shall not be impeached or questioned in any court or place out of Congress; and the members of Congress shall he protected in their persons from arrests and imprisonments, during the time of their going to and from and attendance on Congress, except for treason, felony or breach of the peace.

ARTICLE 6. No state, without the consent of the United States in Congress assembled, shall send any embassy to or receive any embassy from, or enter into any conference agreement, alliance, or treaty, with any king, prince, or state; nor shall any person holding any office of profit or trust under the United States, or any of them, accept of any present, emolument, office or title of any kind whatever, from any king, prince, or foreign state; nor shall the United States in Congress assembled, or any of them, grant any title of nobility.

No two or more states shall enter into any treaty, confederation, or alliance whatever, between them, without the consent of the United States in Congress assembled, specifying accurately the purposes for which the same is to be entered into and how long it shall continue.

No state shall lay any imposts or duties, which may interfere with any stipulations in treaties entered into by the United States in Congress assembled, with any king, prince, or state, in pursuance of any treaties already proposed by Congress to the courts of France and Spain.

No vessel-of-war shall be kept up in time of peace by any state, except such number only as shall be deemed necessary by the United States in Congress assembled for the defence of such state or its trade; nor shall any body of forces be kept up by any state in time of peace, except such number only as in the judgment of the United States in Congress assembled, shall be deemed requisite to garrison the forts necessary for the defence of such state; but every state shall always keep up a well-regulated and disciplined militia, sufficiently armed and accoutred, and shall provide and have constantly ready for use, in public stores, a due number of field-pieces and tents, and a proper quantity of arms, ammunition, and camp equipage.

No state shall engage in any war without the consent of the United States in Congress assembled, unless such state be actually invaded by enemies or shall have received certain advice of a resolution being formed by some nation of Indians to invade such state, and the danger is so imminent as not to admit of a delay till the United States in Congress assembled can be consulted; nor shall any state grant commissions to any ships or vessels-of-war, nor letters of marque or reprisal, except it be after a declaration of war by the United States in Congress assembled, and then only against the kingdom or state, and the subjects thereof, against which war has been so declared, and under such regulations as shall be established by the United States in Congress assembled, unless such state be infested by pirates, in which case vessels-of-war may be fitted out for that occasion, and kept so long as the danger shall continue, or until the United States in Congress assembled shall determine otherwise.

ATICLE 7. When land forces are raised by any state for the common defence, all officers of or under the rank of colonel, shall be appointed by the legislature of each state respectively, by whom such forces shall be raised or in such manner as such state shall direct, and all vacancies shall be filled up by the state which first made the appointment.

ARTICLE 8. All charges of war, and all other expenses that shall be incurred for the common defence or general welfare, and allowed by the United States in Congress assembled, shall be defrayed out of a common treasury, which shall be supplied by the several states in proportion to the value of all land within each state granted to or surveyed for any person, as such land and the buildings and improvements thereon shall be estimated according to such mode as the United States in Congress assembled shall from time to time direct and appoint.

The taxes for paying that proportion shall be laid and levied by the authority and direction of the legislatures of the several states, within the time agreed upon by the United States in Congress assembled.

ARTICLE 9. The United States in Congress assembled shall have the sole and exclusive right and power of determining on peace and war, except in the cases mentioned in the sixth article—of sending and receiving ambassadors—entering into treaties and alliances; provided that no treaty of commerce shall be made whereby the legislative power of the respective states shall be restrained from imposing such imposts and duties on foreigners as their own people are subjected to, or from prohibiting exportation or importation of any species of goods or commodities whatsoever—of establishing rules for deciding in all cases, what captures on land or water shall be legal, and in what manner prizes taken by land or naval forces in the service of the United States shall be divided or appropriated—of granting letters of marque and reprisal in times of peace—appointing courts for the trial of piracies and felonies committed on the high seas, and establishing courts for receiving and determining finally appeals in all cases of captures: provided, that no member of Congress shall be appointed a judge of any of the said courts.

The United States in Congress assembled shall also be the last resort on appeal in all disputes and differences now subsisting or that hereafter may arise between two or more states concerning boundary, jurisdiction or any other cause whatever; which authority shall always be exercised in the manner following: whenever the legislative or executive authority or lawful agent of any state in controversy with another shall present a petition to Congress, stating the matter in question, and praying for a hearing, notice thereof shall be given by order of Congress to the legislative or executive authority of the other state in controversy, and a day assigned for the appearance of the parties, by their lawful agents, who shall then be directed to appoint by joint consent commissioners or judges to constitute a court for hearing and determining the matter in question; but if they cannot agree, Congress shall name three persons out of each of the United States, and from the list of such persons each party shall alternately strike out one, the petitioners beginning, until the number shall be reduced to thirteen; and from that number not less than seven nor more than nine names, as Congress shall direct, shall, in in the presence of Congress, be drawn out by lot; and the persons whose names shall be so drawn, or any five of them, shall be commissioners or judges, to hear and finally determine the controversy, so always as a major part of the judges, who shall hear the cause, shall agree in the determination; and if either party shall neglect to attend at the day appointed, without showing reasons which Congress shall judge sufficient, or being present shall refuse to strike, the Congress shall proceed to nominate three persons out of each state, and the secretary of Congress shall strike in behalf of such party absent or refusing; and the judgment and sentence of the court to be appointed in the manner before prescribed, shall be final and conclusive; and if any of the parties shall refuse to submit to the authority of such court, or to appear, or defend their claim or cause, the court shall nevertheless proceed to pronounce sentence or judgment, which shall in like manner he final and decisive, the judgment or sentence and other proceedings being in either case transmitted to Congress, and lodged among the acts of Congress for the security of the parties concerned; provided, that every commissioner, before he sits in judgment, shall take an oath, to be administered by one of the judges of the supreme or superior court of the state, where the cause shall be tried, "well and truly to hear and determine the matter in question, according to the best of his judgment, without favor, affection, or hope of reward:" provided also, that no state shall be deprived of territory for the benefit of the United States.

All controversies concerning the private right of soil, claimed under different grants of two or more states, whose jurisdiction as they may respect such lands, and the states which passed such grants are adjusted, the said grants or either of them being at the same time claimed to have originated antecedent to such settlement of jurisdiction, shall, on the petition of either party to the Congress of the United States, be finally determined as near as may be, in the same manner as is before prescribed for deciding disputes respecting territorial jurisdiction between different states.

The United States in Congress assembled shall also have the sole and exclusive right and power of regulating the alloy and value of coin struck by their own authority, or by that of the respective states—fixing the standard of weights and measures throughout the United States— regulating the trade and managing all affairs with the Indians not members of any of the states; provided that the legislative right of any state within its own limits be not infringed or violated—establishing and regulating post-offices from one state to another throughout all the United States, and exacting such postage on the papers passing through the same, as may be requisite to defray the expenses of the said office—appointing all officers of the land forces in the service of the United States excepting regimental officers—appointing all the officers of the naval forces, and commissioning all officers whatever in the service of the United States—making rules for the government and regulation of the said land and naval forces and directing their operations.

The United States in Congress assembled shall have authority to appoint a committee to sit in the recess of Congress, to be denominated "a committee of the states," and to consist of one delegate from each state; and to appoint such other committees and civil offices as may be necessary for managing the general affairs of the United States, under their direction—to appoint one of their number to preside, provided that no person be allowed to serve in the office of president more than one year in any term of three years—to ascertain the necessary sums of money to be raised for the service of the United States, and to appropriate and apply the same for defraying the public expenses—to borrow money or emit bills on the credit of the United States, transmitting every half year to the respective states an account of the sums of money so borrowed or emitted—to build and equip a navy—

to agree upon the number of land forces, and to make requisitions from each state for its quota, in proportion to the number of white inhabitants in such state: which requisition shall be binding, and thereupon, the legislature of each state shall appoint the regimental officers, raise the men, and clothe, arm, and equip them, in a soldier-like manner, at the expense of the United States; and the officers and men so clothed, armed and equipped, shall march to the place appointed, and within the time agreed on by the United States in Congress assembled: but if the United States in Congress assembled, shall on considera-tion of circumstances judge proper that any state should not raise men or should raise a smaller number than its quota and that any other state should raise a greater number of men than the quota thereof, such extra number shall be raised, officered, clothed, armed, and equipped, in the same manner as the quota of such state, unless the legislature of such state shall judge that such extra number can not safely be spared out of the same; in which case they shall raise, officer, clothe, arm and equip, as many of such extra number as they judge can be safely spared. And the officers and men so clothed, armed and equipped, shall march to the place appointed, and within the time agreed on by the United States in Congress assembled.

The United States in Congress assembled shall never engage in a war, nor grant letters of marque and reprisal in time of peace, nor enter into any treaties or alliances, nor coin money, nor regulate the value thereof, nor ascertain the sums and expenses necessary for the defence and welfare of the United States or any of them, nor emit bills, nor borrow money on the credit of the United States, nor appropriate money, nor agree upon the num-ber of vessels-of-war to be built or purchased, or the number of land or sea forces to be raised, nor ap-point a commander-in-chief of the army or navy unless

21

nine states assent to the same; nor shall a question on any other point, except for adjourning from day to day, be determined unless by the votes of a majority of the United States in Congress assembled.

The Congress of the United States shall have power to adjourn to any time within the year, and to any place within the United States, so that no period of adjournment be for a longer duration than the space of six months; and shall publish the journal of their proceedings monthly, except such parts thereof relating to treaties, alliances, or military operations, as in their judgment require secrecy; and the yeas and nays of the delegates of each state on any question, shall be entered on the journal when it is desired by any delegate; and the delegates of a state or any of them, at his or their request, shall be furnished with a transcript of the said journal, except such parts as are above excepted, to lay before the legislatures of the several states.

ARTICLE 10. The committee of the states, or any nine of them, shall be authorized to execute, in the recess of Congress, such of the powers of Congress as the United States in Congress assembled, by the consent of nine states, shall from time to time, think expedient to vest them with; provided that no power be delegated to the said committee, for the exercise of which, by the articles of confederation, the voice of nine states in the Congress of the United States assembled is requisite.

ARTICLE 11. Canada, acceding to this confederation, and joining in the measures of the United States, shall be admitted into, and entitled to, all the advantages of this Union; but no other colony shall be admitted into the same, unless such admission be agreed to by nine states.

ARTICLE 12. All bills of credit emitted, moneys borrowed, and debts contracted, by or under the authority of Congress, before the assembling of the United States.

in pursuance of the present confederation, shall be deemed and considered as a charge against the United States, for payment and satisfaction whereof the said United States and the public faith are hereby solemnly pledged.

ARTICLE 13. Every state shall abide by the decision of the United States in Congress assembled, on all questions which, by this confederation, are submitted to them. And the articles of this confederation shall be inviolably observed by every state, and the Union shall be perpetual; nor shall any alteration at any time hereafter be made in any of them, unless such alteration be agreed to in a Congress of the United States, and be afterward confirmed by the legislature of every state.

And whereas it has pleased the great Governor of the world to incline the hearts of the legislatures we respectively represent in Congress, to approve of and to authorize us to ratify the said articles of confederation and perpetual Union: *know ye,* that we, the undersigned delegates, by virtue of the power and authority to us given for that purpose, do, by these presents, in the name and in behalf of our respective constituents, fully and entirely ratify and confirm each and every of the said articles of confederation and perpetual Union, and all and singular the matters and things therein contained; and we do further solemnly plight and engage the faith of our respective constituents, that they shall abide by the determinations of the United States in Congress assembled, on all questions which, by the said confederation, are submitted to them; and that the articles thereof shall be inviolably observed by the states we respectively represent; and that the union be perpetual.

In witness whereof, we have hereunto set our hands, in Congress. Done at Philadelphia, in the state of Penn sylvania, the ninth day of July, in the year of our Lord one thousand seven hundred and seventy-eight, and in the third year of the independence of America.

New Hampshire.

JOSIAH BARTLETT,
JOHN WENTWORTH, JR.

Massachusetts Bay.

JOHN HANCOCK,
SAMUEL ADAMS,
ELBRIDGE GERRY,
FRANCIS DANA,
JAMES LOVELL,
SAMUEL HOLTEN,

Rhode Island.

WILLIAM ELLERY,
HENRY MARCHANT,
JOHN COLLINS.

Connecticut.

ROGER SHERMAN,
SAMUEL HUNTINGTON,
OLIVER WOLCOTT,
TITUS HOSMER,
ANDREW ADAMS.

New York.

JAMES DUANE,
FRANCIS LEWIS,
WILLIAM DUER,
GOUVERNEUR MORRIS.

New Jersey.

JOHN WITHERSPOON,
NATH. SCUDDER.

Pennsylvania.

ROBERT MORRIS,
DANIEL ROBERDEAU,
JONATHAN BAYARD SMITH,
WILLIAM CLINGAN,
JOSEPH REED.

Delaware.

THOMAS M'KEAN,
JOHN DICKINSON,
NICHOLAS VAN DYKE.

Maryland.

JOHN HANSON,
DANIEL CARROLL.

Virginia.

RICHARD HENRY LEE,
JOHN BANISTER,
THOMAS ADAMS,
JOHN HARVIE,
FRANCIS LIGHTFOOT LEE,

North Carolina.

JOHN PENN,
CONSTABLE HARNETT,
JOHN WILLIAMS.

South Carolina.

HENRY LAURENS,
WILLIAM HENRY DRAYTON
JOHN MATTHEWS,
RICHARD HUTSON,
THOMAS HEYWARD, JR.

Georgia.

JOHN WALTON,
EDWARD TELFAIR,
EDWARD LANGWORTHY

After the Articles of Confederation were adopted by Congress, that body directed a copy of them to be sent to the speakers of the various state legislatures to be laid before them for action. They were accompanied by a communication, requesting the several legislatures, in case they approved of them, to instruct their delegates in Congress to vote for a ratification of them, which last act should be final and conclusive. On the twenty-ninth of November, a committee of three was appointed to procure the translation of the Articles of Confederation into the French language; and also to prepare and report an address to the people of Canada, urging them to become a portion of the confederacy.

The letter which accompanied the Articles of Confederation when they were sent to the several state legislatures, was in the form of an urgent appeal for immediate and united action. A direful necessity called for some strong bond of union, for the clangor of arms was heard on every side. Foes without, and traitors within, were everywhere sowing the seeds of jealousy between the states, and using every effort to sunder the ligaments of a common interest and repress a common aspiration which united them. It was easily foreseen that the conflicting interests of thirteen distinct states would necessarily clash, and that the idea of sovereignty which each possessed would interpose many objections to a general confederation, such as was proposed. Therefore, the letter was an argumentative one, and endeavored to show them that the plan proposed was the best which could be adapted to the circumstances of all. It concluded with the following impressive admonition:—

"We have reason to regret the time which has elapsed in preparing this plan for consideration. With additional solicitude, we look forward to that which must be necessarily spent before it can be ratified. Every motive loudly calls upon us to hasten its conclusion. More than any other consideration it will confound our foreign enemies, defeat the flagitious practices of the disaffected, strengthen and confirm our friends, support our public credit, restore the value of our money, enable us to maintain our fleets and armies, and add weight and respect to our councils at home, and to our treaties abroad. In short, this salutary measure can no longer be deferred. It seems essential to our very existence as a free people; and without it, we may soon be constrained to bid adieu to independence, to liberty, and to safety—blessings which from the justice of our cause, and the favor of our Almighty Creator visibly manifested in our protection, we have reason to expect, if in an humble dependence on his divine providence, we strenuously exert the means which are placed in our power."

Notwithstanding this pathetic appeal, and the general feeling that *something* must be speedily done, the state legislatures were slow to adopt the Articles. In the first place, they did not seem to accord with the prevailing sentiment of the people, as set forth in the Declaration of Independence; and in many things that Declaration and the Articles of Confederation were manifestly antipodent. The former was based upon declared *right;* the foundation of the latter was asserted *power.* The former was based upon a superintending Providence, and the inalienable rights of man; the latter rested upon the "sovereignty of declared power—one ascending for the foundation of human government, to the laws of nature and of nature's God, written upon the heart of man—the other resting upon the basis of human institutions, and prescriptive law, and colonial charters."* Again, the system of representation proposed, was highly objectionable,

---

* John Quincy Adams' Jubilee Discourse, 1839.

because each state was entitled to the same voice in Congress, whatever might be the difference in population. But the most objectionable feature of all was, that the question of the *limits* of the several states, and also in whom was vested the control or possession of the Crown-lands, was not only unadjusted, but wholly unnoticed. These and other defects, caused most of the states to hesitate at first, to adopt the Articles, and several of them for a long time utterly refused to accept them.

On the twenty-second of June, 1778, Congress proceeded to consider the objections of the states to the Articles of Confederation, and on the twenty-seventh of the same month, a form of ratification was adopted and ordered to be engrossed upon parchment, with a view that the same should be signed by such delegates as were instructed so to do by their respective legislatures.

On the ninth of July, the delegates of New Hampshire, Massachusetts, Rhode Island, Connecticut, New York, Pennsylvania, Virginia and South Carolina, signed the Articles. The delegates from New Jersey, Delaware and Maryland were not yet empowered to ratify and sign. Georgia and North Carolina were not represented, and the ratification of New York was conditional that all the other states should ratify. The delegates from North Carolina signed the articles on the twenty-first of July, those of Georgia on the twenty-fourth of the same month, those of New Jersey on the twenty-sixth of November, and those of Delaware on the twenty-second of February and fifth of May, 1779. Maryland still firmly refused to ratify, until the question of the conflicting claims of the Union and of the separate state to the Crown-lands, should be fully adjusted. This point was finally settled by cessions of the claiming states to the United States, of all the unsettled and unappropriated lands for the benefit of the whole Union. This cession of the Crown-lands to the Union, originated the Territorial System, and the erection of the North Western Territory into a distinct government similar to the existing states, having a local legislature of its own. The insuperable objection of Maryland having been removed by the settlement of this question, her delegates signed the Articles of Confederation on the first day of March, 1781, four years and four months after they were adopted by Congress. By this act of Maryland, they became the organic law of the Union, and on the second of March, Congress assembled under the new powers.

THE FEDERAL CONSTITUTION.

IT was early perceived that the Articles of Confederation conferred powers upon Congress quite inadequate to the objects of an effective National Government. That body, according to the terms of those Articles, possessed no power to liquidate debts incurred during the war,* it had the privilege only of recommending to the several States, the payment thereof. This recommendation was tardily complied with,† and Congress possessed no power to compel the States to obey its mandates. To a great extent, the people lost all regard for the authority of Congress, and the commercial affairs of the country became wretchedly deranged. In truth, everything seemed to be tending toward utter chaos soon after peace in 1783, and the leading minds of the Revolution, in view of increasing and magnified evils, and the glaring defects of the Articles of Confederation, were turned to a consideration of a plan for a closer union of the states, and for a general government founded on the principles of the Declaration of Independence, from which the Confederation in question widely departed.

The sagacious mind of Washington perceived with intense anxiety the tendency toward ruin of that fair fabric which his prowess had helped to rear, and he took the initial step toward the adoption of measures which

---

* The general government at the close of the Revolution, was burdened with a foreign debt of eight millions of dollars, and a domestic debt of about thirty millions, due to the army and to other American citizens.

† During fourteen months, only $482,890 were paid into the public treasury and the foreign interest was paid by a fresh loan from Holland.

finally resulted in the formation of the present Constitution of the United States. Washington had contemplated a scheme for uniting the Potomac with the Ohio, and through his influence, the legislatures of Virginia and Maryland were induced to send commissioners to Alexandria in March, 1785, to deliberate upon the subject. During their stay at Mount Vernon they devised another commission to establish a general tariff on imports, and to mature other commercial regulations. This convention was held at Annapolis, in September, 1786, but only five states were represented—Virginia, Delaware, Pennsylvania, New Jersey and New York.* The chief object of the convention was to consult on the best means of remedying the defects of the Federal government. The delegates met on the eleventh, and by a unanimous vote, chose John Dickinson chairman. After a full interchange of sentiments, they agreed that a committee should be appointed to prepare a draft of a report to be made to the legislatures of the several states then represented. On the fourteenth of September, the following report was submitted:—

To the honorable the legislatures of Virginia, Delaware, Pennsylvania, New Jersey, and New York, the commissioners from the said states respectively, assembled at Annapolis, humbly beg leave to report:—

That, pursuant to their several appointments, they met at Annapolis, in the state of Maryland, on the eleventh day of September instant, and having proceeded to a communication of their powers, they found that the states of New York, Pennsylvania, and Virginia, had, in sub-

---

* The names of the members of the Convention were as follows:—*New York,* Alexander Homilton, Egbert Benson; *New Jersey,* Abraham Clark, William C. Houston, James Schureman; *Pennsylvania,* Tench Coxe; *Delaware,* George Read, John Dickinson, Richard Basset; *Virginia,* Edmund Randolph, James Madison jr. St. George Tucker.

stance, and nearly in the same terms, authorized their respective commissioners "to meet such commissioners as were or might be appointed by the other states in the Union, at such time and place as should be agreed upon by the said commissioners, to take into consideration the trade and commerce of the United States, to consider how far a uniform system in their commercial intercourse and regulations might be necessary to their common interest and permanent harmony, and to report to the several states such an act relative to this great object, as, when unanimously ratified by them, would enable the United States, in Congress assembled, effectually to provide for the same."

That the state of Delaware had given similar powers to their commissioners, with this difference only, that the act to be framed in virtue of these powers, is required to be reported "to the United States, in Congress assembled, to be agreed to by them, and confirmed by the legislature of every state."

That the state of New Jersey had enlarged the object of their appointment, empowering their commissioners "to consider how far a uniform system in their commercial regulations, and *other important matters,* might be necessary to the common interest and permanent harmony of the several states;" and to report such an act on the subject, as, when ratified by them, "would enable the United States, in Congress assembled, effectually to provide for the exigencies of the Union."

That appointments of commissioners have also been made by the states of New Hampshire, Massachusetts, Rhode Island, and North Carolina, none of whom, however, have attended: but that no information has been received by your commissioners of any appointment having been made by the states of Connecticut, Maryland, South Carolina, or Georgia.

That the express terms of the powers to your commissioners supposing a deputation from all the states, and having for object the trade and commerce of the United States, your commissioners did not conceive it advisable to proceed on the business of their mission under the circumstances of so partial and defective a representation.

Deeply impressed, however, with the magnitude and importance of the object confided to them on this occasion, your commissioners cannot forbear to indulge an expression of their earnest and unanimous wish, that speedy measures may be taken to effect a general meeting of the states, in a future convention, for the same and such other purposes as the situation of public affairs may be found to require.

If, in expressing this wish, or in intimating any other sentiment, your commissioners should seem to exceed the strict bounds of their appointment, they entertain a full confidence, that a conduct dictated by an anxiety for the welfare of the United States, will not fail to receive an indulgent construction,

In this persuasion, your commissioners submit an opinion, that the idea of extending the powers of their deputies to other objects than those of commerce, which has been adopted by the state of New Jersey, was an improvement on the original plan, and will deserve to be incorporated into that of a future convention. They are the more naturally led to this conclusion, as, in the course of their reflections on the subject, they have been induced to think that the power of regulating trade is of such comprehensive extent, and will enter so far into the general system of the federal government, that to give it efficacy, and to obviate questions and doubts concerning its precise nature and limits, may require a correspondent adjustment of other parts of the federal system.

That there are important defects in the system of the

federal government, is acknowledged by the acts of all those states which have concurred in the present meeting; that the defects, upon a closer examination, may be found greater and more numerous than even these acts imply, is at least so far probable, from the embarrassments which characterize the present state of our national affairs, foreign and domestic, as may reasonably be supposed to merit a deliberate and candid discussion, in some mode which will unite the sentiments and councils of all the states. In the choice of the mode, your commissioners are of opinion that a convention of deputies from the different states, for the special and sole purpose of entering into this investigation, and digesting a plan for supplying such defects as may be discovered to exist, will be entitled to a preference, from considerations which will occur without being particularized.

Your commissioners decline an enumeration of those national circumstances on which their opinion respecting the propriety of a future convention, with more enlarged powers, is founded; as it would be a useless intrusion of facts and observations, most of which have been frequently the subject of public discussion, and none of which can have escaped the penetration of those to whom they would, in this instance, be addressed. They are, however, of a nature so serious, as, in the view of your commissioners, to render the situation of the United States delicate and critical, calling for an exertion of the united virtue and wisdom of all the members of the confederacy.

Under this impression, your commissioners, with the most respectful deference, beg leave to suggest their unanimous conviction, that it may essentially tend to advance the interests of the Union, if the states, by whom they have been respectively delegated, would themselves concur, and use their endeavors to procure the concur.

rence of the other states, in the appointment of commissioners, to meet at Philadelphia, on the second Monday in May next, to take into consideration the situation of the United States, to devise such further provisions as shall appear to them necessary, to render the constitution of the federal government adequate to the exigencies of the Union; and to report such an act for that purpose, to the United States, in Congress assembled, as, when agreed to by them, and afterward confirmed by the legislature of every state, will effectually provide for the same.

Though your commissioners could not, with propriety, address these observations and sentiments to any but the states they have the honor to represent, they have nevertheless concluded, from motives of respect, to transmit copies of this report to the United States, in Congress assembled, and to the executives of the other states.

By order of the Commissioners.

Dated at Annapolis, September 14th, 1786.

—————

This report was adopted, and transmitted to Congress. On the twenty-first of February, the committee of that body, consisting of Messrs. Dane, Varnum, S. M. Mitchell, Smith, Cadwallader, Irvine, N. Mitchell, Forrest, Grayson, Blount, Bull, and Few, to whom the report of the commissioners was referred, reported thereon, and offered the following resolutions, viz.—

Congress having had under consideration the letter of John Dickinson, Esq., chairman of the commissioners who assembled at Annapolis, during the last year; also the proceedings of the said commissioners, and entirely coinciding with them, as to the inefficiency of the federal government, and the necessity of devising such further provisions as shall render the same adequate to the exigencies of the Union, do strongly recommend to the dif ferent legislatures to send forward delegates, to meet the proposed convention, on the second Monday in May next, at the city of Philadelphia.

The delegates for the state of New York thereupon laid before Congress instructions which they had received from their constituents, and in pursuance of the said instructions, moved to postpone the further consideration of the report, in order to take up the following proposition, viz.—

"That it be recommended to the states composing the Union, that a convention of representatives from the said states respectively, be held at——, on——, for the purpose of revising the articles of confederation and perpetual union between the United States of America, and reporting to the United States, in Congress assembled, and to the states respectively, such alterations and amendments of the said articles of confederation, as the representatives, met in such convention, shall judge proper and necessary, to render them adequate to the preservation and support of the Union."

On taking the question, only three states voted in the affirmative, and the resolution was negatived.

A motion was then made by the delegates for Massachusetts, to postpone the further consideration of the report, in order to take into consideration a motion which they read in their place; this being agreed to, the motion of the delegates for Massachusetts was taken up, and being amended was agreed to, as follows:—

"Whereas, there is provision in the articles of confederation and perpetual union, for making alterations therein, by the assent of a Congress of the United States, and of the legislatures of the several states; and whereas, experience hath evinced that there are defects in the present confederation, as a mean to remedy which, several of the states and particularly the state of New York, by express instructions to their delegates in Congress, have suggested a convention for the purposes expressed in the following resolution; and such convention appearing to be the most probable means of establishing in these states, a firm national government:—

"*Resolved,* That, in the opinion of Congress, it is expedient that, on the second Monday in May next, a convention of delegates who shall have been appointed by the several states, be held at Philadelphia, for the sole and express purpose of revising the articles of confederation, and reporting to Congress and the several legislatures, such alterations and provisions therein, as shall, when agreed to in Congress, and confirmed by the states, render the federal constitution adequate to the exigencies of the government, and the preservation of the Union."

This preamble and resolution were immediately transmitted to the several speakers of State legislative assemblies, and they were laid before the representatives of the people in all the States of the confederacy. While a feeling prevailed generally that *something* must be done to avert the threatened anarchy, toward which governmental operations were tending, great caution was observed in the delegation of powers and in instruction to those who should be appointed members of the proposed convention. However, in compliance with the recommendation of Congress, delegates were chosen in the several states, for the purpose of revising the Articles of Confederation, and assembled in Philadelphia on the second Monday in May, 1787. All the states were represented except Rhode Island.* Washington who was a delegate from Virginia, was chosen president of the convention. Able statesmen were his associates, and they entered earnestly upon their

* For the names of the Delegates to the constitutional convention, see Appendix.

duties. They had not proceeded far, however, before they perceived that the Articles of Confederation were so radically defective and their powers so inadequate to the wants of the country, that instead of trying to amend the code of the old Confederation, they went diligently at work to form a new Constitution. Edmund Randolph submitted a series of resolutions on the twenty-ninth of May, which embodied the plan of a new Constitution. It was proposed to form a general government consisting of a legislature, executive, and judiciary; and a revenue, army and navy independent of the control of the several states. It was to have power to conduct war, establish peace, make treaties; to have the exclusive privilege of coining money, and the supervision of all national transactions. Upon general principles this plan was highly approved, but in that convention there were many ardent and pure patriots, who looked upon the preservation of State Sovereignty as essential, and regarded this proposed form of government, as a radical infringement upon those rights. They therefore violently opposed it.

Another plan was proposed by Mr. Patterson, a delegate from New Jersey. It enlarged the power of Congress, but left it resources and supplies to be found through the medium of the State governments. This plan had that serious defect of the Articles of Confederation,—a dependence of the general government upon the several states, for its vitality. On the 12th of September, the committee to "revise the Articles," submitted the following resolution to Congress, which was adopted

"*Resolved unanimously,* That the said report, with the resolutions and letters accompanying the same, be transmitted to the several legislatures, in order to be submitted to a convention of delegates chosen in each State by the people thereof, in conformity to the resolves of the convention, made and provided in that case."

22

The following is a certified copy of the Constitution ent to the various states for ratification, together with all its amendments subsequently made, and profusely annotated. It is copied from, and compared with, the Roll in the Department of State.

———

We the people of the United States, in order to form a more perfect union, establish justice, insure domestic tranquillity, provide for the common defence, promote the general welfare, and secure the blessings of liberty to ourselves and our posterity, do ordain and establish this Constitution for the United States of America.

ARTICLE I.

Section 1. All legislative powers herein granted shall be vested in a Congress of the United States, which shall consist of a senate and house of representatives.

Section 2. The house of representatives shall be composed of members chosen every second year by the people of the several states, and the electors in each state shall have the qualifications requisite for electors of the most numerous branch of the state legislature.

No person shall be a representative who shall not have attained to the age of twenty-five years, and been seven years a citizen of the United States, and who shall not, when elected, be an inhabitant of that state in which he shall be chosen.

Representatives and direct taxes shall be apportioned among the several states which may be included within this Union, according to their respective numbers,* which

* The constitutional provision, that direct taxes shall be apportioned among the several States according to their respective numbers, to be ascertained by a census, was not intended to restrict the power of imposing direct taxes to States only.—*Loughborough vs. Blake*, 5, *Wheaton*, 319.

shall be determined by adding to the whole number of free persons, including those bound to service for a term of years, and excluding Indians not taxed, three fifths of all other persons. The actual enumeration shall be made within three years after the first meeting of the Congress of the United States, and within every subsequent term of ten years, in such manner as they shall by law direct. The number of representatives shall not exceed one for every thirty thousand,* but each state shall have at least one representative; and until such enumeration shall be made, the state of New Hampshire shall be entitled to choose three, Massachusetts eight, Rhode Island and Providence Plantations one, Connecticut five, New York six, New Jersey four, Pennsylvania eight, Delaware one, Maryland six, Virginia ten, North Carolina five, South Carolina five, and Georgia three.

When vacancies happen in the representation from any state, the executive authority thereof shall issue writs of election to fill such vacancies.

The house of representatives shall choose their speaker and other officers; and shall have the sole power of impeachment.

SECTION 3. The senate of the United States shall be composed of two senators from each state, chosen by the legislature thereof, for six years; and each senator shall have one vote.†

Immediately after they shall be assembled in consequence of the first election, they shall be divided as equally as may be into three classes. The seats of the senators of the first class shall be vacated at the expiration of the second year, of the second class at the expiration of the fourth year, and of the third class at the ex-

---

* See laws United States, vol. ii., chap. 124; iii., 261; iv., 332. Acts of 17th Congress, 1st session, chap. x.; and of the 22d and 27th Congress.

† See art. v., clause 1.

piration of the sixth year, so that one third may be chosen every second year; and if vacancies happen by resignation or otherwise, during the recess of the legislature of any state, the executive thereof may make temporary appointments until the next meeting of the legislature, which shall then fill such vacancies.

No person shall be a senator who shall not have attained to the age of thirty years, and been nine years a citizen of the United States, and who shall not, when elected, be an inhabitant of that state for which he shall be chosen.

The vice-president of the United States shall be president of the senate, but shall have no vote unless they be equally divided.

The senate shall choose their other officers, and also a president, pro tempore, in the absence of the vice-president, or when he shall exercise the office of president of the United States.

The senate shall have the sole power to try all impeachments; When sitting for that purpose they shall be on oath or affirmation. When the president of the United States is tried, the chief justice shall preside; And no person shall be convicted without the concurrence of two thirds of the members present.

Judgment in cases of impeachment shall not extend further than to removal from office, and disqualification to hold and enjoy any office of honor, trust or profit under the United States; but the party convicted shall nevertheless be liable and subject to indictment, trial, judgment and punishment, according to law.

SECTION 4. The times, places and manner of holding elections for senators and representatives, shall be prescribed in each state by the legislature thereof: but the Congress may at any time, by law, make or alter such regulations, except as to the places of choosing senators

The Congress shall assemble at least once in every year, and such meeting shall be on the first Monday in December, unless they shall by law appoint a different day.

SECTION 5. Each house shall be the judge of the elections, returns and qualifications of its own members, and a majority of each shall constitute a quorum to do business; but a smaller number may adjourn from day to day, and may be authorized to compel the attendance of absent members, in such manner, and under such penalties as each house may provide.

Each house may determine the rules of its proceedings,* punish its members for disorderly behavior, and, with the concurrence of two thirds, expel a member.

Each house shall keep a journal of its proceedings, and from time to time publish the same, excepting such parts as may in their judgment require secrecy; and the yeas and nays of the members of either house on any question shall, at the desire of one fifth of those present, be entered on the journal.

---

* To an action of trespass against the sergeant-at-arms of the house of representatives of the United States for assault and battery and false imprisonment, it is a legal justification and bar to plead that a Congress was held and sitting during the period of the trespasses complained, and that the house of representatives had resolved that the plaintiff had been guilty of a breach of the privileges of the house, and of a high contempt of the dignity and authority of the same; and had ordered that the speaker should issue his warrant to the sergeant-at-arms, commanding him to take the plaintiff into custody wherever to be found, and to have him before the said house to answer to the said charge; and that the speaker did accordingly issue such a warrant, reciting the said resolution and order, and commanding the sergeant-at-arms to take the plaintiff into custody, &c., and deliver the said warrant to the defendant: by virtue of which warrant the defendant arrested the plaintiff; and conveyed him to the bar of the house, where he was heard in his defence touching the matter of said charge, and the examination being adjourned from day to day, and the house having ordered the plaintiff to be detained in custody, he was accordingly detained by the defendant until he was finally adjudged to be guilty and convicted of the charge aforesaid, and ordered to be forthwith brought to the bar and reprimanded by the speaker, and then discharged from custody, and after being thus reprimanded, was actually discharged from the arrest and custody aforesaid.— *Anderson* vs *Dunn, 6 Wheaton,* 204.

Neither house, during the session of Congress shall, without the consent of the other, adjourn for more than three days, nor to any other place than that in which the two houses shall be sitting.

SECTION 6. The senators and representatives shall receive a compensation for their services, to be ascertained by law, and paid out of the treasury of the United States. They shall in all cases, except treason, felony and breach of the peace, be privileged from arrest during their attendance at the session of their respective houses, and in going to and returning from the same; and for any speech or debate in either house, they shall not be questioned in any other place.

No senator or representative shall, during the time for which he was elected, be appointed to any civil office under the authority of the United States, which shall have been created, or the emoluments whereof shall have been increased during such time; and no person holding any office under the United States, shall be a member of either house during his continuance in office.

SECTION 7. All bills for raising revenue shall originate in the house of representatives; but the senate may propose or concur with amendments as on other bills.

Every bill which shall have passed the house of representatives and the senate, shall, before it become a law, be presented to the president of the United States; if he approve he shall sign it, but if not he shall return it, with his objections to that house in which it shall have originated, who shall enter the objections at large on their journal, and proceed to reconsider it. If after such reconsideration two thirds of that house shall agree to pass the bill, it shall be sent, together with the objections, to the other house, by which it shall likewise be reconsidered, and if approved by two thirds of that house, it shall become a law. But in all such cases the votes of both houses shall be determined by yeas and nays, and the names of the persons voting for and against the bill shall be entered on the journal of each house respectively. If any bill shall not be returned by the president within ten days (Sunday excepted) after it shall have been presented to him, the same shall be a law, in like manner as if he had signed it, unless the Congress by their adjournment prevent its return, in which case it shall not be a law.

Every order, resolution, or vote to which the concurrence of the senate and house of representatives may be necessary (except on a question of adjournment) shall be presented to the president of the United States; and before the same shall take effect, shall be approved by him, or being disapproved by him shall be repassed by two thirds of the senate and house of representatives, according to the rules and limitations prescribed in the case of a bill.

SECTION 8. The Congress shall have power to lay and collect taxes,* duties, imposts and excises, to pay the debts and provide for the common defence and general welfare of the United States; but all duties, imposts and excises, shall be uniform throughout the United States;

To borrow money on the credit of the United States;

To regulate commerce with foreign nations, and among the several states, and with the Indian tribes;

To establish a uniform rule of naturalization,† and uniform laws on the subject of bankruptcies‡ throughout the United States;

+ The power of Congress to *lay and collect taxes, duties,* &c., extends to the District of Columbia, and to the territories of the United States, as well as to the states.—*Loughborough,* vs. *Blake, 5 Wheaton,* 318. But Congress are not bound to extend a direct tax to the district and territories. — *Id.,* 318.

† Under the constitution of the United States, the power of naturalization is exclusively in Congress— *Chivac* vs. *Chivac, 2 Wheaton,* 259.

See laws United States, vol. ii., chap. 30; ii., 261; iii., 71; iii., 288; iii., 400; iv., 564; vi., 32.

' Since the and adoption of the constitution of the United States, a state has authority

To coin money, regulate the value thereof, and of foreign coin, and fix the standard of weights and measures;

To provide for the punishment of counterfeiting the securities and current coin of the United States;

To establish post-offices and post-roads,

To promote the progress of science and useful arcs, by securing for limited times to authors and inventors, the exclusive right to their respective writings and discoveries;

To constitute tribunals inferior to the supreme court;

To define and punish piracies and felonies committed on the high seas, and offences against the law of nations;*

To declare war, grant letters of marque and reprisal, and make rules concerning captures on land and water;

To raise and support armies, but no appropriation of money to that use shall be for a longer term than two years;

To provide and maintain a navy;

To make rules for the government and regulation of the land and naval forces;

To provide for calling forth the militia to execute the laws of the Union, suppress insurrections and repel invasions;

to pass a bankrupt law, provided such law does not impair the obligation of con tracts within the meaning of the constitution (art. i., sect. 10), and provided there be no act of Congress in force to establish a uniform system of bankruptcy conflicting with such law.— *Sturgess* vs. *Crowninshield, 4 Wheaton,* 122, 192.

See laws United States, vol. ii., chap. 368, sect. 2; iii., 66; iii., 158.

* The act of the 3d March, 1819, chap. 76, sect. 5, referring to the law of nations for a definition of the crime of piracy, is a constitutional exercise of the power of Congress to define and punish that crime.— *United States* vs. *Smith, 5 Wheaton,* 153, 157.

Congress have power to provide for the punishment of offences committed by persons on board a ship-of-war of the United States, wherever that ship may lie. But Congress have not exercised that power in the case of a ship lying in the waters of the United States, the words within fort, arsenal, dockyard, magazine, or in *any other place or district of country under the sole and exclusive jurisdiction of the United States,* in the third section of the act of 1790, chap. 9, not extending to a ship-of-war, but only to objects in their nature, fixed and territorial.— *United States* vs. *Bevans,* 3 *Whenton,* 890.

To provide for organizing, arming, and disciplining the militia, and for governing such part of them as may be employed in the service of the United States, reserving to the states respectively, the appointment of the officers, and the authority of training the militia according to the discipline prescribed by Congress;*

To exercise exclusive legislation in all-cases whatsoever, over such district (not exceeding ten miles square) as may, by cession of particular states, and the acceptance of Congress, become the seat of the government of the United States,† and to exercise like authority over all places purchased by the consent of the legislature of the state in which the same shall be, for the erection of forts, magazines, arsenals, dockyards, and other needful buildings;—And

To make all laws which shall be necessary and proper for carrying into execution the foregoing powers, and all other powers vested by this constitution in the government of the United States, or in any department or officer thereof.‡

* Vide amendments, art. ii.

† Congress has authority to impose a direct tax on the District of Columbia in proportion to the census directed to be taken by the constitution.— *Loughborough* vs. *Blake*, 5 *Wheaton*, 317.

But Congress are not bound to extend a direct tax to the district and territories.—*Id.*, 322.

The power of Congress to exercise exclusive jurisdiction in all cases whatsoever within the District of Columbia, includes the power of taxing it.—*Id*, 324

‡ Whenever the terms in which a power is granted by the constitution to Congress, or whenever the nature of the power itself requires that it should be *exercised* exclusively by Congress, the subject is as completely taken away from the state legislatures as if they had been expressly forbidden to act on it.—*Sturgess* vs. *Crominshield*, 4 *Wheaton*, 193.

Congress has power to incorporate a bank.—*McCulloch* vs. *State of Maryland*, 4 *Wheaton*, 316.

The power of establishing a corporation is not a distinct sovereign power or *end* of government, but only the means of carrying into effect other powers which are sovereign. Whenever it becomes an appropriate means of exercising any of the powers given by the constitution to the government of the Union, it may be exercised by that government.—*Id.*, 411, 421.

If a certain means to carry into effect any of the powers expressly given by the

SECTION 9. The migration or importation of such persons as any of the states now existing shall think proper to admit, shall not be prohibited by the Congress prior to

constitution to the government of the Union, be an appropriate measure, not prohibited by the constitution. the degree of its necessity is a question of legislative discretion, not of judicial cognizance—*Id,*   421.

The act of the 19th of April, 1816, chap. 44, to incorporate the subscribers to the bank of the United States is a law made in pursuance of the constitution.—*Id.,* 424.

The bank of the United States has constitutionally a right to establish its branches or offices of discount and deposite within any state.—*Id.,* 424.

There is nothing in the constitution of the United States similar to the articles of confederation, which excludes incidental or implied powers .—*Id.,* 403.

If the *end* be legitimate, and within the scope of the constitution, all the *means* which are appropriate, which are plainly adapted to that end, and which are not prohibited, may constitutionally be employed to carry it into effect.—*Id.,421.*

The powers granted to Congress are not exclusive of similar powers existing in the states, unless where the constitution has expressly in terms given an exclusive power to Congress, or the exercise of a like power is prohibited to the states, or there is a direct repugnancy or incompatibility in the exercise of it by the states—*Houston*   vs *Moore,   5 Wheaton*   49.

The example of the first class is to be found in the exclusive legislation delegated to Congress over places purchased by the consent of the legislature of the state in which the same shall be for forts, arsenals, dockyards, &c. Of the second class, the prohibition of a state to coin money or emit bills of credi. Of the third class, the power to establish a uniform rule of naturalization, and the delegation of admiralty and maritime jurisdiction.—*Id.,* 49.

In all other classes of cases the states retain concurrent authority with Congress.— Id.,48.

But in cases of concurrent authority, where the laws of the states and of the Union are in direct and manifest collision on the same subject, those of the Union being the supreme law of the land, are of paramount authority, and the state so far, and so far only as such incompatibility exists, must necessarily yield—*Id.,* 49.

The state within which a branch of the United States bank may be established, can not, without violating the constitution, tax that branch.—*McCulloch*   vs *State of Maryland,* 4 *Wheaton,* 425.

The state governments have no right to tax any of the constitutional means employed by the government of the Union to execute its constitutional powers.— *Id.,* 427.

The states have no power by taxation, or otherwise, to retard, impede, burden, or in any manner control, the operation of the constitutional laws enacted by Congress, to carry into effect the powers vested in the national government.— *Id.,* 436.

This principle does not extend to a tax paid by the real property of the bank of the United States, in common with the other real property in a particular state, nor to a tax imposed on the proprietary which the citizens of that state may hold in common with the other property of the same description throughout the state —*Id.* 436.

the year one thousand eight hundred and eight, but a tax or duty may be imposed on such importation, not exceeding ten dollars for each person.

The privilege of the writ of habeas corpus shall not be suspended, unless when in cases of rebellion or invasion the public safety may require it.

No bill of attainder or ex post facto law shall be passed.

No capitation, or other direct tax shall be laid, unless in proportion to the census or enumeration hereinbefore directed to be taken.

No tax or duty shall be laid on articles exported from any state.

No preference shall be given by any regulation of commerce or revenue to the ports of one state over those of another: nor shall vessels bound to, or from, one state, be obliged to enter, clear, or pay duties in another.

No money shall be drawn from the treasury, but in consequence of appropriations made by law; and a regular statement and account of the receipts and expenditures of all public money shall be published from time to time.

No title of nobility shall be granted by the United States: And no person holding any office of profit or trust under them, shall, without the consent of the Congress, accept of any present, emolument, office, or title, of any kind whatever, from any king, prince, or foreign sate.

SECTION 10. No state shall enter into any treaty, alliance, or confederation; grant letters of marque and reprisal; coin money; emit bills of credit; make anything but gold and silver coin a tender in payment of debts; pass any bill of attainder, ex postfacto law, or law impairing the obligation of contracts,* or grant any title of nobility.

* Where a law is in its nature a *contract,* where absolute rights have vested

No state shall, without the consent of the Congress, lay any imposts or duties on imports or exports, except what may be absolutely necessary for executing its inspection laws: and the net produce of all duties and im posts, laid by any state on imports or exports, shall be for the use of the treasury of the United States; and all such laws shall be subject to the revision and control of the Congress.

No state shall, without the consent of Congress, lay any duty of tonnage, keep troops, or ships-of-war in time of peace, enter into any agreement or compact with another

under that contract, a repeal of the law can not divest those rights.—*Fletcher* vs. *Peck,* 6 *Cranch,* 88.

A party to a contract can not pronounce its own deed invalid, although that party be a *sovereign state.—Id.,* 88.

A *grant* is a *contract executed.—Id.,* 89.

A law annulling conveyance is unconstitutional, because it is a law impairing the obligation of contracts within the meaning of the constitution of the United States. *—Id.*

The court will not declare a law to be unconstitutional, unless the opposition between the constitution and the law be clear and plain.—*Id.,* 87.

An act of the legislature of *a* state, declaring that certain lands which should be purchased for the Indians should not thereafter be subject to any tax, constituted a contract which could not, after the adoption of the constitution of the United States, be rescinded by a subsequent legislative act; such rescinding act being void under the constitution of the United States.—*State of New Jersey* vs. *Wilson,* 7 *Cranch,* 164.

The present constitution of the United States did not commence its operation until the first Wednesday in March, 1789, and the provision in the constitution, that "no state shall make any law impairing the obligation of contracts," does not extend to a state law enacted before that day, and operating upon rights of property vesting before that time.—*Owings* vs. *Speed,* 5 *Wheaton,* 420, 421.

An act of a state legislature, which discharges a debtor from all liability for debts contracted previous to his discharge, on his surrendering his property for the benefit of his creditors, is a law impairing "the obligations of contracts," within the meaning of the constitution of the United States, so far as it attempts to discharge the contract; and it makes no difference in such a case, that the suit was brought in a state court of the state of which both the parties were citizens where the contract was made, and the discharge obtained, and where they continued to reside until the suit was brought.—*Farmers and Mechanics' Bank* vs. *Smith,* 6 *Wheaton,* 131.

The act of New York, passed on the 3d of April, 1811 (which not only liberates the person of the debtor, but discharges him from all liability for any debt contracted previous to his discharge, on his surrendering his property in the manner

state, or with a foreign power, or engage in war, unless actually invaded, or in such imminent danger as will not admit of delay.

ARTICLE II.

Section 1. The executive power shall be vested in a president of the United States of America. He shall hold his office during the term of four years,* and, together with the vice-president, chosen for the same term, be elected, as follows:

Each state shall appoint, in such manner as the legislature thereof may direct,† a number of electors, equal to the whole number of senators and representatives to which the state may be entitled in the Congress: but no senator or representative, or person holding an office of trust or profit under the United States, shall be appointed an elector.

---

it prescribes,) so far as it attempts to discharge the contract, is a law impairing the obligation of contracts within the meaning of the constitution of the United States, and is not a good plea in bar of an action brought upon such contract.— *Sturgess* vs. *Crowinshield,* 4 *Wheaton,* 122, 197.

Statutes of limitation and usury laws, unless retroactive in their effect, do not impair the obligation of contracts, and are constitutional.—*Id.,* 206.

A state bankrupt or insolvent law (which not only liberates the person of the debtor, but discharges him from all liability for the debt,) so far as it attempts to discharge the contract, is repugnant to the constitution of the United States, and it makes no difference in the application of this principle, whether the law was passed *before* or *after* the debt was contracted.—*McMillan* vs. *McNeill,* 4 *Wheaton,* 209.

The charter granted by the British crown to the trustees of Dartmouth college, in New Hampshire, in the year 1769, is a contract within the meaning of that clause of the constitution of the United States (art. i., sect. 10) which declares, that no state shall make any law impairing the obligation of contracts. The charter was not dissolved by the revolution.—*College* vs. *Woodard,* 4 *Wheaton,* 518

An act of the state legislature of New Hampshire, altering the charter of Dart. mouth College in a material respect, without the consent of the corporation, is an act impairing the obligation of the charter, and is unconstitutional and void.– *Id.,* 518.

* See laws United States, vol. ii., chap. 109, sect. 12.

† See laws United States, vol. ii., chap. 109.

[*The electors shall meet in their respective states, and vote by ballot for two persons, of whom one at least shall not be an inhabitant of the same state with themselves. And they shall make a list of all the persons voted for, and of the number of votes for each; which list they shall sign and certify, and transmit sealed to the the seat of the government of the United States, directed to the president of the senate. The president of the senate shall in the presence of the senate and house of representatives, open all the certificates, and the votes shall then be counted. The person having the greatest number of votes shall be the president, if such number be a majority of the whole number of electors appointed; and if there be more than one who have such majority, and have an equal number of votes, then the house of representatives shall immediately choose by ballot one of them for president; and if no person have a majority, then from the five highest on the list the said house shall in like manner choose the president. But in choosing the president, the votes shall be taken by states, the representation from each state having one vote; a quorum for this purpose shall consist of a member or members from two thirds of the states, and a majority of all the states shall be necessary to a choice. In every case, after the choice of the president, the person having the greatest number of votes of the electors shall be the vice-president. But if there should remain two or more who have equal votes, the senate shall choose from them by ballot the vice-president.†]

The Congress may determine the time of choosing the electors,‡ and the day on which they shall give their votes; which day shall be the same throughout the United States.§

No person except a natural born citizen, or a citizen of the United States, at the time of the adoption of this constitution, shall be eligible to the office of president

* Vide amendments, art. xii.
† This clause is annulled. See amendments, art. xii.
‡ See laws United Ststes, vol. ii., chap. 104, sect. 1; also law 28th Congress.
§ See laws United States, vol. ii., chap. 109, sect. 2.

neither shall any person be eligible to that office who shall not have attained to the age of thirty-five years, and been fourteen years a resident within the United States.

In case of the removal of the president from office, or of his death, resignation,* or inability to discharge the powers and duties of the said office, the same shall devolve on the vice-president, and the Congress may by law provide for the case of removal, death, resignation or inability, both of the president and vice-president, declaring what officer shall then act as president, and such officer shall act accordingly, until the disability be removed, or a president shall be elected.†

The president shall, at stated times, receive for his services, a compensation, which shall neither be increased nor diminished during the period for which he shall have been elected, and he shall not receive within that period any other emolument from the United States, or any of them.

Before he enter on the execution of his office, he shall take the following oath or affirmation:—"I do solemnly swear (or affirm) that I will faithfully execute the office of president of the United States, and will, to the best of my ability, preserve, protect and defend the constitution of the United States."

SECTION 2. The president shall be commander-in-chief of the army and navy of the United States, and of the militia of the several states, when called into the actual service of the United States;‡ he may require the opinion, in wri-

---

* See laws United States, vol. ii., chap. 104, sect. 11.

† See laws United States, vol. ii., chap. 109, sect. 9; and vol iii. chap. 403.

‡ The act of the state of Pennsylvania, of the 28th March, 1814 (providing, sect. 21, that the officers and privates of the militia of that state neglecting or refusing to serve when called into actual service, in pursuance of any order or requisition of the president of the United States, shall be liable to the penalties defined in the act of Congress of 28th February, 1795, chap. 277, or to any penalty which may have been prescribed since the date of that act, or which may hereafter be prescribed by any law of the United States, and also providing for the

ting, of the principal officer in each of the executive departments, upon any subject relating to the duties of their respective offices, and he shall have power to grant reprieves and pardons for offences against the United States, except in cases of impeachment.

He shall have power, by and with the advice and consent of the senate, to make treaties, provided two thirds of the senators present concur; and he shall nominate, and by and with the advice and consent of the senate, shall appoint ambassadors, other public ministers and consuls, judges of the supreme court, and all other officers of the United States, whose appointments are not herein otherwise provided for, and which shall be established by law; but the Congress may by law vest the appointment of such inferior officers, as they think proper, in the president alone, in the courts of law, or in the heads of departments.

The president shall have power to fill up all vacancies that may happen during the recess of the senate, by granting commissions which shall expire at the end of their next session.

SECTION 3. He shall from time to time give to the Congress information of the state of the Union, and recommend to their consideration such measures as he shall judge necessary and expedient; he may, on extraordinary occasions, convene both houses, or either of them, and in case of disagreement between them, with respect to the time of adjournment, he may adjourn them to such time as he shall think proper; he shall receive ambassadors and other public ministers; he shall take care that

---

trial of such delinquents by a state court-martial, and that a list of the delinquents fined by such court should be furnished to the marshal of the United States, &c.; and also to the comptroller of the treasury of the United States, in order that the further proceedings directed to be had thereon by the laws of the United States might be completed), is not repugnant to the constitution and laws of the United States.—*Houston,* vs. *Moore,* 5 *Wheaton.* 1, 12.

the laws be faithfully executed, and shall commission all the officers of the United States.

SECTION 4. The president, vice-president, and all civil officers of the United States, shall be removed from office on impeachment for, and conviction of, treason, bribery, or other high crimes and misdemeanors.

ARTICLE III.

SECTION 1. The judicial power of the United States, shall be vested in one supreme court, and in such inferior courts as the Congress may from time to time ordain and establish.* The judges, both of the supreme and inferior courts, shall hold their offices during good behavior, and shall, at stated times, receive for their services, a compensation, which shall not be diminished during their continuance in office.†

SECTION 2. The judicial power shall extend to all cases in law and equity, arising under this constitution, the laws of the United States, and treaties made, or which shall be made, under their authority;—to all cases affecting ambassadors, other public ministers and consuls;—to all cases of admiralty and maritime jurisdictions;—to controversies to which the United States shall be a party;—to controversies between two or more states;—between a state and citizens of another state;—between citizens of different states,‡—between citizens of the same state claiming lands under grants of different states, and be tween a state, or the citizens thereof, and foreign states, citizens or subjects.§

---

* Congress may constitutionally impose upon the judges of the supreme court of the United States the burden of holding circuit courts.—*Stuart* vs. *Laird* 1 *Cranch,* 299.

† See laws of the United States, vol. ii., chap. 20.

‡ A citizen of the District of Columbia is not a citizen of a state within the meaning of the constitution of the United States.—*Hepburn et al* vs. *Ellzin* 2 *Cranch,* 445.

§ The supreme court of the United States has not power to issue a *mandam*

23

In all cases affecting ambassadors, other public ministers and consuls, and those in which a state shall be party, the supreme court shall have original jurisdiction. In all the other cases before mentioned, the supreme court shall have appellate jurisdiction, both as to law and fact, with such exceptions, and under such regulations as the Congress shall make.*

to a *secretary of state* of the United States, it being an exercise of original jurisdiction not warranted by the constitution, notwithstanding the act of Congress.— *Marbury,* vs. *Madison,* 1 *Cranch,* 137.

See a restriction of this provision.—Amendments; art. xi.

*The appellate jurisdiction of the supreme court of the United States extends to a final judgment or decree in any suit in the highest court of law, or equity or a state. where is drawn in question the validity of a treaty, &c.—*Martin* vs. *Hunter's lessee,* 1 *Wheaton,* 304.

Such judgment, &c., may be re-examined by writ of error, in the same manner as if rendered in a circuit court.—*Id.*

If, the cause has been once remanded before, and the state court decline or refuse to carry into effect the mandate of the supreme court thereon, this court will proceed to a final decision of the same, and award execution thereon.

Quere.—Whether this court has authority to issue a mandamus to the state court to enforce a former judgment?—*Id.,* 362.

If the validity or construction of a treaty of the United States is drawn in question, and the decision is against its validity, or the title specially set up by either party under the treaty, this court has jurisdiction to ascertain that title, and determine its legal validity, and is not confined to the abstract construction of the treaty itself.—*Id.,* 362.

Quere.—Whether the courts of the United States have jurisdiction of offences at common law against the United States?—*United States* vs. *Coolidge,* 1 *Wheaton,* 415.

The courts of the United States have exclusive jurisdiction of all seizures made on land or water for a breach of the laws of the United States, and any intervention of a state authority, which by taking the thing seized out of the hands of the United States' officer, might obstruct the exercise of this jurisdiction, is illegal.—*Slocum* vs. *Mayberry et al,* 2 *Wheaton,* 1,9.

In such a case the court of the United States have cognizance of the seizure, may enforce a re-delivery of the thing by attachment or other summary process.— *Id.,* 9.

The question under such a seizure, whether a forfeiture has been actually incurred, belongs exclusively to the courts of the United States, and it depends upon the final decree of such courts, whether the seizure is to be deemed rightful or tortuous.—*Id.,* 9, 10.

If the seizing officer refuse to institute proceedings to ascertain the forfeiture, the district court may, on application of the aggrieved party, compel the officer to proceed to adjudication, or to abandon the seizure.—*Id.,* 10.

The jurisdiction of the circuit court of the United States extends to a case

The trial of all crimes, except in cases of impeachment, shall be by jury; and such trial shall be held in the state where the said crimes shall have been committed; but

between citizens of Kentucky, claiming lands exceeding the value of five hundred dollars, under different grants, the one issued by the state of Kentucky and the other by the state of Virginia, upon warrants issued by Virginia, and locations founded thereon, prior to the separation of Kentucky from Virginia. It is the grant which passes the *legal* title to the land, and if the controversy is founded upon the conflicting grants of different states, the judicial power of the courts of the United States extends to the case, whatever may have been the equitable title of the parties prior to the grant.—*Colson et al* vs. *Lewis,* 2 *Wheaton,* 377.

Under the judiciary of 1789, chap. 20, sect. 25, giving appellate juridiction to the supreme court of the United States, from the final judgment or decree of the highest court of law or equity of a state, in certain cases the writ of error may be directed to any court in which the record and judgment on which it is to act may be found; and if the record has been remitted by the highest court, &c., to another court of the state, it may be brought by the writ of error from that court.—*Gelston* vs. *Hoyt,* 3 *Wheaton,* 246, 303.

The remedies in the courts of the United Sates at common law and in equity are to be, not according to the practice of state courts, but according to the principles of common law and equity as defined in England. This doctrine reconciled with the decisions of the courts of Tennessee, permitting an equitable title to be asserted in an action at law.—*Robinson* vs. *Campbell,* 3 *Wheaton,* 221.

Remedies in respect to real property, are to be pursued according to the *lex loci rei sitae.—Id.,* 2,9.

The courts of the United States have *exclusive* cognizance of questions of forfeitures upon all seizures made under the laws of the United States, and it is not competent for a state court to entertain or decide such question of forfeiture. If a sentence of condemnation be definitively pronounced by the proper court of the United States, it is conclusive that a forfeiture is incurred; if a sentence of acquittal, it is equally conclusive against the forfeiture, and in either case the question cannot be again litigated in any common law for ever.—*Gelston* vs. *Hoyt,* 3 *Wheaton,* 246, 311.

Where a seizure is made for a supposed forfeiture under a law of the United States, no action of trespass lies in any common-law tribunal, until a final decree is pronounced upon the proceeding *in rem* to enforce such forfeiture: for it depends upon the final decree of the court proceeding *in rem,* whether such seizure is to be deemed rightful or tortuous, and the action, if brought before such decree is made, is brought too soon.—*Id.,* 313.

If a suit be brought against the seizing officer for the supposed trespass while the suit for the forfeiture is depending, the fact of such pending may be pleaded in abatement, or as a temporary bar of the action. If after a decree of condemnation, then that fact may be pleaded as a bar: if after an acquittal with a certificate of reasonable cause of seizure, then that may be pleaded as a bar. If after an acquittal without such certificate, then the officer is without any justification for the seizure, and it is definitively settled to be a tortuous act. If to an action of trespass in a state court for a seizure, the seizing officer plead the fact of for

when not committed within any state, the trial shall be at such place or places as the Congress may by law have directed.*

feiture in his defence without averring a *lis pendens,* or a condemnation, or an acquittal, with a certificate of reasonable cause of seizure, the plea is bad: for it attempts to put in this issue the question of forfeiture in a state court.—*Id.,* 314.

Supposing that the third article of the constitution of the United States which declares, that "the judicial power shall extend to all cases of admiralty and maritime jurisdiction" vested in the United States exclusive jurisdiction of all such cases, and that a murder committed in the waters of a state where the tide ebbs and flows, is a case of admiralty and maritime jurisdiction; yet Congress have not, in the 8th section of the act of 1790, chap. 9, "for the punishment of certain crimes against the United States," so exercised this power, as to confer on the courts of the United States jurisdiction over such murder.—*United States* vs. *Bevans,* 3 *Wheaton,* 336, 387.

Quere.—Whether courts of common law have concurrent jurisdiction with the admiralty over murder committed in bays, &c., which are enclose parts of the sea?—*Id.,* 387.

The grant to the United States in the constitution of all cases of admiralty and maritime jurisdiction, does not extend to a cession of the waters in which those cases may arise, or of general jurisdiction over the same. Congress may pass all laws which are necessary for giving the most complete effect to the exercise of the admiralty and maritime jurisdiction granted to the government of the Union; but the general jurisdiction over the place subject to this grant, adheres to the territory as a portion of territory not yet given away, and the residuary powers of legislation still remain in the state.—*Id.,* 389.

The supreme court of the United States has constitutionally appellate jurisdiction under the judiciary act of 1789, chap. 20, sect. 25, from the final judgment or decree of the highest court of law or equity of a state having jurisdiction of the subject matter of the suit, where is drawn in question the validity of a treaty or statute of, or an authority exercised under, the United States and the decision is against their validity: or where is drawn in question the validity of a statute of, or an authority exercised under any state, on the ground of their being repugnant to the constitution, treaties, or laws of the United States, and the decision is in favor of such their validity: or of the constitution or of a treaty, or statute of, or commission held under the United States, and the decision is against the title, right, privilege, or exemption, specially set up or claimed by either party under such clause of the constitution, treaty statute, or commission.—*Cohens* vs. *Virginia,* 6 *Wheaton,* 264, 375.

It is no objection to the exercise of this appellate jurisdiction, that one of the parties is a state, and the other a citizen of that state.—*Id.*

The circuit courts of the Union have chancery jurisdiction in every state; they have the same chancery powers, and the same rules of decision in equity cases, in all the states.—*United States* vs. *Howland,* 4 *Wheaton,* 108, 115.

Resolutions of the legislature of Virginia of 1810, upon the proposition from Pennsylvania to amend the constitution, so as to provide an impartial tribunal to

* See amendments, art. vi.

SECTION 3. Treason against the United States, shall consist only in levying war against them, or in adhering to their enemies, giving them aid and comfort.

No person shall be convicted of treason unless on the testimony of two witnesses to the same overt act, or on confession in open court.

The Congress shall have power to declare the punishment of treason, but no attainder of treason shall work

decide disputes between the State and federal judiciaries.—*Note to Cohens* vs. *Virginia. Note* 6 *Wheaton,* 358.

Where a cause is brought to this court by writ of error, or appeal from the highest court of law, or equity of a state, under the 25th section of the judiciary act of 1789, chap. 20, upon the ground that the validity of a statute of the United States was drawn in question, and that the decision of the state court was against its validity, &c., or that the validity of the statute of a state was drawn in question as repugnant to the constitution of the United States, and the decision was in favor of Its validity, it must appear from the record, that the act of Congress, or the constitutionality of the state law, was drawn in question.—*Miller* vs. *Nicholls,* 4 *Wheaton,* 311, 315.

But it is not required that the record should in terms state a misconstruction of the act of Congress, or that it was drawn into question. It is sufficient to give this court jurisdiction of the cause, that the record should show that an act of Congress was applicable to the case.—*Id.,* 315.

The supreme court of the United States has no jurisdiction under the 25th section of the judiciary act of 1789, chap. 20, unless the judgment or decree of the state court be a final judgment or decree. A judgment reversing that of an inferior court, and awarding a *venire facias de novo,* is not a final judgment.—*Houston* vs. *Moore,* 3 *Wheaton,* 433.

By the compact of 1802, settling the boundary line between Virginia and Tennessee, and the laws made in pursuance thereof, it is declared that all claims and titles to land derived from Virginia, or North Carolina, or Tennessee, which have fallen into the respective states, shall remain as secure to the owners thereof, as if derived from the government within whose boundary they have fallen, and shall not be prejudiced or affected by the establishment of the line. Where the titles of both the plaintiff and defendant in ejectment were derived under grant from Virginia to lands which fell within the limits of Tennessee, it was held that a prior settlement right thereto, which would in *equity* give the party a title, could not be asserted as a sufficient title in an action of ejectment brought in the circuit court of Tennessee.—*Robinson* vs. *Campbell,* 3 *Wheaton,* 212.

Although the state courts of Tennessee have decided that, under their statutes (declaring an elder grant founded on a junior entry to be void), a junior patent, founded on a prior entry, shall prevail *at law* against a senior patent founded on a junior entry, this doctrine has never been extended beyond cases within the express provision of the statute of Tennessee, and could not apply to titles deriving all their validity from the laws of Virginia, and confirmed by the compact between the two states.—*Id.* 212

corruption of blood, or forfeiture except during the life of the person attainted.*

ARTICLE IV.

SECTION 1. Full faith and credit shall be given in each state to the public acts, records, and judicial proceedings of every other state.† And the Congress may by general laws prescribe the manner in which such acts, records and proceedings shall be proved, and the effect thereof.‡

SECTION 2. The citizens of each state shall be entitled to all privileges and immunities of citizens in the several states.

A person charged in any state with treason, felony, or other crime, who shall flee from justice, and be found in another state, shall on demand of the executive authority of the state from which he fled, be delivered up, to be removed to the state having jurisdiction of the crime.

No person held to service or labor in one state, under the laws thereof, escaping into another, shall, in consequence of any law or regulation therein, be discharged from such service or labor, but shall be delivered up on claim of the party to whom such service or labor may be due.

SECTION 3. New states may be admitted by the Congress into this Union; but no new state shall be formed or erected within the jurisdiction of any other state; nor any state be formed by the junction of two or more states.

---

* See laws of the United States, vol. ii., chap. 36.

† A judgment of a state court has the same credit, validity, and effect, in every other court within the United States, which it had in the court where it was rendered; and whatever pleas would be good to a suit thereon in such state, and none others can be pleaded in any other court within the United States.—*Hampton* vs. *McConnell,* 3 *Wheaton,* 234.

The record of a judgment in one state is conclusive evidence in another, although it appears that the suit in which it was rendered, was commenced by an attachment of property, the defendant having afterward appeared and taken defence.—*Mayhew* vs. *Thacher,* 6 *Wheaton,* 129.

‡ see laws United States, vol. ii., chap, 38; and vol, iii., chap. 409.

or parts of states, without the consent of the legislatures of the states concerned as well as of the Congress.

The Congress shall have power to dispose of and make all needful rules and regulations respecting the territory or other property belonging to the United States; and nothing in this constitution shall be so construed as to prejudice any claims of the United States, or of any particular state.

SECTION 4. The United States shall guaranty to every state in this Union a republican form of government, and shall protect each of them against invasion; and on application of the legislature, or of the executive (when the legislature can not be convened) against domestic violence.

ARTICLE V.

The Congress, whenever two thirds of both houses shall deem it necessary, shall propose amendments to this constitution, or, on the application of the legislatures of two thirds of the several states, shall call a convention for proposing amendments, which, in either case, shall be valid to all intents and purposes, as part of this constitution, when ratified by the legislatures of three fourths of the several states, or by conventions in three fourths thereof, as the one or the other mode of ratification may be proposed by the Congress; provided that no amendment which may be made prior to the year one thousnnd eight hundred and eight shall in any manner affect the first and fourth clauses in the ninth section of the first article; and that no state, without its consent, shall be deprived of its equal suffrage in the senate.*

ARTICLE VI.

All debts contracted and engagements entered into, before the adoption of this constitution, shall be as valid

* See ante art. i., sect. 3, clause 1.

against the United States under this constitution, as under the confederation.

This constitution, and the laws of the United States which shall be made in pursuance thereof; and all treaties made, or which shall be made, under the authority of the United States, shall be the supreme law of the land;* and the judges in every state shall be bound thereby, anything in the constitution or laws of any state to the contrary notwithstanding.†

The senators and representatives before mentioned, and the members of the several state legislatures, and all executive and judicial officers, both of the United States and of the several states, shall be bound by oath or affirmation, to support this constitution;‡ but no religious test shall ever be required as a qualification to any office or public trust under the United States.

ARTICLE VII.

The ratification of the conventions of nine states, shall be sufficient for the establishment of this constitution between the states so ratifying the same.

Done in convention by the unanimous consent of the states present, the seventeenth day of September, in the year of our Lord one thousand seven hundred and eighty-seven and of the independence of the United

---

* An act of Congress repugnant to the constitution can not become a law.— *Marbury* vs. *Madison,* 1 *Cranch,* 176.

† The courts of the United States are bound to take notice of the constitution.— *Marbury* vs. *Madison,* 1 *Cranch,* 178.

A contemporary exposition of the constitution, practised and acquiesced under for a period of years, fixes its construction.—*Stuart* vs. *Laird,* 1 *Cranch,* 299.

The government of the Union, though limited in its powers, is supreme within its sphere of action, and its laws, when made in pursuance of the constitution, form the supreme law of the land.—*McCulloch* vs. *State of Maryland,* 4 *Wheaton.* 405.

‡ See laws of the United States, vol. ii., chap. 1.

States of America the twelfth. In witness whereof we
have hereunto subscribed our names.

Go. WASHINGTON,

President, and deputy from Virginia.

New Hampshire.

JOHN LANGDON,

NICHOLAS GILMAN.

Massachusetts.

NATHANIEL GORHAM.

RUFUS KING.

Connecticut.

WILLIAM SAMUEL JOHNSON,

ROGER SHERMAN.

New York.

ALEXANDER HAMILTON.

New Jersey.

WILLIAM LIVINGSTON,

DAVID BREARLEY,

WILLIAM PATERSON,

JONATHAN DAYTON.

Pennsylvania.

BENJAMIN FRANKLIN,

THOMAS MIFFLIN,

ROBERT MORRIS,

GEORGE CLYMER,

THOMAS FITZSIMONS,

JARED INGERSOLL,

JAMES WILSON,

GOUVERNEUR MORRIS.

Attest:

Delaware.

GEORGE REED,

GUNNING BEDFORD, JR.,

JOHN DICKINSON,

RICHARD BASSETT,

JACOB BROOM.

Maryland.

JAMES M'HENRY,

DANIEL OF ST. THO. JENIFER,

DANIEL CARROLL.

Virginia.

JOHN BLAIR,

JAMES MADISON, JR.

North Carolina.

WILLIAM BLOUNT,

RICHARD DOBBS SPAIGHT,

HUGH WILLIAMSON.

South Carolina.

JOHN RUTLEDGE,

CHARLES C. PINCKNEY,

CHARLES PINCKNEY,

PIERCE BUTLER.

Georgia.

WILLIAM FEW,

ABRAHAM BALDWIN.

WILLIAM JACKSON, *Secretary.*

AMENDMENTS*

To the Constitution of the United States, ratified according to the Provisions of the fifth Article of the foregoing Constitution.

Article the first. Congress shall make no law respecting an establishment of religion, or prohibiting the free exercise thereof; or abridging the freedom of speech, or of the press; or the right of the people peaceably to assemble, and to petition the government for a redress of grievances.

Article the second. A well regulated militia being necessary to the security of a free state, the right of the people to keep and bear arms, shall not be infringed.

Article the third. No soldier shall, in time of peace, be quartered in any house, without the consent of the owner; nor in a time of war, but in a manner to be prescribed by law.

Article the fourth. The right of the people to be secure in their persons, houses, papers, and effects, against unreasonable searches and seizures, shall not be violated, and no warrants shall issue, but upon probable cause, supported by oath or affirmation, and particularly describing the place to be searched, and the persons or things to be seized.

Article the fifth. No person shall be held to answer for a capital, or otherwise infamous crime, unless on a presentment or indictment of a grand jury, except in cases arising in the land or naval forces, or in the militia, when in actual service in time of war or public danger; nor shall any person be subject for the same offence to be twice

---

* Congress, at its first session, begun and held in the city of New York, on Wednesday, the 4th of March, 1789, proposed to the legislatures of the several states twelve amendments to the constitution, ten of which, only, were adopted.

put in jeopardy of life or limb; nor shall be compelled in any criminal case to be a witness against himself, nor be deprived of life, liberty or property, without due process of law; nor shall private property be taken for public use, without just compensation.

Article the sixth. In all criminal prosecutions, the accused shall enjoy the right to a speedy and public trial, by an impartial jury of the state and district wherein the crime shall have been committed, which district shall have been previously ascertained by law, and to be informed of the nature and cause of the accusation; to be confronted with the witnesses against him; to have compulsory process for obtaining witnesses in his favor, and to have the assistance of counsel for his defence.

Article the seventh. In suits at common law, where the value in controversy shall exceed twenty dollars, the right of trial by jury shall be preserved, and no fact tried by a jury, shall be otherwise re-examined in any court of the United States, than according to the rules of the common law.*

Article the eighth. Excessive bail shall not be required, nor excessive fines imposed, nor cruel and unusual punishments inflicted.

Article the ninth. The enumeration in the constitution of certain rights, shall not be construed to deny or disparage others retained by the people.

Article the tenth. The powers not delegated to the United States, by the constitution, nor prohibited by it to the

* The act of assembly of Maryland, of 1793, chap. 30, incorporating the bank of Columbia, and giving to the corporation a summary process by execution in the nature of an attachment against its debtors who have, by an express consent in writing, made the bonds, bills, or notes, by them drawn and endorsed, negotiable at the bank, is not repugnant to the constitution of the United States or of Maryland.—*Bank of Columbia* vs. *Okely,* 4 *Wheaton,* 246, 249.

But the last provision in the act of incorporation, which gives this summary process to the bank, is no part of its corporate franchise, and may be repealed or altered at pleasure by the legislative will.—*Id.,* 245.

states, are reserved to the states respectively, or to the people.*

Article the eleventh.† The judicial power of the United States shall not be construed to extend to any suit in law or equity, commenced or prosecuted against one of the United States by citizens of another state, or by citizens or subjects of any foreign state.

Article the twelfth.‡ The electors shall meet in their respective states, and vote by ballot for president and vice-president, one of whom, at least, shall not be an inhabitant of the same state with themselves; they shall name

* The powers granted to Congress are not exclusive of similar powers existing in the states, unless where the constitution has expressly in terms given an exclusive power to Congress, or the exercise of a like power is prohibited to the states, or there is a direct repugnancy or incompatibility in the exercise of it by the states.—*Houston* vs. *Moore*, 5 *Wheaton*, 1, 12.

The example of the first class is to be found in the exclusive legislation delegated to Congress over places purchased by the consent of the legislature of the state in which the same shall be for forts, arsenals, dock-yards, &c. Of the second class, the prohibition of a state to coin money or emit bills of credit. Of the third class, the power to establish a uniform rule of naturalization, and the delegation of admiralty and maritime jurisdiction.—*Id.,* 49.

In all other classes of cases, the states retain concurrent authority with Congress.—*Id.,* 49.

But in cases of concurrent authority, where the laws of the states and the Union are in direct and manifest collision on the same subject, those of the Union being the supreme law of the land are of paramount authority, and the state laws so far, and so far only as such incompatibility exists, must necessarily yield.—*Id.,* 49.

There is nothing in the constitution of the United States similar to the articles of confederation, which excludes incidental or implied powers.—*McCulloch* vs. *State of Maryland,* 4 *Wheaton,* 406.

If the end be legitimate, and within the scope of the constitution, all the *means* which are appropriate, which are plainly adapted to that end, and which are not prohibited, may constitutionally be employed to carry it into effect.—*Id.,* 421.

The act of Congress of 4th May, 1812, entitled, "An act further to amend the charter of the city of Washington," which provides (sect. 6) that the corporation of the city shall be empowered for certain purposes and under certain restrictions, to authorize the drawing of lotteries does not extend to authorize the corporation to force the sale of the tickets in such lottery in states where such sale may be prohibited by the state laws.—*Cohens* vs. *Virginia,* 6 *Wheaton,* 264, 375.

† This amendment was proposed at the first session of the third Congress, See ante art, iii., sect. 2, clause 1.

‡ Proposed at the first session of the eighth Congress. See ante art, sect. 1, clause 3. Annulled by this amendment.

in their ballots the person voted for as president, and in distinct ballots the person voted for as vice-president, and they shall make distinct lists of all persons voted for as president, and of all persons voted for as vice-president, and of the number of votes for each, which lists they shall sign and certify, and transmit sealed to the seat of the government of the United States, directed to the president of the senate;*—the president of the senate shall, in the presence of the senate and house of representatives, open all the certificates, and the votes shall then be counted;— the person having the greatest number of votes for president, shall be the president, if such number be a majority of the whole number of electors appointed; and if no person have such majority, then from the persons having the highest numbers not exceeding three on the list of those voted for as president, the house of representatives shall choose immediately, by ballot, the president. But in choosing the president, the votes shall be taken by states, the representation from each state having one vote; a quorum for this purpose shall consist of a member or members from two thirds of the states, and a majority of all the states shall be necessary to a choice. And if the house of representatives shall not choose a president whenever the right of choice shall devolve upon them, before the fourth day of March next following, then the vice president shall act as president, as in the case of the death or other constitutional disability of the president. The persons having the greatest number of votes as vice-president, shall be the vice-president, if such number be a majority of the whole number of electors appointed, and if no person have a majority, then from the two highest numbers on the list, the senate shall choose the vice-president; a quorum for the purpose shall consist of two thirds of the whole number of senators, and a majority of the

* See laws of the United States, vol. ii., chap. 109, sect. 5.

whole number shall be necessary to a choice. But no person constitutionally ineligible to the office of president shall be eligible to that of vice-president of the United States.

NOTE.—Another amendment was proposed as article xiii., at the second session of the eleventh Congress, but not having been ratified by a sufficient number of states, has not yet become valid as a part of the constitution of the United States. It is erroneously given as a part of the constitution, in page 74, vol, i., laws of the United States.

I have examined and compared the foregoing print of the constitution of the United States, and the amendments thereto, with the rolls in this office, and find it a faithful and literal copy of the said constitution and amendments, in the text and punctuation thereof. It appears that the first ten amendments, which were proposed at the first session of the first Congress of the United States, were finally ratified by the constitutional number of states, on the 15th day of December, 1791; that the eleventh amendment, which was proposed at the first session of the third Congress, was declared, in a message from the president of the United States to both houses of Congress, dated 8th January, 1798, to have been adopted by three fourths, the constitutional number of states; and that the twelfth amendment, which was proposed at the first session of the eighth Congress, was adopted by three fourths, the constitutional number of states, in the year one thousand eight hundred and four, according to a public notice thereof, by the secretary of state, under date the 25th of September, of the same year.

DANIEL BRENT, *Chief Clerk.*

Department of State, Washington, 25th Feb., 1828.

As soon as the Constitution was presented to Congress, that body adopted a resolution, by which it was recommended to the several states, to call conventions within their respective jurisdictions to consider it, and adopt or reject it. It was agreed that when nine of the thirteen states should ratify it, it should become the fundamental law of the land.

In every state in the Union, there was a strong party opposed to the constitution, and frequently the leaders in the opposition were men whose patriotism was beyond reproach. Among these was Patrick Henry, of Virginia, who opposed its ratification by the Assembly of his state, with all his gigantic powers. The annulling, to a great extent, of State Rights, and basing the sovereignty too absolutely upon the popular will, were the chief objections to the instrument; for the experience of all former ages had shown, that of all human governments, demo cracy was the most unstable, fluctuating, and short-lived. Despotism, arising from a centralization of power in the general government, on one hand, and anarchy incident to the instability of democracy, on the other, were the Scylla and Charybdis, between which the republic would, in the opinion of these opponents, be placed, with almost a certainty of destruction. Long and stormy sessions were therefore had in the several state conventions, and in most of them, the majorities in favor of the constitution were small.* It was not until the twenty first of June, 1788, that New Hampshire, the ninth state, ratified it, and it became the law of the land. Rhode Island did not give its sanction until the twenty ninth of May, 1790.

The friends of the new Constitution greatly rejoiced when its ratification was secured by a majority of the states; and it was gratifying to see many of the patriotic leaders of the opposition, submit cheerfully to the will of the majority, and lend their aid in carrying its provisions into operation. Steps were immediately taken to organize the government under it, the most important of which was, the election of a Chief Magistrate. The friends of the new constitution turned their eyes upon Washington; —indeed his name seemed first to occur to the mind

---

* A periodical, devoted to the advocacy of the principles and doctrines of the constitution, was started, under the auspices of Hamilton, Madison and others. It was called *"The Federalist."* and was filled with essays, arguing in favor of the proposed change in the government. Those opposed to the constitution styled themselves *"Anti-Federalists,"* and this was the origin of those party names, one of which is familiar to the ear even in our day. Washington belonged to the Federal party, and, although he saw many defects in the constitution, yet it was so much better than all that preceded it, that he gave it his hearty support. It was during his administration, that the *"Republican"* party came into being, with Mr Jefferson at its head.

of the whole nation. The first Presidential Electors were chosen in February, 1789, and on the first Wednesday of March, the Electoral College met to vote for Chief Magistrate. Washington received the unanimous vote of the electors, and John Adams was chosen Vice-President.

But one act more remained to complete the glorious work begun in 1776, by declaring the colonies "free and independent states." That act was the inauguration of the first President of the Republic, now placed upon a stable basis. It took place in the city of New York, on the thirtieth day of April, 1789. As soon as Washington was apprized of his election, he proceeded to the seat of the general government, at New York. His journey was one triumphant procession, grander far, because of its noble moral aspect, than any that ever attended the return to the capital of the proudest of Rome's many victors. No sorrowing captives; no spoils of palaces and temples; no gorgeous display of banners and spears, and all the dreadful pomp of barbarous War, attended the Hero's march; but through busy towns and smiling fields his pathway to highest exaltation was laid out, and the shouts of a grateful people, mingled with the songs of children and the sweet hosannas of women, greeted him at every step.

At nine o'clock on the morning of his inauguration, Washington attended divine service, a fit preparation for the solemn scene in which he was about to engage. He then proceeded to the old Federal Hall, and upon the balcony, in the presence of assembled thousands, Chancellor Livingston administered to him the oath of office, and proclaimed him the President of the United States. The Revolution was complete, the divine truth of Man's Equality was vindicated, and our Republic—the pride and glory of the earth, started upon its wondrous career.

In the language of that lamented statesman and sage John Quincy Adams, we say to our countrymen,—

"And now the future is all before us, and Providence our guide.

"When the children of Israel, after forty years of wanderings in the wilderness, were about to enter upon the promised land, their leader, Moses, who was not permitted to cross the Jordan with them, just before his removal from among them, commanded that when the Lord their God should have brought them into the land, they should put the curse upon Mount Ebal, and the blessing upon Mount Gerizim. This injunction was faithfully fulfilled by his successor Joshua. Immediately after they had taken possession of the land, Joshua built an altar to the Lord, of whole stones, upon Mount Ebal. And there he wrote upon the stones a copy of the law of Moses, which he had written in the presence of the children of Israel: and all Israel, and their elders and officers, and their judges, stood on the two sides of the ark of the covenant, borne by the priests and Levites, six tribes over against Mount Gerizim, and six over against Mount Ebal. And he read all the words of the law, the blessings and cursings, according to all that was written in the book of the law.

"Fellow-citizens, the ark of *your* covenant is the Declaration of Independence. Your Mount Ebal, is the confederacy of separate state sovereignties, and your Mount Gerizim is the Constitution of the United States. In that scene of tremendous and awful solemnity, narrated in the Holy Scriptures, there is not a curse pronounced against the people, upon Mount Ebal, not a blessing promised them upon Mount Gerizim, which your posterity may not suffer or enjoy, from your and their adherence to, or departure from, the principles of the Declaration of Independence, practically interwoven in

24

the Constitution of the United States. Lay up these principles, then, in your hearts, and in your souls—bind them for signs upon your hands, that they may be as frontlets between your eyes—teach them to your children, speaking of them when sitting in your houses, when walking by the way, when lying down and when rising up—write them upon the doorplates of your houses, and upon your gates—cling to them as to the issues of life—adhere to them as to the cords of your eternal salvation."

APPENDIX.

STAMP ACT.*

W HEREAS , by an act made in the last session of Parliament, several duties were granted, continued, and appropriated toward defraying the expenses of defending, protecting, and securing the British colonies and plantations
in America: and whereas it is first necessary, that provision be made for raising a further revenue within your
majesty's dominions in America, towards defraying the
said expenses; we, your majesty's most dutiful and loyal
subjects, the *Commons of Great Britain,* in parliament
assembled, have therefore resolved to give and grant unto
your majesty the several rights and duties hereinafter
mentioned; and do most humbly beseech your majesty
that it may be enacted, And be it enacted by the king's
most excellent majesty, by and with the advice and consent of the lords spiritual and temporal, and commons, in
this present parliament assembled, and by the authority
of the same, That from and after the first day of November, one thousand seven hundred and sixty-five, there
shall be raised, levied, collected, and paid unto his
majesty, his heirs, and successors, throughout the colonies
and plantations in America, which now are, or hereafter
may be, under the dominion of his majesty, his heirs and
successors

1. For every skin of vellum or parchment, or sheet or
piece of paper, on which shall be engrossed, written, or

* Received the royal signature, March 27th, 1765.

printed, any declaration, plea, replication, rejoinder, demurrer, or other pleading, or any copy thereof, in any court of law within the British colonies and plantations in America, a stamp duty of *three pence.*

2. For every skin or piece of vellum or parchment, or sheet or piece of paper, on which shall be engrossed, written, or printed, any special bail, and appearance upon such bail in any such court, a stamp duty of *two shillings.*

3. For every skin or piece of vellum or parchment, or sheet or piece of paper, on which may be engrossed, written, or printed, any petition, bill, or answer, claim, plea, replication, rejoinder, demurrer, or other pleading, in any court of chancery or equity within the said colonies and plantations, a stamp duty of *one shilling and six pence.*

4. For every skin or piece of vellum or parchment, or sheet or piece of paper, on which shall be engrossed, written, or printed, *any copy* of any petition, bill, answer, claim, plea, replication, rejoinder, demurrer, or other pleading, in any such court, a stamp duty of *three pence.*

5. For every skin or piece of vellum or parchment, or sheet or piece of paper, on which shall be engrossed, written, or printed, any monition, libel, answer, allegation, inventory, or renunciation, in ecclesiastical matters, in any court of probate, court of the ordinary, or other court exercising ecclesiastical jurisdiction within the said colonies and plantations, a stamp duty of *one shilling.*

6. For every skin or piece of vellum or parchment, or sheet or piece of paper, on which shall be engrossed, written, or printed, any copy of any will (other than the probate thereof,) monition, libel, answer, allegation, inventory, or renunciation, in ecclesiastical matters, in any such court, a stamp duty of *six pence.*

7. For every skin or piece of vellum or parchment, or sheet or piece of paper, on which shall be engrossed,

written, or printed, any donation, presentation, collation or institution, of or to any benefice, or any writ or instrument for the like purpose, or any register, entry, testimonial, or certificate of any degree taken in any university, academy, college, or seminary of learning, within the said colonies and plantations, a stamp duty of *two pounds.*

8. For every skin or piece of vellum or parchment, or sheet or piece of paper, on which shall be engrossed, written, or printed, any monition, libel, claim, answer, allegation, information, letter of request, execution, renunciation, inventory, or other pleading, in any admiralty court within the said colonies and plantations, a stamp duty of *one shilling.*

9. For every skin or piece of vellum or parchment, or sheet or piece of paper, on which any copy of any such monition, libel, claim, answer, allegation, information, letter of request, execution, renunciation, inventory, or other pleading, shall be engrossed, written, or printed, a stamp duty of *six pence.*

10. For every skin or piece of vellum or parchment, or sheet or piece of paper, on which shall be engrossed, written, or printed, any appeal, writ of error, writ of dower, *ad quod damnum,* certiorari, statute merchant, statute staple, attestation, or certificate, by any officer, or exemplification of any record or proceeding, in any court whatsoever, within the said colonies and plantations (except appeals, writs of error, certiorari, attestations, certificates, and exemplifications, for, or relating to the removal of any proceedings from before a single justice of the peace,) a stamp duty of *ten shillings.*

11. For every skin or piece of vellum or parchment, or sheet or piece of paper, on which shall be engrossed, written, or printed, any writ of covenant for levying fines, writ of entry for suffering a common recovery, or attachment issuing out of, or returnable into any court within

the said colonies and plantations, a stamp duty of *five shillings.*

12. For every skin or piece of vellum or parchment, or sheet or piece of paper, on which shall be engrossed, written, or printed, any judgment, decree, or sentence, or dismission, or any record of *nisi prius* or *postea,* in any court within the said colonies and plantations, a stamp duty of *four shillings.*

13. For every skin or piece of vellum or parchment, or sheet or piece of paper, on which shall be engrossed, written, or printed, any affidavit, common bail, or appearance, interrogatory, deposition, rule, order or warrant of any court, or any *dedimus potestatem, capias subpœna,* summons, compulsory citation, commission, recognisance, or any other writ, process, or mandate, issuing out of, or returnable into, any court, or any office belonging thereto, or any other proceeding therein whatsoever, or any copy thereof, or of any record not herein before charged, within the said colonies and plantations (except warrants relating to criminal matters, and proceedings thereon, or relating thereto,) a stamp duty of *one shilling.*

14. For every skin or piece of vellum or parchment, or sheet or piece of paper, on which shall be engrossed, written, or printed, any note or bill of lading, which shall be signed for any kind of goods, wares, or merchandise, to be exported from, or any cocket or clearance granted within the said colonies and plantations, a stamp duty of *four pence.*

15. For every skin or piece of vellum or parchment, or sheet or piece of paper, on which shall be engrossed, written, or printed, letters of mart or commission for private ships of war, within the said colonies and plantations, a stamp duty of *twenty shillings.*

16. For every skin or piece of vellum or parchment, or sheet or piece of paper, on which shall be engrossed,

written, or printed, any grant, appointment, or admission of, or to any public beneficial office or employment, for the space of one year, or any lesser time, of or above *twenty pounds per annum* sterling money, in salary, fees, and perquisites, within the said colonies and plantations (except commissions and appointments of officers of the army, navy, ordnance, or militia, of judges, and of justices of the peace,) a stamp duty of *ten shillings.*

17. For every skin or piece of vellum or parchment, or sheet or piece of paper, on which any grant, of any liberty, privilege, or franchise, under the seal or sign manual, of any governor, proprietor, or public officer, alone, or in conjunction with any other person or persons, or with any council, or any council and assembly, or any exemplification of the same, shall be engrossed, written, or printed, within the said colonies and plantations, a stamp duty of *six pounds.*

18. For every skin or piece of vellum or parchment, or sheet or piece of paper, on which shall be engrossed, written, or printed, any license for retailing of spirituous liquors, to be granted to any person who shall take out the same, within the said colonies and plantations a stamp duty of *twenty shillings.*

19. For every skin or piece of vellum or parchment, or sheet or piece of paper, on which shall be engrossed, written, or printed, any license for retailing of wine, to be granted to any person who shall not take out a license for retailing of spirituous liquors, within the said colonies and plantations, a stamp duty of *four pounds.*

20. For every skin or piece of vellum or parchment, or sheet or piece of paper, on which shall be engrossed, written, or printed, any license for retailing of wine, to be granted to any person who shall take out a license for retailing of spirituous liquors, within the said colonies and plantations, a stamp duty of *three pounds.*

21. For every skin or piece of vellum or parchment, or sheet or piece of paper, on which shall be engressed, written, or printed, any probate of will, letters of administration, or of guardianship for any estate above the value of twenty pounds sterling money, within the British colonies and plantations upon the continent of America, the islands belonging thereto, and the Bermuda and Bahama islands, a stamp duty of *five shillings.*

22. For every skin or piece of vellum or parchment, or sheet or piece of paper, on which shall be engrossed, written, or printed, any such probate, letters of administration or of guardianship, within all other parts of the British dominions in America, a stamp duty of *ten shillings.*

23. For every skin or piece of vellum or parchment, or sheet or piece of paper, on which shall be engrossed, written, or printed, any bond for securing the payment of any sum of money, not exceeding the sum of ten pounds sterling money, within the British colonies and plantations upon the continent of America, the islands belonging thereto, and the Bermuda and Bahama islands, a stamp duty of *six pence.*

24. For every skin or piece of vellum or parchment, or sheet or piece of paper, on which shall be engrossed, written, or printed, any bond for securing the payment of any sum of money, above ten pounds, and not exceeding twenty pounds sterling money, within such colonies, plantations, and islands, a stamp duty of *one shilling.*

25. For every skin or piece of vellum or parchment, or sheet or piece of paper, on which shall be engrossed, written, or printed, any bond for securing the payment of any sum of money above twenty pounds, and not exceeding forty pounds sterling money, within such colonies, plantations, and islands, a stamp duty of *one shilling and six pence.*

26. For every skin or piece of vellum or parchment or

sheet or piece of paper, on which shall be engrossed, written, or printed, any order or warrant for surveying or setting out any quantity of land, not exceeding one hundred acres, issued by any governor, proprietor, or any public officer, alone, or in conjunction with any other person or persons, or with any council, or any council and assembly, within the British colonies and plantations in America, a stamp duty of *six pence.*

27. For every skin or piece of vellum or parchment, or sheet or piece of paper, on which shall be engrossed, written, or printed, any such order or warrant for surveying or setting out any quantity of land above one hundred and not exceeding two hundred acres, within the said colonies and plantations, a stamp duty of *one shilling.*

28. For every skin or piece of vellum or parchment, or sheet or piece of paper, on which shall be engrossed, written, or printed, any such order or warrant for surveying or setting out any quantity of land above two hundred and not exceeding three hundred and twenty acres, and in proportion for every such order or warrant for surveying or setting out every other three hundred and twenty acres, within the said colonies and plantations, a stamp duty of *one shilling and six pence.*

29. For every skin or piece of vellum or parchment, or sheet or piece of paper, on which shall be engrossed, written, or printed, any original grant, or any deed, mesne conveyance, or other instrument whatsoever, by which any quantity of land, not exceeding one hundred acres, shall be granted, conveyed or assigned, within the British colonies and plantations upon the continent of America, the islands belonging thereto, and the Bermuda and Bahama islands (except leases for any term not exceeding the term of twenty-one years), a stamp duty of *one shilling and six pence.*

30 For every skin or piece of vellum or parchment, or

sheet or piece of paper, on which shall be engrossed written, or printed, any such original grant, or any such deed, mesne conveyance, or other instrument whatsoever, by which any quantity of land, above one hundred and not exceeding two hundred acres, shall be granted, conveyed, or assigned, within such colonies, plantations, and islands, a stamp duty of *two shillings.*

31. For every skin or piece of vellum or parchment, or sheet or piece of paper, on which shall be engrossed, written, or printed, any such original grant, or any such deed, mesne conveyance, or other instrument whatsoever, by which any quantity of land, above two hundred, and not exceeding three hundred and twenty acres, shall be granted, conveyed, or assigned, and in proportion for every such grant, deed, mesne conveyance, or other instrument, granting, conveying, or assigning, every other three hundred and twenty acres, within such colonies, plantations, and islands, a stamp duty of *two shillings and six pence.*

32. For every skin or piece of vellum or parchment, or sheet or piece of paper, on which shall be engrossed, written, or printed, any such original grant, or any such deed, mesne conveyance, or other instrument whatsoever, by which any quantity of land, not exceeding one hundred acres, shall be granted, conveyed, or assigned, within all other parts of the British dominions in America, a stamp duty of *three shillings.*

33. For every skin or piece of vellum or parchment, or sheet or piece of paper, on which shall be engrossed, written, or printed, any such original grant, or any such deed, mesne conveyance, or other instrument whatsoever, by which any quantity of land, above one hundred and not exceeding two hundred acres, shall be granted, conveyed or assigned, within the same parts of the said dominions a stamp duty of *four shillings.*

34. For every skin or piece of vellum or parchment, or sheet or piece of paper, on which shall be engrossed, written, or printed, any such original grant, or any such deed, mesne conveyance, or other instrument whatsoever, by which any quantity of land, above two hundred and not exceeding three hundred and twenty acres, shall be granted, conveyed, or assigned, and in proportion for every such grant, deed, mesne conveyance, or other instrument, granting, conveying, or assigning every other three hundred and twenty acres, within the same parts of the said dominions, a stamp duty of *five shillings.*

35. For every skin or piece of vellum or parchment, or sheet or piece of paper, on which shall be engrossed, written, or printed, any grant, appointment, or admission, of or to any beneficial office or employment, not herein before charged, above the value of twenty pounds per annum sterling money, in salary, fees, and perquisites, or any exemplification of the same, within the British colonies and plantations upon the continent of America, the islands belonging thereto, and the Bermuda and Bahama islands (except commissions of officers of the army, navy, ordnance, or militia, and of justices of the peace), a stamp duty of *four pounds.*

36. For every skin or piece of vellum or parchment, or sheet or piece of paper, on which shall be engrossed, written, or printed, any such grant, appointment, or admission, of or to any such public beneficial office or employment, or any exemplication of the same, within all other parts of the British dominions in America, a stamp duty of *six pounds.*

37. For every skin or piece of vellum or parchment, or sheet or piece of paper, on which shall be engrossed, written, or printed, any indenture, lease, conveyance, contract, stipulation, bill of sale, charter party, protest, articles of apprenticeship or covenant (except for the hire

of servants not apprentices, and also except such other matters as herein before charged), within the British colonies and plantations in America, a stamp duty of *two shillings and six pence.*

38. For every skin or piece of vellum or parchment, or sheet or piece of paper on which any warrant or order for auditing any public accounts, beneficial warrant, order, grant, or certificate, under any public seal, or under the seal or sign manual of any governor, proprietor, or public officer, alone, or in conjunction with any person or persons, or with any council, or any council and assembly, not herein before charge, or any passport or letpass, surrender of office, or policy of assurance, shall be engrossed, written or printed within the said colonies and plantations (except warrants or orders for the service of the army, navy, ordnance, or militia, and grants of offices under twenty pounds per annum, in salary, fees, and perquisites) a stamp duty of *five shillings.*

39. For every skin or piece of vellum or parchment, or sheet or piece of paper, on which shall be engrossed, written or printed, any notarial act, bond, deed, letter of attorney, procuration, mortgage, release, or other obligatory instrument, not herein before charged, within the said colonies and plantations, a stamp duty of *two shillings and three pence.*

40. For every skin or piece of vellum or parchment, or sheet or piece of paper, on which shall be engrossed, written, or printed, any register, entry, or enrolment of any grant, deed, or other instrument whatsoever, herein before charged, within the said colonies and plantations, a stamp duty of *three pence.*

41. For every skin or piece of vellum or parchment, or sheet or piece of paper, on which shall be engrossed, written, or printed, any register, entry, or any enrolment of any grant, deed, or other instrument whatsoever, not

herein before charged, within the said colonies and plantations, a stamp duty of *two shillings.*

42. And for and upon every pack of playing cards, and all dice, which shall be sold or used within the said colonies and plantations, the several stamp duties following (that is to say);

43. For every pack of such cards, one shilling.

44. And for every pair of such dice, ten shillings.

45. And for and upon every paper called a *pamphlet,* and upon every newspaper, containing public news, or occurrences, which shall be printed, dispersed, and made public, within any of the said colonies and plantations, and for and upon such advertisements as are hereinafter mentioned, the respective duties following (that is to say);

46. For every such pamphlet and paper, contained in a half sheet, or any lesser piece of paper, which shall be so printed, a stamp duty of one half-penny for every printed copy thereof.

47. For every such pamphlet and paper (being larger than half a sheet, and not exceeding one whole sheet), which shall be printed, a stamp duty of one penny for every printed copy thereof.

48. For every pamphlet and paper, being larger than one whole sheet, and not exceeding six sheets in octavo, or in a lesser page, or not exceeding twelve sheets in quarto, or twenty sheets in folio, which shall be so printed, a duty after the rate of one shilling for every sheet of any kind of paper which shall be contained in one printed copy thereof.

49. For every advertisement to be contained in any gazette, newspaper, or other paper, or any pamphlet which shall be so printed, a duty of two shillings.

50. For every *almanac,* or calendar, for any one particular year, or for any time less than a year, which shall be written or printed on one side only of any one sheet, skin,

or piece of paper, parchment, or vellum, within the said colonies and plantations, a stamp duty of *two pence.*

51. For every other almanac or calendar, for any one particular year, which shall be written or printed within the said colonies and plantations, a stamp duty of *four pence.*

52. And for every almanac or calendar, written or printed in the said colonies and plantations, to serve for several years, duties to the same amount respectively shall be paid for every such year.

53. For every skin or piece of vellum or parchment, or sheet or piece of paper, on which any instrument, proceeding, or other matter or thing aforesaid, shall be engrossed, written, or printed, within the said colonies and plantations, in any other than the English language, a stamp duty of double the amount of the respective duties before charged thereon.

54. And there shall be also paid, in the said colonies and plantations, a duty of six pence for every twenty shillings, in any sum not exceeding fifty pounds sterling money, which shall be given, paid, contracted, or agreed for, with or in relation to any clerk or apprentice, which shall be put or placed to or with any master or mistress, to learn any profession, trade, or employment. II. And also a duty of one shilling for every twenty shillings, in any sum exceeding fifty pounds, which shall be given, paid, contracted, or agreed for, with, or in relation to, any such clerk or apprentice.

55. Finally, the produce of all the aforementioned duties shall be paid into his majesty's treasury; and there held in reserve, to be used from time to time by the parliament, for the purpose of defraying the expenses necessary for the defence, protection, and security of the said colonies and plantations.

CONSTITUTIONAL CONVENTION.

THE NAMES OF THE DELEGATES TO THE CONVENTION
WHICH MET AT PHILADELPHIA, IN MAY, 1787, TO FRAME
A NEW CONSTITUTION, WERE AS FOLLOWS:—

New Hampshire, on the 27th of June, 1787, appointed John Langdon, John Pickering, Nicholas Gilman, and Benjamin West.

Massachusetts, on the 9th of April, 1787, appointed Francis Dana, Elbridge Gerry, Nathaniel Gorham, Rufus King, and Caleb Strong.

Connecticut, on the second Thursday of May, 1786, appointed William Samuel Johnson, Roger Sherman, and Oliver Ellsworth.

New York, on the 6th of March, 1787, appointed Robert Yates, John Lansing, jr., and Alexander Hamilton.

New Jersey, on the 23d of November, 1780, appointed David Brearley, William Churchill Houston, William Paterson, and John Neilson; and on the 8th of May, 1787, added William Livingston, and Abraham Clark; and on the 5th of June, 1787, added Jonathan Dayton.

Pennsylvania, on the 30th of December, 1786, appointed Thomas Mifflin, Robert Morris, George Clymer, Jared Ingersoll, Thomas Fitzsimons, James Wilson, and Gouverneur Morris; and on the 28th of March, 1787, added Benjamin Franklin.

Delaware, on the 3d of February, 1787, appointed George Reed, Gunning Bedford, jr., John Dickinson, Richard Bassett, and Jacob Broom.

Maryland, on the 26th of May, 1787, appointed James M'Henry, Daniel of St. Thomas Jenifer, Daniel Carroll, John Francis Mercer, and Luther Martin.

Virginia, on the 16th of October, 1786, appointed George Washington, Patrick Henry, Edmund Randolph, John Blair, James Madison, jr., George Mason, and George Wythe. Patrick Henry having declined his appointment as deputy, James M'Clure was nominated to supply his place.

North Carolina, in January, 1787, elected Richard Caswell, Alexander Martin, William Richardson Davie, Richard Dobbs Spaight, and Willie Jones. Richard Caswell having resigned, William Blount was appointed a deputy in his place. Willie Jones having also declined his appointment, was supplied by Hugh Williamson.

South Carolina, on the 8th of March, 1787, appointed John Rutledge, Charles Pinckney, Charles Cotesworth Pinckney, and Pierce Butler.

Georgia, on the 10th of February, 1787, appointed William Few, Abraham Baldwin, William Pierce, George Walton, William Houston, and Nathaniel Pendleton

THE END.

www.ingramcontent.com/pod-product-compliance
Lightning Source LLC
Chambersburg PA
CBHW031231090426
42742CB00007B/155